The Cassell Dictionary of
Literary and Language Terms

CASSELL PUBLISHERS LIMITED
Villiers House, 41/47 Strand
London WC2N 5JE

First published 1992

British Library Cataloguing in Publication Data
Ruse, Christina
   The Cassell dictionary of literary and language terms.
   1. English language – Dictionaries
   I. Title   II. Hopton, Marilyn
   403

   ISBN 0-304-31927-9 hbk
   ISBN 0-304-31932-5 pbk

Typeset by Fakenham Photosetting Limited, Fakenham, Norfolk
Printed in Great Britain by Biddles Ltd, Guildford and King's Lynn

THE CASSELL DICTIONARY OF

Literary and Language Terms

Christina Ruse and Marilyn Hopton

CASSELL

Introduction

This dictionary is not another academic reference to literary terms. It has been compiled and written by teachers for students who are studying English at an advanced level. The wordlist was assembled after a careful analysis of set texts, syllabuses, textbooks, glossaries, literary essays and reviews.

This book is intended as a straightforward and readable explanation of literary and language terms together with examples from literary works likely to be met in course material or almost certainly available from libraries. The authors have deliberately avoided rare or obscure references and the language of the entries has been kept as straightforward as possible. The information is introductory but is intended to encourage students by offering suggestions for further reading and including many cross-references that direct students on an interesting journey in a particular area of interest.

Unlike other references, this book does not assume any classical education or any knowledge of British cultural history. Therefore, essential information is provided about personalities, historical contexts, social and economic influences and the links between one period or movement and another. Whenever it is relevant, the relationships between English literary heritage and other countries in Europe and elsewhere are described and discussed.

The contents deal with traditional as well as modern grammatical terms and there are numerous examples to help understanding and illustrate correct usage. Language and literature are inextricably linked, for example in considerations of style, and a reference work combining the two aspects is particularly desirable.

Vocabulary items that may not be readily identifiable as literary terms but are common in course work and essays are explained in the dictionary, often with cross-references to related items. Examples are *abridge* and *adapt* or *essay* and *thesis*. Informal vocabulary such as *waffle* is also included.

In entries directly associated with literature courses and examinations detailed guidance is provided for good essay writing. Examples of this can be seen under *appreciation*, *character sketch* and *detective fiction*.

Finally, the authors have mentioned influences of other art forms such as film, television, light entertainment and popular song. The connections between these and the literary heritage are obvious but are all too often neglected.

This dictionary, then, is very useful for

- Students who are studying literature at school and college. It will be particularly useful for those taking a module in literature as part of a wider course of study.

- Overseas students who are studying English in situations where English is the language of education and examination but is not the mother tongue.

- Foreign students who are studying English language and literature at an advanced level.

Saying the words

Many words in this dictionary are unusual or difficult to say. These words are shown with a special spelling to help you.

Example: aesthetic /ees-theet/ or motif /moh-**teef**/

The darker letters show that this part of the word is spoken more strongly. The hyphens separate spoken parts of the word.

There are sounds that have many different spellings in English.

Example: 'ee' can be f<u>ee</u>t, b<u>ea</u>t, p<u>ie</u>ce, athl<u>e</u>te etc.

For these sounds the following spellings are used:

ee	*as in*	f<u>ee</u>t, b<u>ea</u>t, m<u>e</u>tre, mot<u>if</u>
i	*as in*	pr<u>i</u>nt, com<u>i</u>c, s<u>y</u>llable, m<u>y</u>th
e	*as in*	t<u>e</u>nse, h<u>ea</u>d, addr<u>e</u>ss, <u>e</u>dit
a	*as in*	<u>a</u>ct, bl<u>a</u>ck, ad<u>a</u>pt, p<u>a</u>rable
aa	*as in*	h<u>a</u>rd, dr<u>a</u>ma, <u>a</u>rchive, contr<u>a</u>st
o	*as in*	s<u>o</u>ft, c<u>o</u>medy, n<u>o</u>vel, w<u>a</u>ffle
aw	*as in*	cl<u>au</u>se, s<u>aw</u>, b<u>oa</u>rds, v<u>au</u>deville
oo	*as in*	m<u>oo</u>d, bl<u>ue</u>, m<u>o</u>vement, tr<u>ou</u>badour
yoo	*as in*	n<u>ew</u>, m<u>u</u>se, rev<u>iew</u>, masc<u>u</u>line
u	*as in*	p<u>u</u>n, t<u>o</u>ngue, c<u>ou</u>plet, con<u>u</u>ndrum
er	*as in*	v<u>er</u>b, h<u>ea</u>rd, f<u>ir</u>st, w<u>or</u>d
a	*as in*	dr<u>a</u>ma, <u>a</u>side, howl<u>er</u>, iron<u>y</u>
ay	*as in*	c<u>a</u>se, <u>a</u>pron, gr<u>ai</u>l, d<u>ei</u>sm
oh	*as in*	t<u>o</u>ne, h<u>er</u>o, fol<u>io</u>, f<u>o</u>lk
ie	*as in*	l<u>igh</u>t, m<u>i</u>me, var<u>ie</u>ty, rh<u>y</u>me
ou	*as in*	n<u>ou</u>n, <u>ow</u>l, cr<u>ow</u>n, uml<u>au</u>t
oi	*as in*	v<u>oi</u>ce, t<u>oy</u>, f<u>oi</u>l, tabl<u>oi</u>d
ere	*as in*	n<u>ear</u>, h<u>er</u>o, coh<u>er</u>ent, ballad<u>eer</u>
air	*as in*	b<u>are</u>, f<u>ai</u>ry, p<u>ear</u>, w<u>er</u>ewolf
yur	*as in*	c<u>ure</u>, <u>Eu</u>rope, P<u>u</u>ritan, c<u>ae</u>sura
ur	*as in*	s<u>ure</u>, all<u>ure</u>, r<u>u</u>ral, broch<u>ure</u>
k	*as in*	<u>c</u>all, <u>ch</u>orus, <u>k</u>ey, baro<u>que</u>
g	*as in*	<u>g</u>loss, ta<u>g</u>, fi<u>g</u>ure, a<u>g</u>ony
dg	*as in*	<u>j</u>oy, <u>g</u>ender, tra<u>g</u>edy, con<u>j</u>unction
th	*as in*	<u>th</u>rill, <u>th</u>eatre, my<u>th</u>, diph<u>th</u>ong

th	*as in*	that, with, the, other
ch	*as in*	chain, each, question, posthumous
sh	*as in*	short, fiction, brochure, ancient
zh	*as in*	measure, version, genre, montage
ng	*as in*	song, English, blank, function
y	*as in*	yarn, year, yellow, your
ks	*as in*	index, climax, axiom, lexis

A

abbreviation

formal style requires full stops, as in *B.A.*, *p.m.*, but not after *Dr*, *Mrs*, *Ltd*, *Pty* etc (which include the last letter of the original word). It is a modern trend to leave out full stops altogether especially for frequently used abbreviations such as *BBC*, *TV*, *eg*, *etc*, and when the abbreviation is an acronym, such as *AIDS* or *OPEC*.

ab initio   /ab i-**nish**-ee-oh/

a Latin phrase meaning 'from the beginning'.

abridge

to shorten a novel etc by leaving out parts, but without changing the main story. Some of Shakespeare's plays are published in abridged editions for schools; the parts considered unsuitable for children have been removed. See ADAPT. **abridgement** noun.

absolute

1 describes a grammatical construction that is independent of the main clause, as in *Seriously though, shouldn't you write and apologize?*
2 describes a transitive verb used without a direct object, as in *Her loud voice is likely to disconcert*.

abstract

a summary of the main details of a piece of writing or a speech, particularly when these have a scientific or academic content.

abstract noun

the name of anything we experience as an idea or quality, not something we experience by sight, touch, smell etc, e.g. *beauty*, *doubt*, *history*. See CONCRETE NOUN.

absurd, theatre of the

any dramatic work that portrays the concept of life as being meaningless and the universe as having no real purpose.

In order to show this, these plays include almost no development or motivation in the characters, each of whom is unable to communicate successfully with others. There is also no significance to the dialogue, and the total effect is to portray an irrational, often illogical, set of episodes without a definite or conventional plot. Samuel Beckett, with works such as *Waiting for Godot* (1956), and Harold Pinter, with works such as *The Birthday Party* (1960), are two of several modern playwrights who have written such drama. See EXISTENTIALISM.

academy

an official association of literary, scientific or artistic men and women formed to promote culture and learning, especially one of national importance, such as *The Royal Society* (1662) (for sciences) in England; *L'Académie française* (1635) (for language) in France. The word comes from the place near Athens where Plato's Academia was founded, one of the five chief schools of philosophy in Ancient Greece (c. 387 BC to AD 529).

acatalectic   /*a*-kat-*a*-lek-tik/

describes a line of verse that is 'complete' because it includes all the syllables necessary to maintain a uniform metrical pattern (i.e. all the feet are complete), as in this opening line of Wole Soyinka's *Night* (1967):

Your hand | is heav|y, Night, | upon | my brow |

See CATALECTIC.

accent

to stress or emphasize particular syllables in a line of verse in order to produce a metrical pattern or rhythm. The symbol ⌐ or ´ indicates an accented (stressed) syllable, as in

I wan|dered lone|ly as | a cloud |

See UNACCENTED.

account

a written or spoken report, description etc, especially one produced for official use.

accusative = OBJECTIVE.

acknowledgement

an author's or publisher's statement, with thanks, at the beginning of a book that other writers, books, illustrations etc have been used when preparing a book.

acronym

a word (a type of abbreviation) formed from the first letters of other words, such as BASIC (**B**eginner's **A**ll-purpose **S**ymbolic **I**nstruction **C**ode) or AIDS (**A**cquired **I**mmune **D**eficiency **S**yndrome).

acrostic

(usually) a poem written so that the initial letters of the lines produce a word or phrase relevant to the theme, such as in Ben Jonson's *The Alchemist* (1610). Acrostics are also used as memory devices, such as *Every Good Boy Deserves Fun* (EGBDF, the notes on the lines in written music). See MNEMONIC.

act

1 a major division of a play. Shakespeare used the classical model of five acts (although there is no conclusive evidence that he actually divided his plays into scenes and acts; in 1709, Nicholas Rowe provided the divisions we know), but in modern times three acts are usual. One-act plays form a newer, separate dramatic category.

2 a short performance, especially one of several in light entertainment, such as *a comedian's act, a juggler's act*.

3 (**Acts**) a formal report on the proceedings, decisions etc of a learned society, formal meeting etc.

action

the events which take place in a plot or performance of a dramatic work. An *action-packed* drama is one which includes a lot of physical activity.

active

a form of a verb in which the grammatical subject is the person or thing that performs the action or is responsible for it. The active forms of the verb *break* are *break, breaks, broke*. In *Richard breaks/broke the stick*, *breaks* and *broke* are in the active form. See PASSIVE.

active vocabulary

the words, expressions etc used by an individual in speech or writing. See IDIOLECT, PASSIVE VOCABULARY.

acute accent

the mark ´ placed above a vowel, usually 'e', to show how the vowel should be spoken, as in *cliché*.

adage   /ad-idg/

a proverb or saying that is often quoted, e.g. *Waste not, want not*.

adapt

to rewrite a literary work for another purpose, such as a play for filming or a novel for a television dramatization. E M Forster's *A Passage to India* (1924) has been adapted for filming. See ABRIDGE.
adaptation noun.

adapter or adaptor

a person who writes adaptations.

addendum

(two *addenda*)
1 an appendix or supplement in a book, journal etc.
2 a comment or statement that is added later.

address

a formal speech given by an important person to an audience, for example by the principal to the parents and children of a school.

adjective

a word used to describe people, objects, ideas, events etc and used (usually) with nouns and pronouns, such as *a ridiculous excuse, up-to-date information*. Adjectives can also be used with verbs such as *appear, taste, feel* as in *Her idea seems impossible* or *That cake tastes sweet*. They can also be used with verbs such as *become* or *turn* to show how the object changes, as in *He washed his hands clean*. Also, adjectives can be used to replace a noun, as in *I'd like two large and one small, please* (when shopping), or *I'm the youngest in the class*. Some adjectives are used with 'the' as a noun as in *the wealthy, the British, the forgotten* (all used with a plural verb). Past and present participles can be used as adjectives, e.g. *a torn page* or *a smiling baby*.

Finally, a few adjectives which end in -ed have a special pronunciation /-id/, as in *a learned society, an aged relative*. See ATTRIBUTIVE, PREDICATIVE. **adjectival** adjective.

An **adjectival clause** is a clause that functions as an adjective and it is always introduced by a relative pronoun, as in *a teacher who is very popular*.

An **adjectival participial clause** is a participial clause that functions as an adjective, as in *Students requiring tickets for the bus must buy them now*.

adjunct

an adverb or adverbial phrase that is an integral part of a clause or sentence, as in *explain it slowly*. It can often be contrasted with another adverb in questions or statements expressing alternatives, as in *Did you see him outside the house or was he inside?* and *I can join you afterwards but not before the meeting*.

An adjunct is not separated by commas. See CONJUNCT, DISJUNCT.

ad-lib

to make a speech or comment without any preparation or planning. **ad-lib** adjective.

adverb

a word used to say when, where or how something happens, or to give information about the verb, as in *She laughed loudly*. An adverb can also give more information about adjectives, as in *an extremely loud laugh*, about other adverbs, as in *I laughed very loudly*, or about a prepositional phrase, as in *I was absolutely over the moon with joy*.

Many adjectives can become adverbs by adding -*ly*, e.g. *greatly*, *happily*. But some words ending in -*ly* are adjectives, not adverbs, e.g. *lovely*, *ugly*. A few words such as *early* function as both adverbs and adjectives, as in *I got up early* (adverb) and *I'm an early riser* (adjective). See DEGREE (adverb of degree). **adverbial** adjective.

An **adverbial clause** is a clause that functions as an adverb, as in *Stop writing when the bell rings*. *Please ask if you want me to come* is an adverbial clause of condition; *I came because I got your message* is an adverbial clause of reason. See ADJUNCT, CONJUNCT, DISJUNCT.

adverbial particle

an adverb used as part of a phrasal verb, e.g. *go away*, *keep out*.

aesthete   /ees-theet/

a person who greatly appreciates literature, especially verse, and beauty in the visual arts.

aestheticism   /ees-thet-i-sizm/

great respect and love for the importance of the arts and beauty, especially the belief that this is how we should judge the value of existence. See PRE-RAPHAELITES.

aesthetics   /ees-thet-iks/

the philosophical study of the science of beauty, using logic to judge the essence of beauty and truth; the psychological study of the processes of artistic creation and appreciation. See BELLES-LETTRES.

affectation

the use of an artificial style or method of writing or speaking which is inappropriate to the subject or context, such as Mrs Elton's response in Jane Austen's *Emma* (1816) to Mr Knightley's invitation to visit him and spend the day picking strawberries:

> It is a morning scheme, you know, Knightley; quite a simple thing. I shall wear a large bonnet, and bring one of my little baskets hanging on my arm. Here, – probably this basket with pink ribbon ... (and a few minutes later) ... I wish we had a donkey. The thing would be for us all to come on donkeys, Jane, Miss Bates, and me, and my *caro sposo* walking by.

affirmative

describes a verb form in a sentence without *not*, e.g. *I like it* or *She won't tell, will she? They worked hard today* is an affirmative sentence. See NEGATIVE.

affix

a group of letters put at the beginning (*prefix*) or at the end (*suffix*) of a word to make a new word which either has a new meaning or is a different part of speech, as in *anti-nuclear, disassociate, likely, African*.

Africanism

a word or expression which is characteristic of an African culture or language and is used in a non-African context, e.g. *safari*.

Afro-American

describes people who are of African and American origin and their culture, language and history.

Afro-Caribbean

describes people of African descent who were born in, or whose families come from, the islands of the Caribbean and their culture and language. See RAP.

agent

the part of a passive sentence which states the person or thing performing the action, as in *The cup was won by the reserve team*.

Age of Reason = ENLIGHTENMENT.

agitprop   /adg-it-prop/

propaganda in literature, especially supporting Communism.

agony column

a part of a newspaper or magazine in which readers write letters describing personal problems and someone (an *agony aunt*, or rarely *agony uncle*) replies.

agrapha

the sayings of Jesus Christ that are not recorded in the official Gospels.

agraphia

the loss of ability to write, caused by damage to the brain. See ALEXIA, APHASIA.

agreement

the forms of a verb, noun, pronoun etc used to show the relationship between the subject and verb etc according to number, gender etc, as in *Women and elephants never forget an injury* or *You that love England, that have an ear for her music....*

aide mémoire   /ed mem-**waa**/

1 a document that summarizes the main points in an agreement or proposal.
2 any device used to help a person to remember something, e.g. a mnemonic.

album

1 a file or book with blank pages, used to keep photographs, newspaper clippings etc.
2 a book with a wide variety of stories, illustrations etc, especially one produced for children.

Alexandrine

a line of verse with six iambic feet, such as in this line from Spenser's *The Faerie Queene* (1589 and 1596):

Ease af|ter war, | death af|ter life, | does great|ly please.|

It is rare in English poetry.

alexia

the lack of ability to learn how to read caused by damage to the central nervous system. See AGRAPHIA, APHASIA, DYSLEXIA.

allegory

a form of narrative writing in which the people, objects or events are used symbolically to put across a particular (usually moral or religious) meaning. Parables and fables are allegories.

John Lyly's *Endimion* (1591) is an allegorical drama, but John Bunyan's *The Pilgrim's Progress* (1678) is the outstanding allegory in English. Orwell's *Animal Farm* (1945) is probably the best-known modern example. See APOLOGUE, DREAM ALLEGORY, BEAST EPIC.
allegorical adjective.

alliteration

the deliberate repetition of the first consonant in associated words or next to stressed syllables, as in W B Yeats' *The Fisherman* (1914):

> The clever man who cries
> The catch-cries of the clown

or in D H Lawrence's *Snake* (1923):

> He sipped with his straight mouth,
> Softly drank through his straight gums, into his slack, long
>   body,
> Silently.

Alliteration was a prominent feature of Old English verse and has continued to be widely used. It is often used in everyday expressions such as *then and there* or *heaven and hell*. **alliterative** adjective.

allocution

a formal speech, especially one that gives advice or tries to persuade a person to agree or believe something.

allonym

someone's name used by another writer. See PSEUDONYM.

allophone

a speech sound that is a variant of a phoneme, e.g. one that is aspirated and one that is not.

allusion

the device of making a reference to a well-known person, place etc, the significance of which the reader or audience is expected to recognize and understand. Thomas Hardy's novels are full of classical allusions.

almanac

a reference book that gives historical and statistical information.

In medieval times, an almanac was used to calculate and record the movements of the planets, moon and stars. During the 16th century, an almanac would forecast weather, disasters such as wars and the outbreak of disease. Today some almanacs continue to predict good and bad fortune.

alphabet

a set of letters or symbols used in a writing system. The Greek alphabet has 24 letters, and the English alphabet has 26.

altar poem

a poem written in the shape of the topic. George Herbert's *The Altar* (1633) is the best-known example.

alternate rhyme

lines of verse with the rhyme scheme *a b a b . . .*

ambiguity

a written or spoken statement that can have more than one interpretation, as in *Watch the blackboard while I go through it again.* It is often unintentional, but it is sometimes used deliberately for fun or for dramatic effect. See DOUBLE ENTENDRE.

Americanism

a word or expression that is characteristic of American English, e.g. *railroad* for *railway*, *gas* for *petrol*, *different than* for *different from.*

ampersand

the symbol & and & used to replace 'and' in writing, usually in names of business companies, such as *Green & Son Ltd.*

amphigory   /am-fi-gree/

a piece of writing that has no sense or meaning.

amplifier

an adverb or adverbial phrase (an *intensifier*) that affects the meaning of a sentence by increasing the force of part of it. See BOOSTER, MAXIMIZER. The opposite of an amplifier is a *downtoner.*

anachronism

the mention or use of a person or object in a context when the person or thing could not have existed. In *Chaucer looked at his watch and picked up the telephone* there are two anachronisms. In Shakespeare's *Julius Caesar* any reference to clocks striking is an anachronism since striking clocks had not been invented in Roman times. **anachronistic** adjective.

anacoluthon   /an-*a*-ka-**loo**-thon/

a sentence in which one grammatical construction changes to another, as in *If I meet him this evening, what do you want me to say?*

anagram

a word or phrase made from the letters of a different word or phrase, often used in crossword puzzles, e.g. *plum* is an anagram of *lump* and *eat no ants* is an anagram of *annotates*. See PALINDROME.

analects or analecta

excerpts or fragments from a longer piece of writing.

analogue

1 a word in one language with the same origin as a word in another language. The English word *calculate* is an analogue of the Latin word *calculus*.
2 two versions of the same story can be called analogues; part of the story in Shakespeare's *Twelfth Night* is an analogue of a novella (a tale) in French by Bandello (c. 1554).
analogous adjective.

analyse

to divide a sentence into its grammatical parts and label them.

anapaest or anapest   /an-*a*-pest/

a metrical foot that contains two unstressed syllables followed by a stressed (accented) syllable (˘ ˘ ‾). See DACTYL, METRE. **anapaestic** adjective.

anaphora   /*a*-naf-*a*-r*a*/

the use of *a/an/the* or pronouns to refer back to previous information with the implication that the reader or listener understands the reference (i.e. which one), as in *We visited **the** museum on Wednesday*. See ANTECEDENT. **anaphoric** adjective.

anastrophe   /*a*-nas-tr*a*-fee/

the act of changing the usual or logical order of words in a sentence to obtain a rhythm or for emphasis, as in the third line of this extract from Byron's *Don Juan* (1819–1824):

> The isles of Greece, the isles of Greece!
> Where burning Sappho loved and sung,
> Where grew the arts of war and peace,

ancient

describes, in literature, the 'classical' as opposed to the 'modern' thinkers and writers.

During the neoclassical period, there was a lot of argument about the relative qualities of ancient and modern approaches. Swift's *The Battle of the Books* (1704) is the most significant work on the topic in English.

anecdote

a brief account of an interesting or amusing event, especially an incident in a person's life. **anecdotal** adjective.

angle brackets

brackets shaped < >.

Anglicism

a word or expression which is characteristically English in the United Kingdom or British internationally, e.g. *roundabout*.

Anglo-French

(of) the French language as used in England between 1066 and 1350, and (of) the literature produced (mainly in monasteries). See MIDDLE ENGLISH.

Anglo-Indian

(of) a word or expression in English that has its origin in an Indian language, e.g. *chutney* or *pukka*.

Anglo-Irish

(of) the English language spoken in Ireland, or literature written in English by Irish writers such as George Moore and George Bernard Shaw.

Anglo-Norman = ANGLO-FRENCH.

Anglophone

a person who speaks English from birth.

Anglo-Saxon

(of) the language of Anglo-Saxon England (also called Old English which is now the preferred term), the earliest phase of the English language, between 450 and 1066. Aelfric, a monk who lived at the end of the 10th century (he is also called Grammaticus) is considered the greatest Anglo-Saxon prose writer but the poem *Beowulf* (late 10th century) is the most significant work. See OLD ENGLISH.

The second part of the period of Middle English (about 1350–1500) is also referred to as the Anglo-Saxon period. See MIDDLE ENGLISH.

angry young man

a British writer in the 1950s especially of plays, e.g. John Osborne, who criticized traditional social values and customs and people in authority.

anisometric   /an-ie-soh-**met**-rik/

describes verse with lines of unequal length, as in Adrian Mitchell's *To Whom it may Concern* (1969):

> I was run over by the truth one day
> Ever since the accident I've walked this way
> So stick my legs in plaster
> Tell me lies about Vietnam.

anisomorphic   /an-ie-soh-**maw**-fik/

describes languages that have different semantic categories when describing reality. For example, the English language describes many colours, e.g. pink and rose, as shades of a particular one, red, while some other languages consider them as separate colours.

annals

a record of historical events produced annually, now mainly used to describe historical narrative and records of scientific and artistic organizations. See CHRONICLE.

annotate

to produce a textual comment (an *annotation*) in a book; it may include explanations, informative notes and other comments.

annual

a book produced in a different edition each year. Today, children's annuals are very popular.

anon

an abbreviation meaning 'anonymous', used in texts when the author is not known.

anonym = PSEUDONYM.

anonymous

by an author who is not known.

antagonist

a main character in a play, novel etc, or part of one, who is in conflict with the hero or heroine. In William Golding's *Lord of the Flies* (1954), Jack becomes Piggy's antagonist. See PROTAGONIST.

antecedent

a noun replaced by a pronoun in the same sentence or a following sentence, as in *I heard **the football match** on the radio – it must have been exciting to watch* (*the football match* is replaced by *it*). It can also be a noun related to a relative clause, as in *Can you name **the man** who discovered America?* See ANAPHORA.

antecedent action

the action that occurred before the plot of a literary work begins.

anthem

a song of praise or reverence, especially *a national anthem*.

anthology

a collection of poems or other writings, either by one author or about a particular topic or theme. F T Palgrave's anthology *The Golden Treasury of Songs and Lyrics* (1861) is a classic example.

anthropomorphic

describes a literary work that gives human form or human qualities to gods or animals, as in Greek mythology.

anticlimax

1 any insignificant event that follows an important or serious one.
2 a sudden change from something serious or important to something trivial, often used for effects such as surprise or humour. See BATHOS.

antihero

a main character of a novel or play who has none of the traditional qualities of a hero such as bravery, strength, morals. Heathcliff in Emily Brontë's *Wuthering Heights* (1847) has been described as an antihero. In Tom Stoppard's *Rosencrantz and Guildenstern are dead* (1966), both main characters are antiheroes. See ANTINOVEL.

antinovel

a novel that has none of the traditional qualities or structure, such as a recognizable plot and clear development of characters. These novels often use experimental techniques and language such as those developed by Surrealists. See STREAM OF CONSCIOUSNESS, IMPRESSIONISM. Virginia Woolf's *The Waves* (1931) is often called an antinovel.

antiphrasis /an-**tif**-r*a*-sis/

the intentional use of a satirical description to convey the opposite meaning. In Shakespeare's *Julius Caesar*, Antony describes the murderers as *honourable men* using antiphrasis. In Evelyn Waugh's *A Handful of Dust* (1934), the lawyer Mr Graceful is not at all graceful!

antistrophe /an-**tis**-tr*a*-fee/

the second of three sections of a Pindaric ode (see ODE) based on the movement and chants of the Chorus in classical Greek tragedy. During the antistrophe, the Chorus moved in a circle from left to right. See EPODE, STROPHE.

antithesis /an-**tith**-*a*-sis/

a literary technique when opposite or contrasting statements are used for emphasis, as in *and down they forgot as up they grew* (e e cummings). **antithetical** adjective.

antonomasia /an-t*a*-n*a*-**may**-zi*a*/

1 the use of a title to replace a well-known person's name, as in *the Bard of Avon* for William Shakespeare.
2 the use of a well-known name to express an idea, as in *a Machiavellian politician* for an 'unscrupulous' one.

antonym

a word that is opposite in meaning to another word. *In* and *out* are antonyms. See SYNONYM.

aphaeresis /*a*-**fere**-*a*-sis/

the removal of the first part of the word to make another word with the same meaning, as in *phone* for *telephone*. See APOCOPE.

aphasia /*a*-**fay**-zi*a*/

the loss of ability to speak or write caused by damage to the central nervous system. See AGRAPHIA, ALEXIA.

aphesis /**af**-i-sis/

the gradual omission as a language develops of a part of the beginning of a word, usually of a short, unaccented letter or syllable, such as *specially* from *especially*. See APOCOPE.

aphorism   /af-*a*-rizm/

a statement of an important, general truth using a few well-chosen words; it is usually attributable to an author. Samuel Taylor Coleridge's treatise *Aids to Reflection* (1825) is filled with spiritual and moral aphorisms.

T S Eliot's splendid aphorism on writers is *Immature poets imitate; mature poets steal.*

apocope   /*a*-**pok**-*a*-pee/

the removal of final letters or syllables of a word in the natural development of a language, to create a new word, such as *cinema* from *cinematography*. See APHAERESIS.

apocrypha   /*a*-**pok**-ri-f*a*/

works of doubtful or unknown authorship, especially some Biblical texts. See CANON (2). **apocryphal** adjective.

apologia = APOLOGY.

apologue   /**ap**-*a*-log/

a fable with a moral. Aesop's *Fables* (6th century BC) are the best-known examples.

apology

a formal defence or explanation in literature. Sir Philip Sidney's *Apologie for Poetrie* (1595) is a well-known example.

apophasis   /*a*-**pof**-*a*-sis/

1 a statement which asserts something but also appears to deny the truth of it, e.g. *If I didn't know better, I'd say you stole that chocolate.*
2 a statement which asserts something that you say you will not mention, e.g. *. . . not to mention her laziness.*

apophthegm or apothegm   /*a*-p*a*-them/

a brief statement of a practical or useful truth, usually attributable to an author, such as Balzac's *It is as easy to dream a book as it is hard to write one.* See MAXIM.

aposiopesis   /*a*-p*a*-sie-*a*-**pee**-sis/

the intentional failure to finish a statement, used to express exasperation, to threaten etc, e.g. *You do that again and I'll . . . I'll . . .*

apostolic

of or about the Apostles and their teachings.

apostrophe /a-**pos**-tra-fee/

1 the punctuation mark ' used
a to show possession, as in *Anne's books* or *teachers' materials.*
b to show omission of letters or numbers in contractions, as in *I've, o'clock, '86.*
2 in literature, an apostrophe is a poem addressed to a person who is imagined, now dead or not present, such as Gerard Manley Hopkins' *The Windhover, to Christ Our Lord* (1877).

apotheosis /a-**poth**-i-**oh**-sis/

the glorification of a human, elevating her or him to the rank of a god. In ancient Rome, the apotheosis of the emperors was usual. **apotheosize** verb.

appellation

a name, title or distinctive phrase used to identify a person or thing, e.g. *Sir* Walter Scott, *the Bard of Avon* (Shakespeare). **appellative** adjective.

appendix

(two *appendices*)
a set of additional facts, information etc at the end of a literary work.

applied linguistics

the study of linguistics and its practical use, for example when working out methods for learning a foreign language, or looking at the links between grammatical structure and semantic groups.

apposition

a grammatical construction in which a noun or noun phrase is placed after another noun to add information or modify its meaning, as in *Peter, **the son of my boss**, has won the award.*

appreciation

a critical review of a piece of writing, dramatic performance etc. It is also known as *practical criticism.* This is often required in examinations and it is important to examine the following aspects of the text:
a *Content:* what it is about; it may be philosophical, romantic, absurd, scholarly etc.
b *Style:* this considers the manner of expression rather than content; it may be vivid, classical, pompous, vulgar, informative, explicit, fluent etc.
c *Mood* or *atmosphere:* what this is and how it is achieved; it may be cheerful, gloomy, nostalgic, angry etc.

d *Choice and use of vocabulary and figures of speech:* why they are used; whether they are suited to the context.

e *Success of the text:* whether or not the writer achieves her or his intentions and why.

f *Your personal opinion:* it is very important that you engage with the text and record your personal response such as your opinion of the writer's approach or whether you have gained a new understanding about life.

approximator

an adverb or an adverbial phrase (an *intensifier*) that affects the meaning of a sentence by showing or suggesting that the action of the verb has not happened yet or did not actually happen, e.g. *almost* or *as good as* as in *I've **almost** finished* or *She **as good as** said she didn't like it*. See COMPROMISER, DIMINISHER, MINIMIZER.

apron stage

the part of a stage that projects beyond the proscenium arch. The audience can watch a play from the front three sides.

Arcadian

describes verse etc which idealizes rural simplicity and happiness. Sir Philip Sidney's *Arcadia* (1590) is the best-known example. The word comes from *Arcadia* (also called *Arcady*), a beautiful region in Greece.

archaism

a word or expression found in literature that is no longer used in everyday speech. *Quoth, thee* and *thence* are archaisms. **archaize** verb.

archetype

the original model or pattern from which others are created. In literature, it can refer to a recurring theme or symbol. **archetypal** adjective.

archive

(often *archives*)
(a place with) a collection of written records about an organization, institution, family etc.

archivist

a person who works in an archive.

argot

jargon used by a particular group, such as sailors or farmers, in a community.

argument

a summary of the main points to be noted in an essay, novel, play or episode. It is often given in the introduction. In Shakespeare's *Hamlet*, the travelling actors who perform at the palace give a mimed version of their play before the spoken one and Ophelia notes that the mime *imports the argument of the play*.

Ariel

a spiritual being, a character in Shakespeare's last play *The Tempest*. He has the ability to change shape and assume various disguises; because of this, he plays a crucial role in the development of the plot, although acting at all times under his master Prospero's command. See PUCK.

Arthurian

of the legendary deeds of King Arthur and his Knights of the Round Table who represented the best of chivalry in early medieval England. King Arthur's actual existence is not proven. See LEGEND.

article

1 See DEFINITE and INDEFINITE ARTICLE.
2 a piece of writing on one topic in a newspaper, magazine or book. See COLUMN (2), FEATURE (3).
3 a clause in a legal contract.

artificial

describes writing that is highly elaborate or affected as opposed to natural or convincing.

aside

a remark made on the stage to another actor which the audience hears but which is supposedly not heard by other characters on stage.

aspect

verb tenses show whether an action was occurring at a particular time, is completed etc. These verb forms are called aspects, as in *The sun was shining* (**continuous aspect**) or *The sun has shone* (**perfect aspect**). **aspectual** adjective.

assertive

in affirmative statements, words such as *some, someone* (*assertive forms*) can be used. These words cannot be used in negative statements and questions; use *any, anyone* (*nonassertive forms*).

assonance

the repetition of similar vowel sounds used as an approximate rhyme in poetry and prose. *These* and *cheese* are perfect rhymes, but *ships* and *sticks* are examples of assonance. See HALF-RHYME. Wilfred Owen's poem *Exposure* (1920) illustrates the use of assonance:

> Watching, we hear the mad gusts tugging on the wire
> Live twitching agonies of men among its brambles.
> Northward, incessantly, the flickering gunnery rumbles.

asterism

a symbol using three asterisks ⁂ or ⁂, used in printed texts to highlight the material that follows.

asyllabic   /ay-si-**lab**-ik/

not acting as a syllable.

asyndeton   /a-**sin**-di-tan/

the style of deliberately leaving out conjunctions in a phrase or sentence for dramatic effect, as in *It would take me many months – you could do it in a few weeks* (*but* is left out before *you*).

atlas

a published collection of maps (or sometimes graphs etc).

atmosphere

the mood or subjective impression produced by a piece of writing, e.g. romantic, gloomy, joyful or uneasy.

atonic   /ay-**ton**-ik/

describes any unstressed syllable of a word. In *atonic*, *a* and *ic* are atonic. See TONIC. **atony** noun.

attributive

describes an adjective placed immediately in front of the noun it modifies. In **black** *ink*, *black* is in the attributive position.

With a few verbs (*become*, *wash* etc), an adjective that shows how the object changes can be placed after the noun but is still referred to as being in the attributive position, as in *Please keep your books* **clean**. Many adjectives, e.g. *latter* or *ancient* as in **ancient** *Greece*, can only be used in the attributive position; compound adjectives can only be used in the attributive position, as in *a* **second-storey** *window*.

Many nouns can be used as attributive adjectives, e.g. *a* **dawn** *chorus*, *a* **drama** *student*, *an* **essay** *competition*. See PREDICATIVE, PREMODIFIER.

aubade   /aw-**baad**/

a lover's poem or song uttered when parting at dawn, such as in Shakespeare's *Romeo and Juliet*.

Augustan Age

1 the ancient Roman period (c. 50 BC–10 AD) of great classical verse from Virgil, Horace and Ovid (when Augustus Caesar was emperor). **2** any period of great literary achievement in which there is a return to classical values, e.g. the later part of the neoclassical period.

authorial

of or about writers or writing, as in *authorial adjectives* such as *Chaucerian* or *Spenserian*.

autobiography

a personal account of one's life, including memoirs, diaries or letters as well as a formal narrative. In his *The Naked Civil Servant* (1968), Quentin Crisp describes autobiography as *an obituary in serial form with the last instalment missing*. See BIOGRAPHY, MEMOIRS.

Although we usually associate autobiography with prose it may also be written in verse, e.g. John Betjeman's *Summoned by Bells* (1960).

automatism   /aw-**tom**-*a*-tizm/

describes the effects produced by rejecting conscious thought that a writer tries to experience in order to have the benefit of completely free thought.

autotype

an exact copy of a manuscript, illustration etc.

auxiliary verb

a verb, e.g. *be*, *do*, *have*, used with other verbs to make tenses, passive forms and questions, e.g. *I am writing*, *It was hidden*, *Do be quiet! Do you need me?* See MODAL AUXILIARY VERB.

avant-garde

describes writing that contains innovations in form and technique, e.g. Samuel Beckett's *Waiting for Godot* (1956). See ABSURD, THEATRE OF THE.

axiom

a self-evident truth, e.g. *All men are mortal.* **axiomatic** adjective.

B

Babel, the Tower of   /bay-bəl/
a tower built in an attempt to reach heaven but not completed because
of confusion caused by the builders using many different languages. It
is mentioned in the Book of Genesis in the Bible (Genesis 11: 1–9):
God became angry when he saw the tower being built; he caused the
builders to speak different languages so that they could not communicate with each other and the building would not be completed.
    It is thought the city of Babel was in Babylonia, an ancient empire in
the Middle East (the region of modern Iraq near its border with Iran
where the River Euphrates and River Tigris flow towards the Gulf).
    Babel is also used to refer to any noisy confusion of different voices
and sounds.

back-formation
the process of creating a shorter word by deleting part of an existing
word that is mistakenly considered to be an affix. For example, *edit* is a
back-formation from *editor* and *televise* is a back-formation from
television.

background
the physical or social setting of any piece of writing including a poem,
novel, drama or episode. The Brontë sisters used the Yorkshire moors
where they lived as the background to most of their novels.
    Background can also refer to the author's philosophical viewpoint,
particularly when a major purpose of the piece of writing is social
documentary. Critics often refer to the Russian background of Tolstoy's novels; D H Lawrence used the industrial working-class of
northern England as the background to many of his novels; John
Steinbeck used his native state of California and the lives of poor
farming communities as the background to many of his stories and
novels.

back-matter = END-MATTER.

back number
a copy of a newspaper, magazine etc produced at an earlier date.

badinage   /bad-i-naazh/
a short, witty and playful exchange during a conversation.

balance

the inclusion in a literary essay of all points of view that should be considered, even if eventually one point of view is favoured. Balance was very much valued by the neoclassicists. See NEOCLASSICISM.

It is important that essays written for examinations have balance because it prevents the essay from being onesided, which would lose marks, and it also suggests to the examiner that the candidate has arrived at a particular decision or opinion having understood and carefully assessed all the aspects or views in the text.

ballad   /bal-*a*d/

a kind of poem that can be recited or sung, and that describes a dramatic story or episode using simple language and a simple repeated tune. There is often a repeated verse and earliest examples were often accompanied by dancing.

The **traditional** or **folk ballad** dates from about the 15th century in England and was one of the earliest forms of storytelling or narrating historical events. This was a very important way of passing on history, legends and information in illiterate or semiliterate communities. These traditional ballads are anonymous and no doubt changed according to the imaginative talents of the singers or storytellers. Many of them are well known and are sung or recited worldwide, such as the 18th century Scottish ballads *The Work of the Weavers* and *Sir Patrick Spens*, the Australian *Stir the Wallaby Stew* and *Clementine* from North America. In England, the legends of Robin Hood were a rich source of ballads.

In Britain and America, later ballads were carefully composed and written down by known poets, and are described as **literary** or **art ballads**. This poetic form, with its short stanzas and regular rhythm used to tell a dramatic story, has always been popular. S T Coleridge's *The Rime of the Ancient Mariner* (1798) is a typical example. See BROADSIDE.

The ballad's popularity has continued in the 20th century in its written form (Charles Causley has written several including *What Has Happened to Lulu?* and *The Ballad of the Bread Man*) and in song (*The Gresford Disaster* was written after a coalmining disaster in north England in 1934 in which 265 men were killed; it was recorded in 1964 by the folksinger Ewan MacColl who has composed some fine industrial ballads including *Cannily, Cannily*).

ballade   /ba-**laad**/

a French poetic form traditionally with three stanzas followed by a concluding shorter one (see ENVOI). The number of lines in the stanzas varied but the most common used eight lines for the first three stanzas and four lines for the final one, with the rhyme scheme *a b a b b c b c* (three times) and *b c b c*. Each stanza shared the same last line (see REFRAIN).

The ballade was popular in France in the 15th century and poets such as François Villon produced excellent examples. However, it is a complex and difficult form and had lost its popularity by the 17th century.

In England, Chaucer had used this form in his *Truth* (or *Balade de bon conseyl*) (c. 1390) but it did not enjoy any revival until English poets such as Swinburne tried it in the 19th century. Later poets such as Hilaire Belloc also tried it, but the ballade has never been popular outside France.

balladeer   /bal-*a*-dere/
a person who sings traditional ballads.

ballad metre
the metre of a ballad stanza; it is usually iambic and therefore the same as common metre. Here is the last verse of a well-known traditional ballad *The Unquiet Grave*:

> Thĕ stālk | ĭs wīth|ĕred drȳ, | mў lŏve, |
>   Sŏ wīll | ŏur hēarts | dĕcāy; |
> Sŏ māke | yŏursēlf | cŏntēnt, | mў lŏve, |
>   Tĭll Gōd | cālls yŏu | ăwāy. |

Although it is the basic metre of much popular and traditional poetry, it has been used or adapted by later poets like Keats, Coleridge, Wordsworth and even later by Oscar Wilde for his *Ballad of Reading Gaol* (1898):

> Ĭ nēv | ĕr sāw | ă mān | whŏ loōked |
>   Wĭth sūch | ă wĭst|fŭl ēye |
> Ŭpōn | thĕ lītt|lĕ tēnt | ŏf blūe |
>   Whĭch prīs|ŏnĕrs cāll | thĕ skȳ. |

balladmonger
a person who sold traditional ballads printed on one side of a sheet of paper. See BROADSIDE.

ballad stanza
a stanza of four lines, usually with the rhyming scheme *a b c b*, and four metrical feet in the first and third lines and three metrical feet in the

second and fourth lines. This kind of stanza is often used in ballads. See the examples under BALLAD METRE.

barb

a sarcastic comment intended to hurt a person's feelings.

barbarism

a word or expression considered to be substandard, especially one that is a crude or wrong construction, e.g. one that uses a combination of Greek and Latin roots (such as *telecast*), and so offends purists. **barbarize** verb.

bard

a pre-eminent poet. The word was used by the Celts in ancient France and Britain (see CELTIC) to describe a poet who recited poetry that praised heroic deeds, especially in historic campaigns. A bard often accompanied himself on a musical instrument, usually on the harp.

These poets enjoyed a special social status which has its only modern equivalent in Wales where a poet who has taken part in an Eisteddfod is called a *bardd*. Today, bard is used with a capital letter as a term of praise to describe a great poet of national significance – Shakespeare is often called *the Bard of Avon* (Avon is the area in central England where he was born and grew up) and the Scottish poet, Robert Burns, is known simply as *the Bard*. **bardic** adjective.

bare infinitive

the infinitive form of a verb without *to*. It is used when forming the future tense, as in *She'll pay you tomorrow*, and to form the imperative, as in **Come here!** It is most common after verbs such as *can*, *might*, *must*, *should* and *will* (see MODAL AUXILIARY VERB), as in *You can come*, *He mustn't sign* or *I won't pay*, and after verbs such as *hear*, *see*, *help* and *let*, as in *I heard him scream*, *We saw it fall*, *I'll help you clean* and *Let her go*. Note that *to* is essential in the passive, e.g. *He was heard to scream*.

A **bare infinitive clause** can be used with *do*, e.g. *What he did was phone the police*, where *to* can also be used, *What he did was to phone the police*, unless the bare infinitive clause is in the initial position, *Phone the police is what he did*, or the sentence is a command, suggestion or warning, *Do phone the police*.

baroque   /ba-rok/

describes the ornate and elaborate style of 17th century architecture. Because of this, ornate and elaborate writing of the 17th century is also called baroque. A well-known example is the extravagant description of Mary Magdalen's eyes in Crashaw's poem *The Weeper* (1646):

> two faithfull fountains;
> Two walking baths; two weeping motions;
> Portable and compendious oceans.

base or base form

the basic or simplest form of a verb, e.g. *come, put, sing, suffer*.
The other forms are:
    verb + -s (*comes, puts, sings, suffers*)
    the past form (verb + -ed or an irregular form, e.g. *came, put, sang, suffered*)
    verb + -ing (*coming, putting, singing, suffering*)
    the past participle (verb + -ed or an irregular form, e.g. *come, put, sung, suffered*).

bastard title = HALF-TITLE.

bathos   /**bay**-thos/

a sudden fall in the subject-matter of a piece of writing or a speech from something dignified or serious to something ordinary or ridiculous. Often it is not intentional and is therefore an implicit criticism of style or contents. At other times it may be used deliberately to create a humorous effect. Alexander Pope, in an essay *On Bathos, or the Art of Sinking in Poetry* (1727) gave a good example:

> Ye Gods! annihilate but Space and Time
> And make two lovers happy.

His own mock-epic poem *The Rape of the Lock* (1712 and 1714) provides several examples. Here is one:

> And thou, Great Anna, whom three Realms obey
> Dost sometimes counsel take and sometimes tea.

beast epic or beast fable

a story or series of stories using animals as characters. These stories are often fables or parables and they are all allegorical or satirical.
    They were very popular in ancient Greece and Rome and also in medieval Europe. *Roman de Renart*, written in France in the 12th century by Pierre de Saint-Cloud, is a prominent example from this period; it is a collection of fables using Reynard the Fox as the hero. The fox represents a man who deceives others and uses his cunning to escape punishment. Chaucer's *The Nun's Priest's Tale* (c. 1387) is based on one episode and tells of a fox that is outwitted by Chanticleer the cock.

Recent beast epics include Kipling's *Jungle* books (1894 and 1895) and Orwell's *Animal Farm* (1945). They have always formed a popular basis for children's stories. See BESTIARY.

beat

the accent or emphasis in a metrical foot that produces rhythm in poetry. See METRE.

Beat generation

a group of American poets and novelists who wrote in the late 1950s. They rejected contemporary religious, political and cultural values, and sought salvation through drugs, sex and alternative religions such as Buddhism.

Allen Ginsberg's *Howl* (1955) was almost a manifesto for the Beats, celebrating an underworld of drugs, sex and mysticism. Jack Kerouac's novel *On the Road* (1957) was another central text. Other members of the Beat generation were Lawrence Ferlinghetti and William Burroughs whose novel *Naked Lunch* (1959) was avant-garde in structure as well as content. The Beats had a strong influence on the youth culture of the 1960s.

bedroom farce   See FARCE.

belles-lettres

any writing valued because of its artistic and aesthetic qualities rather than because of its factual or moral content. The word is used mainly of essays or literary studies and not of poetry, fiction or scientific writing.

Belles-lettres are judged on characteristics such as elegance of style, the imaginative or witty use of vocabulary, and the suitability of the structure and phrasing to the content. The French essayist Montaigne (1533–1592) was a well-known writer of belles-lettres, and Max Beerbohm (1872–1956) produced notable witty and elegant essays.

belletrist

a person who writes belles-lettres.

bestiary

a moral story or narrative poem that uses the habits of real or mythical animals to illustrate moral values and to explain Christian doctrine. Such literature was very popular in medieval Europe and a collection of about fifty tales was made at that time and translated into many languages.

The bestiary has been responsible for qualities we give to particular animals such as the greedy pig and also for mythical beasts such as the unicorn. See BEAST EPIC.

bestseller

a book sold in large numbers during a particular period. Bestseller can also refer to an author who has written a bestselling book, particularly more than one. See BLOCKBUSTER.

bibliographer

a person who compiles a bibliography. Two noted bibliographers are W T Lowndes, *The Bibliographer's Manual of English Literature* (1838) and R B McKerrow, *Introduction to Bibliography for Literary Students* (1927).

bibliography

1 a list of the works produced by a particular author (or sometimes a publisher or country).
2 a list of the books, essays or articles produced on a particular subject.
3 a list of all the written sources referred to in the writing of a thesis or book.
4 a study of the history of book publishing and book production.
bibliographic or **bibliographical** adjective.

bibliomania

an excessive or irrational desire to possess books. **bibliomaniac** adjective or noun.

bibliophile

a person who loves books and collects them. **bibliophilistic** adjective.

bilge

silly comments or ideas based on weak evidence or poor research.

billet doux   /bil-ay **doo**/

(two *billets doux*)
a love letter.

binder

1 = BOOKBINDER.
2 (also **ringbinder**) a folder used to hold loose sheets of paper, usually with metal rings.

bindery

a place where pages are fastened together and then bound as books.

binding

the cover put round the pages of a book. See BOARDS, CASE (2).

A *whole* or *full binding* is a cover using only one material, e.g. paper, cloth or leather. A *half binding* uses a strong material (e.g. leather) where there is greatest wear, the spine and the corners, and a cheaper material for the rest. The width of the material round the spine covers one quarter of the width of the front or back cover. Another form of half binding has the strong material along the whole of the outside edge. A *quarter binding* uses strong material for the spine only.

biographer

a person who writes a biography. A noted modern biographer is Peter Ackroyd, known especially for his authoritative biography *Dickens* (1990).

biography

an account of someone's life. It is a very popular 20th century genre. Biographers must undertake an enormous amount of research and their aim is not just to describe what happened in the life of their subject but to examine their character and see what sort of personality emerges. **biographical** adjective.

In the Middle Ages and Elizabethan period, biographies tended to centre on the lives of saints but with the publication of Dr Johnson's *Lives of the English Poets* (1779–81) and of James Boswell's *Life of Samuel Johnson* (1791) literary biography was born. It is now accepted that a biographer will attempt to give a full and honest picture of the subject and include both good and bad points, although some biographies are published which are clearly biased in their attitude, e.g. Lytton Strachey's *Eminent Victorians* (1918). See AUTOBIOGRAPHY, MEMOIRS.

In terms of literary criticism, it is not considered essential to know the details of a writer's life in order to understand her or his work (although some knowledge can illuminate); however, students tend to have an interest in the lives of writers they are studying. Many academic biographers combine a study of a writer's life and work. A recent highly acclaimed scholarly biography is Richard Ellmann's *Life of Oscar Wilde* completed just before Ellmann's death in 1987. Michael Holroyd is currently working on what promises to be a massive biography of G B Shaw.

black comedy

a drama that is pessimistic and cynical; the characters have no beliefs, moral values or hope since they live in a universe without purpose and are victims of fate. See SICK VERSE.

Some of these dramas contain a form of witty but ironical humour or mockery – we may as well laugh at ourselves since we have no control of our lives. Joe Orton's *Loot* (1965) is a typical example: the key incident in the play is a young man hiding the loot from a robbery in his mother's coffin. (The government censor, called the Lord Chamberlain, set as a condition for the licensing of *Loot* that 'the corpse must "obviously" be a dummy and not be seen by the audience'!) Stoppard's *Rosencrantz and Guildenstern are Dead* (1966) and Albee's *Who's Afraid of Virginia Woolf?* (1962) are other modern examples.

Some of Shakespeare's tragicomic plays have been described as *dark* or *black comedies* including *Measure for Measure, All's Well that Ends Well* and *A Winter's Tale.* See ABSURD, CRUELTY.

Blackfriars Theatre, the

a section of a former Dominican monastery in the City of London that James Burbage bought in 1596 and used as a small indoor theatre. Shakespeare had a financial share in this theatre and his theatrical company often performed there, especially in winter when the open-air Globe Theatre was closed.

black humour

humour in literature that is unkind or cruel and is opposed to usual ethical values. It often provides the basis for sick jokes or is used in light comic verse, for example in Lewis Carroll's poem *The Walrus and the Carpenter* from his novel *Through the Looking-Glass* (1872). See BLACK COMEDY.

blanket term or blanket phrase

a word or phrase that has a wide range of uses and covers a group of more definite terms. In the modern world *democratic* seems to be a blanket term for any political approach that is not leftwing.

blank verse

unrhymed verse written in iambic pentameters. The lack of rhyme gives the writer a lot of freedom which is perhaps why it has been a favourite form of poetry over many different periods. It was chosen by Shakespeare for his plays (especially his later plays when he abandoned rhymed verse completely), by Milton for *Paradise Lost* (1667) and by Wordsworth for *The Prelude* (1805). Here are the opening four lines of *The Prelude*:

> Oh there is blessing in this gentle breeze,
> A visitant that while it fans my cheek
> Doth seem half conscious of the joy it brings
> From the green fields and from yon azure sky.

Blank verse has been used in the 20th century, as in W B Yeats' *The Second Coming* (1920):

> The best lack all conviction, while the worst
> Are full of passionate intensity ...

blarney

light and pleasant talk used to flatter or persuade. It is a common feature in the dialogues of James Joyce's novels.

blockbuster

a bestseller that sells in very large numbers or a drama, television programme, musical etc that is extremely popular and attracts very large audiences.

Blockbuster referred originally to a large bomb used to demolish buildings over a wide area.

block letters

a form of writing or printing using separated letters that have clear lines without any decoration. It is particularly common as *block capitals* which are often requested on application or request forms.

Bloomsbury Group, the

a group of writers, painters and philosophers who lived and worked in the Bloomsbury district of central London from about 1907 to the mid-1930s.

The group included Virginia and Leonard Woolf, E M Forster, Maynard Keynes, Lytton Strachey and others. They did not represent a particular 'school' but were an intellectual community identified by a delight in conversation and the free expression of ideas, appreciation of beauty, the commitment to achieve excellence and the stimulus of friendship and love. They challenged the strict moral values of the late Victorian period and so influenced their contemporaries and later writers and thinkers.

Interest in the Bloomsbury Group remains undiminished; there have been many books written about them in the last twenty years.

blue book

1 a cheap novel in a blue cover that was popular at the turn of the 18th century in England. These novels were characterized by overdramatic emotions using sentimental themes or thriller plots. See PENNY DREADFUL.

2 an official British government report in a blue cover.

blue pencil

a deletion or alteration in an article, book etc made by an official censor. **blue-pencil** verb.

bluestocking

an intellectual and serious woman. The word was first used in the mid-18th century to describe a group of literary women (who became known as the Blue Stocking club) who met in Mrs Elizabeth Montagu's house in central London. Other famous members of this group were Elizabeth Vesey, Hester Chapone and Elizabeth Carter. Instead of cardgames, they held intellectual conversations with men of letters in order to encourage a general interest in literature. See SALON.

Bluestocking is now used in a pejorative way, suggesting a woman who is interested only in intellectual issues and therefore has a dull personality. Virginia Woolf (1882–1941) is often described as a bluestocking.

blurb

a short description of the contents and purpose of a book printed on the back cover or the inside flap of the dust jacket. It is intended to encourage readers and buyers.

boards

the two pieces of board used as the support for the front and back covers of a book. See CASE (2).

Millboard, a grey cardboard made from printers' waste, is a very suitable material for boards because it can bend without cracking and does not deteriorate easily. *Strawboard*, a brown thicker cardboard, tends to be brittle and is used in cheaper bindings. Other materials, such as *pasteboard* and pulp card, are too weak or unstable to use for good bindings.

Boards is also used interchangeably with 'hardback', as in *a boards edition*.

bohemian

a word originally applied to gypsies who were thought to come from Bohemia in central Europe. In modern times it refers to writers, artists and others who lead unconventional lives and deliberately reject rigid forms and structure.

bombast

the name given originally to material used for stuffing and padding out clothes. Now it is used to describe language which is 'padded out', that is inflated and unnecessarily lengthy, but in fact empty of real worth or sincerity. In Shakespeare's *Othello*, Iago says falsely of Othello:

> But he, as loving his own pride and purposes,
> Evades them, with a bombast circumstance,
> Horribly stuff'd with epithets of war.

bon mot   /bon **moh**/

(two *bons mots*)
a short witty remark or reply. For example, when told of President Coolidge's death the American writer Dorothy Parker's response was *How could they tell?*

book

1 a collection of printed pages fixed inside a cover.
2 a written work, for example a novel, textbook, biography etc.
3 the script for an opera or play.
4 a division of a long novel, epic poem, the Bible etc. Each book is sometimes divided into chapters. Milton's *Paradise Lost* (1667) and Thomas Hardy's *The Return of the Native* (1878) are divided into books.
5 **Book of** ... an authoritative source of knowledge about ..., e.g. the *Book of Martyrs* (1563) that details the sufferings of Christian martyrs, T H White's *Book of Beasts* (1954), an English edition of a 12th century Latin bestiary, and many books that provide detailed practical information, e.g. *A Book of Sports and Games*.

bookbinder

a craftsperson or business that binds books.

bookish

describes a person who is very fond of reading or studying, especially a person whose ideas and opinions come from reading and not from personal experiences.

booklet

a small thin book.

bookplate

a label stuck in a book that bears the owner's name; it often has a personalized design and the words *ex libris* meaning 'from the collection of books belonging to'.

bookworm

a person who has a great or exaggerated desire to study from books.

booster

an adverb or adverbial phrase (an *intensifier*) that affects the meaning of a sentence by increasing the force of part of it, e.g. *enormously, much, a great deal*, as in *I enjoyed his book **enormously*** or *I **much** prefer his novels*. Boosters are not as strong as maximizers. See DIMINISHER.

bowdlerize

to take out words or passages from a play or novel thought to be indecent. **bowdlerization** noun.

The verb is derived from Thomas Bowdler who, with the help of his sister Henrietta, produced his *Family Shakespeare* (1818). This was the beginning of the age of strict Victorian morality in Britain and Bowdler removed references in Shakespeare's plays to any topic or language he considered to be indecent or overexciting.

This used to be done frequently with texts published for use in schools where sexual references, in particular, were removed.

braces

the punctuation marks { and } used to show the groupings of items in a set when parentheses and square brackets have already been used; they are used especially in mathematical expressions.

A single brace often links lines of text.

brackets = SQUARE BRACKETS.

Brackets is also used as a general term for braces and parentheses.

Braille   /brayl/

a system of writing for the blind to read. It uses varying patterns of six raised dots to represent a letter or symbol that can be interpreted by touch. Louis Braille was a blind French teacher and musician who invented this system in the early part of the 19th century.

brickbat

a deliberate and obvious critical comment or insult.

brief

1 a document prepared by a solicitor with the facts and legal points to be used by a barrister in a law case.

2 an official disciplinary letter from a senior Roman Catholic official.

3 a short statement, especially one that is a summary of a large document.

4 a list of information or instructions as preparation for an expedition, campaign etc.

broadsheet

1 a newspaper with a large page size. See TABLOID.

2 = BROADSIDE.

broadside or broadsheet

a large sheet of paper printed on one side. Soon after printing was established in England towards the end of the 15th century, news and information was printed on these sheets and distributed by hand.

At the same time, **broadside ballads** were sold in open-air markets and at fairs. These were printed as two pages each divided into two columns and both pages were printed on one side of the sheet of paper. These ballads were traditional popular ones or new, and often badly-written, songs with melodramatic descriptions of events, recent hangings, moral sermons etc. They were available in Britain even in the 1920s but enjoyed their greatest popularity much earlier.

Broadway

a main street in New York City that crosses Manhattan. It is associated with theatrical productions since most of New York's principal theatres are located on Broadway or in the district nearby.

Because of this, Broadway can also refer to American theatre generally, especially popular shows such as musicals. See OFF-BROADWAY, WEST END.

brochure

a pamphlet or sheet of paper folded several times and used for advertising, providing basic information etc. In earlier times, the word was used of a booklet with pages stitched together but without a cover.

broken rhyme

a rhyme formed by breaking a word

a where one of the rhyme words extends over two lines,

b where more than one word is needed to complete the rhyme, e.g. *estate/their gate.*

bucolic

describes writing, usually verse, about simple innocent life in the countryside, especially as a shepherd. See W H Auden's example at HEXASTICH. See PASTORAL.

bumph

1 official papers, documents etc relating to the daily work of an organization.
2 circulars, leaflets and similar advertising materials, especially those mailed to professional groups such as doctors.
3 cheap novels or magazines considered to have no literary merit.

burlesque

1 comic writing in imitation of a particular author, style of writing or even whole genre with the intention of mocking the original or making it look ridiculous. Burlesque has been a popular form of writing over many periods, in drama, verse and prose. A well-known example in verse is Samuel Butler's *Hudibras* (1663, 1664 and 1678) which makes fun of religious hypocrisy. Another is the play which the 'rude mechanicals' put on in Shakespeare's *A Midsummer Night's Dream*. This very funny play is a burlesque of the theatrical interlude. Sheridan's *The Critic* (1779) also contains a play within a play which burlesques sentimental plays that were popular at the time. See PARODY.
2 a form of light entertainment in North America with bawdy songs and dances, comic acts and striptease. It was very popular in the late 19th and early 20th centuries. Many of the better aspects of burlesque (such as elaborate costumes, excellent comic acts and the expression of passion in clever songs with good melodies) were transferred to the musicals. See VARIETY.

buzz word or buzz phrase

a word or phrase that is current slang or jargon, especially one used in a particular context, e.g. *safe* used by young people to approve of a pop musician. Such words or phrases soon lose their popularity.

by-line

the inclusion of the writer's name on a separate line beneath the title of an article in a newspaper or magazine.

Byronic

describes a passionate, proud and rebellious character who often suffers periods of deep depression. This personality is typical of heroes in Lord Byron's poems, e.g. *Childe Harold* (1812–1818), *The Lament of Tasso* (1817) and *Don Juan* (1819–1824), and was also typical of Byron himself.

byword

a word or name often used as the perfect example of good quality, e.g. *'Cassell' is a byword for reliable dictionaries.*

C

ca. See CIRCA.

cacophony   /ka-**kof**-*a*-nee/

an unpleasant and harsh combination of sounds; it usually relies on short and hard vowels and consonants such as *i*, *e*, *o* and *k*, *ch*, *p*. It is common in tongue twisters, as in *Peter Piper picked a peck of pickled pepper.* See EUPHONY. **cacophonous** adjective.

cadence

the rhythmic pattern of prose or verse. It is formed by the stress on particular syllables and by intonation.

Cadence is a particular feature of each individual writer who often composes sentences that mirror the patterns of her or his own speech. The qualities of cadence are more general than rhythm alone so that the word is used more often when describing larger, irregular pieces of writing than shorter regular verses.

caesura   /si-**zyur**-*a*/

(two *caesuras* or *caesurae*)
a pause in the rhythm of a line of verse. It is similar to a comma or semicolon in prose and is often marked by either symbol in verse. In scansion, the symbol || marks a caesura. See FEMININE and MASCULINE CAESURA.

Caesuras were first used mainly in the middle of the line but from Chaucer's time, they were used at many different points. Here is an example from John Keats' *The Eve of St Agnes* (1820):

> They glide, || like phantoms, || into the wide hall; ||
> Like phantoms, || to the iron porch, || they glide, ||

> Where lay the Porter, || in uneasy sprawl, ||
> With a huge empty flaggon by his side: ||

Blank verse provided even greater opportunities to use caesuras to vary the rhythm and emphasis as in Shakespeare's speeches; here is an example from Macbeth's soliloquy when he is trying to persuade himself to murder Duncan:

> If it were done || when tis done, || then twere well
> It were done quickly; || if th'assassination
> Could trammel up the consequences, || and catch
> With his surcease, || success, || that but this blow ...

Modern poetry allows complete freedom in metrical pattern and there is therefore equal freedom in the use of caesuras, as in this example from Denise Levertov's *Beyond the End* from *Collected Earlier Poems 1940–1960* (1979):

> It's energy: || a spider's thread: || not to
> 'go on living' but to quicken, || to activate: || extend: ||
> Some have it, || they force it – ||
> with work or laughter or even
> the act of buying, || if that's
> all they can lay their hands on – ||

call
a notice in a theatre that tells the actors the times of rehearsals.

calligraphy
an elaborate and formal style of handwriting, especially as an art form. **calligraphic** adjective. **calligrapher** noun.

calumny = SLANDER.
calumnious adjective.

Calvinism
the religious teaching of Jean Calvin (1509–1564) and his followers. Calvinism emphasized the concept of original sin and the need to be forgiven and saved by God. John Milton's *Paradise Lost* (1667) attempts to justify Calvinist teaching and John Bunyan's *The Pilgrim's Progress* (1678) showed the effect of Calvinism on an individual's personality. **Calvinist** adjective or noun.

Camelot   /**kam**-i-lot/
the town in southern England where King Arthur, according to Arthurian legend, held his court. See LEGEND.

The exact position of Camelot has never been settled. Sir Thomas

Malory, in his *Le Morte Darthur* (1469–1470), claimed that it was Winchester. There is also a strong claim to Camelot having been somewhere in Somerset.

canard   /ka-**naa**/
a false rumour, especially one used as a hoax or joke.

canon
1 a list of works of a particular author, especially those recognized as genuine. For example, the play *Henry VIII* is not accepted in the canon of Shakespeare's works.
2 the books in the New Testament accepted as genuinely belonging to the Bible. See APOCRYPHA.

Canon can also refer to a general rule used when making a moral or religious judgement. **canonical** adjective.

cant
1 insincere statements used to give the impression of being religious or moral, or any statements that do not express genuine feelings and are used only for effect. After Goneril, in Shakespeare's *King Lear*, insincerely expresses her love for her father in order to gain his lands, her sister Regan does the same:

> I am made of that self metal as my sister,
> And prize me at her worth. In my true heart
> I find she names my very deed of love;
> Only she comes too short: that I profess
> Myself an enemy to all other joys
> Which the most precious square of sense possesses,
> And find I am alone felicitate
> In your dear highness' love.

2 the jargon used by a particular group, as in *thieves' cant.*

canticle
a short religious song or poem, especially one with words from the Bible sung as a hymn during church services.

canto
(two *cantos*)
a major division of a long poem, as used in Byron's *Childe Harold* (1812–18).

capitals or capital letters
large letters as used to begin a sentence or name.

cardboard character

a character in a novel, drama etc who is typical of a familiar type of person and who is described or presented in a superficial and unimaginative way.

cardinal virtues, the   See VIRTUES.

caricature

a piece of writing that describes a person by exaggerating her or his main physical features and the peculiarities in her or his personality. There are numerous examples of caricature in English literature; in William Thackeray's *Vanity Fair* (1847–1848), The Marquis of Steyne is a caricature of an actual person, Lord Monmouth.

carol

a hymn that is sung at Christmas.

A *carole* began as a dance in medieval France and then the word referred to the song used with the dancing. Later, it was used of any joyous song connected with a festive occasion, then of religious songs of praise and joy.

Today, carol is used only of hymns and songs that celebrate the birth of Jesus Christ.

Caroline

describes the period when Charles I, King of England, Scotland and Ireland was on the throne from 1625 until his execution in 1649 (Caroline is from *Carolus*, Latin for *Charles*).

Sometimes Caroline refers specifically to the Royalist courtiers and soldiers who wrote poems at that time (see CAVALIER) and at other times to all the verse of the period. Edward Herbert, Robert Herrick, Richard Crashaw, Henry Vaughan and Thomas Carew were all Caroline poets, as was John Milton. See COMMONWEALTH.

cartoon

a humorous and satirical sketch describing an event or character. Cartoon is usually used of drawings but can also refer to a piece of descriptive writing.

case

1 the changes in the form of adjectives, nouns and pronouns used to show grammatical functions in a sentence.
2 the complete outer cover of a book. The boards are covered separae from the pages and the lettering and any decoration are put on while the cover is flat. Afterwards, the book is attached to this case with adhesive.

The introduction of *case binding* in the first part of the 19th century made it possible to produce books by hand more quickly and led the way to machine production and modern binding methods.

casebound = HARDBACK.

catachresis /kat-*a*-**kree**-sis/

the misuse of vocabulary, e.g. using *disinterested* for *uninterested*.

catalectic /kat-*a*-**lek**-tik/

describes a line of verse that does not have a completed foot at the end, as in Blake's *Tiger! Tiger!* (1794):

$$\overline{\text{Ti}}\breve{\text{ger}}! \mid \overline{\text{Ti}}\breve{\text{ger}}! \mid \overline{\text{burn}}\breve{\text{ing}} \mid \overline{\text{bright}}$$

See ACATALECTIC.

catalects /kat-*a*-lekts/

literary works that do not form part of the main set of a writer's works.

catalogue

a list including detailed notes. It is often produced as a book or booklet, for example a *sales catalogue* giving information about various products.

A catalogue can also refer to a detailed descriptive list in a piece of writing, as in this excerpt from Shakespeare's *Macbeth*:

> 1st Murderer:
>   We are men, my liege.
> Macbeth:
>   Ay, in the catalogue ye go for men;
>   As hounds, and greyhounds, mongrels, spaniels, curs,
>   Shoughs, water-rugs, and demi-wolves, are clept
>   All by the name of dogs:

or in this extract from John Keats' *The Eve of St Agnes* (1820):

> While he from forth the closet brought a heap
> of candied apple, quince, and plum, and gourd
> With jellies smoother than the creamy curd,
> And lucent syrops, tinct with cinnamon;
> Manna and dates, in argosy transferr'd
> From Fez; and spiced dainties, every one,
> From silken Samarcand to cedar'd Lebanon.

cataphora   /ka-**taf**-*a*-ra/

the use of vocabulary to refer forward to another part of a statement, e.g. *here* in *Here is my decision*. **cataphoric** adjective.

catastrophe

the final part of a tragedy that resolves the conflict, usually the death of the hero or heroine. In Thomas Hardy's *Tess of the D'Urbervilles* (1891), which follows the twisting fortunes of Tess, the catastrophe is Tess's death. See FREYTAG'S PYRAMID.

catch

1 a popular song sung by several voices each beginning at a different time. The best known in Shakespeare's plays is that in *Twelfth Night*. 2 an additional unstressed syllable at the beginning of a line of verse, as in this well-known example from Gray's *On Vicissitude* (c. 1755) in which *forgetful* has an additional unstressed syllable on *for-* when contrasted with *new-born* and *frisking*:

> New-born flocks, in rustic dance,
>   Frisking ply their feeble feet;
> Forgetful of their wintry trance,
>   The birds his presence greet –

catch phrase

a well-known phrase that is often associated with a particular group such as a political party.

catch word

a word that is associated with a particular group, especially a political party during an election campaign.

catechism

a book that contains the set of religious questions and answers used for religious instruction; they summarize the fundamental principles of Christianity. **catechismal** adjective.

catharsis

In his *Poetics* (4th century BC), the ancient Greek philosopher Aristotle gives a definition of tragedy, part of which states that by using feelings such as pity and fear tragedy brings about the proper catharsis (purging or purification) of these emotions.

As Aristotle did not explain this any further, his exact meaning has been open to interpretation ever since; it is generally considered he is suggesting that the pity and fear felt by the audience throughout the tragedy are purged or cleansed by the tragic climax of the hero's downfall. In this way the audience leaves the theatre feeling calm and emptied of emotion. **cathartic** adjective.

causative

describes the group of verbs (all transitive verbs) that have meanings associated with causing or producing an effect, e.g. *cook* in *She cooked a stew.*

causerie

a short informal conversational piece of writing, or a brief chat as part of a dialogue.

cautionary tale

a story or poem intended to warn about the dangers of doing something, having a particular personality etc. Hilaire Belloc's collection of light verse *Cautionary Tales* (1907) are the best known and include classic examples such as tales about Matilda, Henry King and Rebecca. Here is *Henry King*:

> The Chief Defect of Henry King
>   Was chewing little bits of string.
> At last he swallowed some which tied
>   Itself in ugly Knots inside.
> Physicians of the Utmost fame
>   Were called at once; but when they came
> They answered as they took their fees,
> 'There is no cure for this Disease.
> Henry will very soon be dead.'
> His parents stood about his Bed
> Lamenting his Untimely Death,
> When Henry, with his Latest Breath,
> Cried – 'Oh, my Friends, be warned by me,
> That Breakfast, Dinner, Lunch and Tea
> Are all the Human Frame requires ...'
> With that, the wretched Child expires.

cavalier

describes the poets who wrote during the reign of Charles I (1625–1649), King of England, Scotland and Ireland; Thomas Carew, Richard Lovelace and Sir John Suckling were the principal cavalier poets. See CAROLINE. Their poetry is characterized by stylish and witty lyrics and a move away from the sonnet form which for a century had been widely used for love poetry. See TRIBE OF BEN.

caveat   /kay-vee-*at*/

a formal warning, especially of the possible effects of an action or decision, e.g. that if you give an opinion or information about yourself it could be used to imply that you are guilty of an offense.

cedilla

the mark ç placed below a *c*, as in *façade*, to show that the· *c* is pronounced *s* and not *k*.

Celtic

describes the language and literature of the Celts, people who lived in central and western Europe in pre-Roman times. There are two main groups who influenced the British Isles and France:
a the ancient Britons, the Welsh, the Cornish (from Cornwall in England) and the Bretons (from Brittany in France) – the *Brythonic Celts.*
b the Irish and the Scottish – *the Gaelic Celts.*

Celtic revival

from the period of about 1885 to about 1940, several Irish writers, although writing in English, drew inspiration from their work in Ireland's past, its mysticism, legends and folk heroes, as well as its present. Their aim was to promote a national literature.

The poet and playwright W B Yeats (1865–1939) was a leading figure in this Celtic revival, founding the National Literary Society in Dublin in 1892 and becoming a director of the new Abbey Theatre in 1904 in the hope of establishing a national theatre. It was a period of excellent verse, drama and prose; as well as Yeats, the playwright J M Synge (1871–1909) and the novelist James Joyce (1882–1941) were writing at this time.

censor

an official who examines novels, plays etc and who has the authority to order the removal of any part considered to be offensive, obscene or, in some countries, politically unacceptable.

The advent of printing meant that ideas and attitudes that were in opposition to the church and government could be spread much more easily. From the middle of the 16th century, government censorship was introduced in Britain by the requirement to have a licence to print obtainable only from royal officials. John Milton produced his famous attack *Areopagitica* (1644) on this legislation pleading for unrestricted access to information and ideas; this discourse includes the famous statement, 'Give me the liberty to know, to utter, and to argue freely, according to conscience, above all liberties'. His protests were ignored.

Later, parliament censored journalists by forbidding certain kinds of news from abroad. However, independent reporting of events and anti-government pamphlets continued to be widely circulated.

From the end of the 16th century, the Church of England had attempted to censor religious opposition. In 1694 the Licensing Act for the press was withdrawn but censorship continued through government officials who were specially appointed. They imprisoned journalists and printers responsible for a broad and deliberately vague range of offences such as incitement to oppose the government or Church, causing a breach of the peace by encouraging a lack of confidence in government etc. Warrants issued against individuals had to specify the charges but later these warrants were more general and the individual, printed material or printer need not be named. However, through contesting the officials in court actions, by 1766 these warrants had been stopped.

Dramatic performances were also licensed from the middle of the 16th century and the grant of patents to particular theatrical companies controlled the work of playwrights and theatrical managers. In Elizabethan times, the administrative officials of London were hostile towards the flourishing theatrical industry, hostility which brought them into conflict with Elizabeth I and her court. There were periods when these officials banned public performances; for this reason the first purpose-built theatre was erected in Shoreditch outside the City of London's jurisdiction (see THEATRE). A well-known example of the effect of censorship in Shakespeare's time is the incident about the naming of his character Falstaff. Shakespeare had originally named him Sir John Oldcastle for his play *Henry IV* but the Oldcastle family took offence and Shakespeare renamed him Sir John Falstaff.

In 1642, Parliament, dominated by the Puritans (see COMMONWEALTH), ordered the closure of all theatres although there were clandestine performances until the Restoration in 1660 when the theatres were allowed to reopen. As a reaction to the Puritans, censorship was now very slack allowing for bawdy comedy as well as religious and political satire (see RESTORATION). But by the end of the century, public opinion had changed in favour of firm government control. In 1698, a royal order prohibited performances considered to offend morality or public decency.

From the 18th century, a senior government official, the Lord Chamberlain, had the responsibility for controlling drama, and during that century there are many recorded cases of censoring plays for offences involving political, personal and social satire. The Licensing Act of 1737 made it an obligation for theatres to obtain a licence from the Lord Chamberlain for every play and many works were banned on political grounds, or because they were considered obscene or satirized powerful members of the nobility.

From the early 18th century, the novel rapidly established itself as a popular literary genre (see NOVEL). Again, government undertook responsibility for censorship. One of the first instances was the seizure of copies of Cleland's *Fanny Hill* in 1749 on the grounds that it was pornographic.

A revision of the Licensing Act made in 1843 still left the Lord Chamberlain with the power to censor drama. It has been used to prevent performances of works by such writers as G B Shaw. The Lord Chamberlain's Examiner of Plays said of Ibsen: 'I have studied Ibsen's plays pretty carefully; and all the characters ... appear to me to be morally deranged.' A modification of this act, made in 1909, still gives the Lord Chamberlain authority for licensing but lays down conditions for refusal such as libel, insult to Parliament and the law, indecency and blasphemy. The use of laws against immorality is illustrated in two famous cases. In 1923, an edition of James Joyce's novel *Ulysses* that was printed in France was seized by Customs as being obscene. Only after another amendment to the Licensing Act in 1959 were defendants allowed to call evidence concerning the literary qualities of a work. The well-known case brought by government against D H Lawrence's *Lady Chatterley's Lover* in 1960 was defeated after reputable witnesses spoke on the novel's obvious literary merits.

Since 1968, a licence for plays has been optional. However, by using current legislation banning obscenity and power from the threat to withdraw official funding, government continues to censor drama. A recent example is the methods used in 1980 to stop performances by the National Theatre of Howard Brenton's *The Romans in Britain*.

cf.

an abbreviation of the Latin *confer* meaning *compare*, used to cross-refer to a word or statement that is relevant or interesting when compared.

chain verse

verse with lines or stanzas that are linked by repetition of rhymes; it is rare in English poetry. See VILLANELLE.

chanson de geste   /shaan-son da zhest/

(two *chansons de geste*)
a kind of epic verse that describes the deeds of real and legendary heroes and includes chivalry and love as themes. The term is French for 'a song of deeds'.

These epics, which date from the 11th to the 14th centuries, influenced the development of epic verse throughout Europe. About eighty survive, the best known of which is *Chanson de Roland* (c. 1100).

chant

a simple form of melody in which each syllable is sung using one note or a small variation of notes. It is used by the Chorus in classical Greek drama but is now used mainly when reciting a psalm or parts of a church service. See DIRGE, MANTRA (2).

Chanticleer

a character in the form of a cock that appears in certain literature including *Reynard the Fox*, Chaucer's *The Nun's Priest's Tale*, and nursery rhymes. Chanticleer is intelligent and confident and so can escape from dangerous situations even when his adversaries are big and aggressive.

chanty = SHANTY.

chapbook

a pamphlet or small book sold from the 16th to 18th centuries by pedlars at fairs and market places. Chapbooks contained ballads, stories and reports of murders, witchcraft, religious passages, political or national incidents etc. Many were reprinted numerous times and were popular for several decades.

character

1 a person in a literary work.
2 a single letter, punctuation mark or symbol used when writing or printing.

character assassination

a campaign by the media to destroy the reputation of a well-known person. See GUTTER PRESS.

characterization

the portrait of a character in a literary work; her or his personality, personal qualities, actions, ideas etc.

Methods for characterization include direct description, allowing characters to reveal themselves through their actions and statements, or learning about them through the opinion of other characters. Good authors use a mixture of methods. Shakespeare's characters are often complex and he deliberately leaves us to make personal interpretations of them; this is one important way in which he can involve his audience during a performance. In so many of his plays, it is our interest in the characters rather than the plot that makes the play so rewarding.

It is in the novel that characterization has undergone most devel-

opment and authors take great care to present rounded and psycho-
logically credible characters. Novelists known particularly for
characterization include Jane Austen and Charles Dickens. Strong
characterization is also a notable feature of Russian novels.

character sketch or character study

a description of a character in a novel or play, as written for examinations. It is important to include information that can be identified in
five groups:

a *the facts* – place of birth, age, physique, nationality, relatives, good
or poor skills, intelligent or not etc.

b *contribution to the plot* – an account of her or his actions (including
examples of inactivity!). This can include your judgement about the
type and value of these contributions and how the character behaves
during the principal episodes of the plot. Is the character contrasted
with other characters?

c *what he or she says of himself or herself* – include brief quotations or
references to direct statements but also examine the qualities of her or
his speech, e.g. arrogant or sympathetic, amusing or antisocial.

d *what other characters say* – use brief quotations or references for
important statements from others; point out those that seem to contradict others' attitudes, especially those that contradict the character's
feelings and attitudes about herself or himself.

e *a summary* – use information from **a** to **d** above to describe the
character in short general descriptive terms.

A *character sketch* can be less detailed than a *character study*.

Chaucerian

describes the use of verse form (e.g. heroic couplets or rhyme royal) or
structure (e.g. frame story) similar to Chaucer's *The Canterbury Tales*
(c.1387). The best-known example is William Morris' *The Earthly
Paradise* (1868–1870) with a prologue and a set of tales using Chaucerian metre.

The **Scottish Chaucerians** were writers in Scotland in the mid 15th
to mid 16th centuries who showed strong Chaucerian influences.
Robert Henryson's *Testament of Cresseid* (1593) is particularly well
known, as is King James I of Scotland's *Kingis Quair* (1423–1424) (see
RHYME ROYAL). William Dunbar (?1465–1530) and Gavin Douglas
(?1474–1522) are also associated with this group.

chiasmus   /kie-az-mas/

(two *chiasmi*)
a reversal of the word order in the second part of a line of verse or a
statement in prose, as in Milton's *Paradise Lost* (1667) Book IX when

Adam addresses Eve:

> Sole Eve, associate sole

chivalry

the moral qualities and social manners expected of a medieval knight. Knights were expected to serve the King, be faithful to God, show respect for noblewomen, help all women in distress, oppose any unjust or cruel behaviour and destroy monsters. See COURTLY LOVE, FEUDAL. **chivalric** adjective.

choriamb   /kaw-ri-amb/

(two *choriambs* or *choriambi*)
a metrical foot that is a combination of a trochee (‾ ˘) and an iamb (˘ ‾) so that two stressed syllables enclose two unstressed syllables. It is rare in English verse, but there is an example from Ruskin's *Trust Thou thy Love* (1881):

> Trust thou thy Love; | If she be proud, | is she not sweet?

Chorus

a lyrical poem sung by a group of actors (dancers and singers). Chorus can also refer to the actors.

Ancient Greek drama, which reached the height of its brilliance in 400 BC, had its origins in the Chorus. These songs began as the main part of religious festivals and then dramatic performances with the text inserted between them. However, the Chorus gradually became a secondary element with the role of observing, commenting on and judging the action, occasionally offering advice but without the power to alter the course of events. And gradually, the Chorus was spoken rather than sung. See ANTISTROPHE, EPODE, STROPHE and PINDARIC ODE at ODE.

The Chorus usually consisted of ordinary men and women (played by men) and therefore expressed the opinions of ordinary people, not of nobles or those with power and influence. For example, in the ancient Greek dramatist Sophocles' *Electra* (5th century BC), the Chorus is fifteen women of Mycenae, an ancient city in the north eastern part of southern Greece where the action takes place.

In Aeschylus' *The Suppliant Women* (c. 500 BC), one of the oldest ancient Greek tragedies, the Chorus is the central character. In Sophocles' dramas nearly a century later, the Chorus is a commentator. Euripides, the youngest ancient Greek tragedian, experimented with the Chorus; on the one hand it gave its name to his play *The Bacchae* (5th century BC) and on the other it is often reduced to a single character.

The ancient Romans borrowed the device of the Chorus and much later the Elizabethan dramatists made some use of it. By this time, the Chorus was usually a simple character, as in Shakespeare's *Henry V*, who spoke the prologue and epilogue and also made comments during the play that helped to link the action of the episodes.

The Chorus is rarely used in modern times, although T S Eliot's *Murder in the Cathedral* (1935) is a notable example of the effective inclusion of it.

chronicle

a comprehensive record of historical events in order of time. They were often written at the time the events happened. For example *The Anglo-Saxon Chronicles* were begun during the reign of King Alfred in the 9th century and continued to be compiled by monks until the middle of the 12th century.

Chronicles continued to be written until the 17th century when they were replaced with memoirs, diaries, travel books and biographies. A rare modern example is the American John Reed's *Ten Days that Shook the World* (1926), a chronicle of events in Petrograd in November, 1917, the Russian revolution. See ANNALS.

chronicle play or history play

a drama about true historical events rather than myths or legends. The earliest examples were simply enactments of ceremonies such as coronations interspersed with historical battle scenes. By the time of Elizabethan drama, these plays had become serious dramatizations of history.

Marlowe's *Edward II* (1594) preceded Shakespeare's series of plays concerning the history of English kings from Richard II onwards. Much of the material for these plays was taken from contemporary chronicles.

From Shakespeare's time until recently, chronicle plays have been rare. However, there have been modern successes such as T S Eliot's *Murder in the Cathedral* (1935) and Robert Bolt's play about Sir Thomas More, *A Man for All Seasons* (1960). There has always been a strong relationship between chronicle plays and tragedy, since the drama of history so often involves the tragic flaw in a major historical character.

cipher or cypher

any kind of secret writing using symbols for ordinary letters.

circa

a Latin word, often abbreviated to *c.* or *ca.*, meaning 'about' or 'approximately', used before an approximate date.

circular

a printed leaflet produced in large numbers for mass distribution.

circulation

the distribution of a newspaper or magazine, especially the total number distributed.

circumflex

the mark ^ placed above a vowel, to show how the vowel is spoken, as in *fête, rôle*.

circumlocution

a roundabout way of saying or writing something, for example *the daughter of my sister* instead of *my niece*. See PERIPHRASIS. Charles Dickens in his novel *Little Dorrit* (1855–1857) satirized the government's inefficiency in his day by calling 'the most important Department under Government' the *Circumlocution Office* to emphasize that it was all words and no action:

> If another Gunpowder plot had been discovered half an hour before the lighting of the match, nobody would have been justified in saving the parliament until there had been half a score of boards, half a bushel of minutes, several sacks of official memoranda, and a family vault full of ungrammatical correspondence, on the part of the Circumlocution Office.

citation

the act of quoting a writer, book or passage as proof or as an example.

cite

to refer to or quote a writer, book or passage as proof or as an example.

classic

any literary work that is considered to be excellent, particularly one that has remained popular for many years, often centuries, and continues to be highly praised. See MODERN CLASSIC.

classical

describes literature from the period of ancient Greece or Rome. It can also refer to later literature considered to be of an equally high standard.

classical sonnet   See SONNET.

classicism

a form of literature that sprang from an admiration of the style of the literature and philosophy of ancient Greece and Rome and modelled itself on those writers. There is total respect for tradition and an avoidance of anything romantic, humorous or unconventional. The qualities admired and copied are those of uniformity, balance, discipline, moderation and reasoning. In English literature, Ben Jonson (1572–1637), John Dryden (1631–1700) and Alexander Pope (1688–1744) were strongly influenced by classicism. See NEOCLASSICISM.

classicist

1 a person who studies the language, literature, philosophy and art of ancient Greece and Rome.

2 a person who is in favour of classicism.

classics, the

1 the literature of ancient Greece and Rome.

2 the philosophy and culture of ancient Greece and Rome.

3 literary works considered as classics (see CLASSIC).

clause

a section of a sentence with a subject and a verb, as in *Because I arrived late I missed my bus.* See ADJECTIVAL, ADVERBIAL, BARE INFINITIVE, CONDITIONAL, COORDINATE, FINITE, INFINITIVE, MAIN, NONFINITE, NOUN, PARTICIPIAL, RELATIVE and SUBORDINATE CLAUSE; IF-CLAUSE, THAT-CLAUSE. **clausal** adjective.

A **clause modifier** is any modifier that is a clause, as in *I bought a toy that was broken* or *He prefers tomatoes when they have been cooked.*

A **clausal object** is an object that is a clause. If the statement is in the passive, the clausal object comes after the main verb with *it* as the subject, as in *It was agreed that we ought to pay for the damage* or *It was not known whether he had left for ever.* If the clausal object comes before the verb, it is introduced by 'that', as in *That he had stolen the pen was obvious.*

cleft sentence

a sentence used to emphasize the subject or object by dividing the sentence into two parts, each with a verb. A cleft sentence usually begins with *It*, as in *It happens to be my brother you insulted*, but *That* or *Those* is also possible as in *Those were my chocolates you ate last night.*

clerihew

a kind of poem invented by Edmund Clerihew Bentley (1875–1956). It is a short comic poem, of irregular metre, that contains two couplets, often about a person whose name makes up one of the rhymes. Here is one example:

> What I like about Clive
> Is that he is no longer alive.
> There is a great deal to be said
> For being dead.

cliché

any word, or group of words, that has been used so often and become so familiar that it no longer has force, e.g. *in this day and age, it never rains but it pours, the conspiracy theory, democracy* and *last but not least.*

Clichés are used widely in conversation because they convey meanings and attitudes very quickly. Using a cliché can often avoid a lengthy explanation or description. However, in formal writing it is best to avoid them as they usually seem superficial and show a lack of imagination; because they are used so often they have lost most of their strength of meaning.

But clichés can be used effectively in ironical situations and, like idiomatic expressions, they can enjoy a particular freshness if they are adapted, for example *as clear as mud* could be *as clear as a mud-spattered windscreen.*

cliff-hanger

a dramatic situation, usually the signal for a disaster, used to end an episode, chapter, act of a play etc or an instalment of a dramatic serial. This device is meant to make the audience eager to read or see the next part.

climax

the point in any literary work with the greatest emotion for the reader or audience. In the structure of the work it is where the crisis is reached and there is a turning-point in the plot which then brings about a resolution. See CRISIS, FREYTAG'S PYRAMID.

cloak-and-dagger

describes literature about spying or any similar secret plotting that appeals to feelings of curiosity, excitement and adventure.

closed couplet

a couplet in which the two lines make up a complete unit in both grammar and meaning. Alexander Pope was extremely versatile in using the closed couplet. Here are examples from his *Essay in Criticism* (1711):

> In ev'ry work regard the writer's End,
> Since none can compass more than they intend;
> And if the means be just, the conduct true,
> Applause, in spight of trivial faults is due.

See HEROIC COUPLET.

closet drama

a play with strong poetic influences that is written to be read rather than performed on stage. Milton's *Samson Agonistes* (1671) is a well-known example. Some authors have intended their plays for the stage but they are better as reading material; Alfred Lord Tennyson's *Becket* (1884) is a typical example.

close translation   See TRANSLATION.

cockney rhyme

a form of slang used by cockneys who are working-class people born in the eastern areas of central London. In it, rhyming words or phrases are substituted for common words, e.g. *fork and knife* for 'wife', *apples and pears* for 'stairs', *plates of meat* for 'feet'.

coda

a musical term that refers to the final, often most meaningful, part of a composition. Coda is now used in literature to refer to a final passage or part of a literary work that provides an essential summary or conclusion.

coffee house

any fashionable place in London in the 17th and 18th centuries where people could drink coffee and discuss literary and political issues. Some, like the Chapter Coffee House, Paternoster Row, became famous and were frequented by many well-known publishers and writers. The Bedford Coffee House in Covent Garden was also very popular with playwrights and authors.

coffee-table book

an illustrated book, usually large in size, intended to be looked through rather than read completely or seriously.

cognate

a noun used as the object of a verb that has the same etymological origins, e.g. *to think a **thought**.*

cognomen

a family name. Cognomen referred originally to an ancient Roman's third name, often a nickname or epithet, that would later become the family name.

cognoscenti   /kog-n*a*-**shen**-tee/

those people who have great knowledge or experience within a particular artistic or literary field.

coherent

describes a literary work that has a logical and consistent arrangement. This can be the selection and order of words and sentences, the relationship between the action and the personalities of the characters, or even the qualities in one particular character that make her or him credible. **coherence** noun.

cohesive device = CONJUNCT.

coined

describes a word or expression that has been deliberately invented, not one that has emerged naturally. Many coined words e.g. *video*, have been readily adopted but critics are generally opposed to writers who try to invent vocabulary. Lewis Carroll's highly imaginative inventions, e.g. *the Snark*, are exceptions. See also the first example at POETIC DICTION.

collaborate

to produce a literary or artistic work with another person. There have been many successful collaborations, including Beaumont (1584–1616) and Fletcher (1579–1625) and Gilbert (1836–1911) and Sullivan (1842–1900).

collage

a picture created by sticking pieces of paper, cloth etc onto a surface. In literature, collage is also used to refer to a work that is made up of lots of different parts: a variety of references, quotations, bits of foreign languages etc. See ECLECTIC. James Joyce and T S Eliot used this technique; here is the last section of T S Eliot's *The Waste Land* (1922):

London Bridge is falling down falling down falling down
Poi s'ascose nel foco che gli affina
Quando fiam uti chelidon – O swallow swallow
Le Prince d'Aquitaine à la tour abolie
These fragments have I shored against my ruins
Why then Ile fit you. Hieronymo's mad againe.
Datta. Dayadhvam. Damyata.
Shantih shantih shantih.

collect   /kol-ekt/

a short prayer used in church services before the epistle (a passage from one of the Epistles in the New Testament) at Communion. The collect changes at different times of the day.

collective noun

a word that names a group and is considered as a single unit, e.g. *herd, crowd, team, gang.*

If the use of the collective noun represents a general attitude (all the members together), it is used with a singular verb, as in *My family lives in London* or *The herd is in the lower field*. If the use refers more specifically to the individuals who make up the group, a plural verb is possible, as in *The team are willing to play in the rain* or *The majority are in favour* although a singular verb is also acceptable.

The pronoun used to substitute a collective noun can be *it* (when the verb is singular) or *they* (when the verb is plural).

collocation

a word used regularly with another, e.g. *blind* with *justice* as *blind justice* (but *deaf* with *justice* is not possible). **collocate** verb.

colloquial

describes vocabulary or a style of English used in ordinary conversation or informal writing. *Get lost!* is a colloquial equivalent of *Go away!*

colloquialism

a word or phrase used in colloquial English, e.g. *OK.*

colloquy   /kol-*a*-kwee/

a formal conversation, especially on religion, or literary work in the form of a dialogue. It has been used as the title of literary works, e.g. the Dutch humanist Erasmus' *Colloquies* (or *Colloquia*) (1519).

colon

the punctuation mark : used

a to introduce a list, summary or explanation with the meaning 'as follows', as in *Chekhov's Three Sisters are: Olga, Masha and Irena*.

b to introduce the explanation of a general statement, as in *I couldn't stop smiling: I had won the competition*.

c between the numbers in a ratio, e.g. *2:1* (two to one).

A colon can be replaced with a semicolon in **b**.

A colon is also used between the numbers representing the hours and minutes on a digital clock or watch.

colporteur   /**kol**-paw-t*a*/

a pedlar of bibles and other books during the 18th century.

column

1 a row of lines on a printed page. Most dictionaries have two columns of text on each page.

2 an article in a newspaper or magazine written regularly by a particular person or on a particular theme.

3 a vertical line of numbers.

columnist

a person who writes a regular column (2) in a newspaper or magazine.

combining form

a form of a word or prefix used to combine with another word to make compounds, as in *Afro-American*, *ambidextrous*, *multinational*.

Comédie Française, la

the French national theatre in Paris; it was founded in 1680.

comedy

any drama whose general purpose is amusement and entertainment and that ends happily. Comedies usually employ wit and humour to make the audience laugh but they may also simply present a cheerful view of life.

Comedy has a long history and was known in ancient Greece as early as the 5th century BC. Aristophanes is probably the best-known writer of comedies from that period; his plays include *The Birds* and *The Frogs*.

Shakespeare's comedies often end in marriage, a traditional form of happy ending. Ben Jonson, Shakespeare's contemporary, wrote many satirical comedies including *The Alchemist* (1610). Comedy has always remained popular with audiences; Alan Ayckbourn is a successful modern writer of social comedies using his keen perception of human behaviour. *Relatively Speaking* (1967) and *Just Between Ourselves* (1976) are two of his many successes. See BLACK, DRAWING-ROOM, FARCE, HIGH, LOW, MUSICAL, NEW, OLD, RESTORATION, ROMANTIC, SATIRICAL, SENTIMENTAL and SITUATION COMEDY; COMMEDIA DELL'ARTE and COMEDY OF HUMOURS, MANNERS and SITUATION.

comic

1 a comedian.
2 a book or magazine that contains comic strips.
3 'amusing' or 'funny', as in *a comic actor* or *a comic play*.

comic opera

an operetta that is a comedy. The best-known examples are those of W S Gilbert and Sir Arthur Sullivan including *HMS Pinafore* (1878), *The Mikado* (1885) and *The Yeoman of the Guard* (1888). These comic operas include a great deal of social and political satire.

comic relief

comic episodes or characters inserted in a serious, even tragic, literary work with the intention of providing the audience with a few moments of humour as a relief from the tension or suspense of the main action. These incidents, however, often link with the main themes.

A classic example of comic relief is the porter's scene in Shakespeare's *Macbeth*; it is a very welcome interlude after the tension of Duncan's murder. The porter's words, although amusing, still harmonize with the serious themes of the play.

comic strip

a series of drawings with the dialogue in speech bubbles, used to tell a funny story or the adventures of a particular hero or heroine.

comma

the punctuation mark , used
a to separate clauses or phrases, as in *When you get there, please phone me* or *To be honest, I don't like you.*
b to separate units in a list (but not before 'and'), as in *It was a long, difficult and lonely journey.*
c to separate a word, clause or phrase in the middle of a sentence, as in *At nine o'clock, however, I was still working* or *As I crossed the road, which was filled with traffic, a man's voice called my name.*
d when addressing a person, as in *Peter, come here* or *Sit down, all of you.*

e to separate supplementary additions, as in *You're right, of course! That's your mother, isn't it? Frankly, I couldn't care less* or *It was the same year as the strike, 1984.*

f after the first part of a quoted speech divided by *he said, I asked* etc, as in *'I know,' she whispered 'who murdered him'.*

g to write dates, e.g. *1 June, 1992.*

A comma must never separate a subject or object from its verb or an adjective from its noun. An apostrophe is often called a 'raised comma'. See QUOTATION MARKS.

commedia dell'arte   /ko-**mee**-di-*a* del-**aa**-tay/

a kind of popular light comedy or farce that dates from the 16th century in Italy. The dialogues were often improvised using repeated themes for plots, usually about love between familiar pairings such as master and maid and with stock characters including Harlequin and Punchinello. Successful performances depended on the quality of farce, clowning, amusing musical accompaniment and mime.

Travelling players spread commedia dell'arte throughout Europe where it influenced other dramatists including Shakespeare and Molière.

comment

an addition to a text that is an explanation or criticism.

common metre or common measure

a stanza with four lines, two with eight syllables (four iambs, ˘ — ˘ — ˘ — ˘ —) and two with six syllables (three iambs, ˘ — ˘ — ˘ —) with the rhyme scheme *a b a b*. See BALLAD METRE, SHORT MEASURE. It is often used for hymns, as in this one written by Isaac Watts:

> Ŏ Gōd, oŭr hēlp ĭn āgĕs pāst,
> Oŭr hōpe fŏr yēars tŏ cōme,
> Oŭr shēltĕr frōm thĕ stōrmў blāst,
> Ănd oūr ĕtērnăl home.

common noun

any noun used to refer to any one of a group, e.g. *book, city, experience, paper, system.*

commonplace book

a notebook used to keep quotations, notes etc that can be used for reference. Many authors, especially those writing historical or academic material, kept such books although the computer is now replacing them.

Commonwealth, the

the period when England was ruled by a Puritan Parliament led by Oliver Cromwell. It lasted from 1649 when King Charles I was executed until 1660 when King Charles II was restored to the throne. See PURITANISM.

In 1642, Cromwell had closed all theatres on the grounds that they were immoral. Apart from clandestine performances, there were no more drama productions – and no further editions of texts, including Shakespeare's plays. Poetry supported and reflected the Puritan beliefs of the period including early works by John Milton and John Bunyan. Abraham Cowley, Andrew Marvell, Henry Vaughan and Edmund Waller were also publishing poetry. During this period, prose thrived, the chief writers being Sir Thomas Browne, Jeremy Taylor and Izaak Walton. A major literary achievement was the publication of Thomas Hobbes' *Leviathan* (1651). See RESTORATION.

comparative, comparative degree or comparative form

the form of an adjective or adverb used to show that the quality mentioned is greater. When a word is short, especially with one syllable, its comparative form is usually made by adding -*er* (or -*r*, -*ier*), as in *shorter, larger, earlier*. For other words, use *more . . .* as in *more enthusiastic*. Some words have irregular forms such as *better* or *worse*.

comparison or degree of comparison

the positive, comparative and superlative forms of an adjective or adverb.

compendium

(two *compendiums* or *compendia*)
1 a book with informal and useful hints about an activity, especially sports and games.
2 an extensive summary of a larger piece of writing.

complaint

a kind of lament, often about the state of the world as well as personal misfortune. *Complaint of Deor*, written in Old English, is an early example. Chaucer wrote several. See JEREMIAD, LAMENT, PLAINT.

complement

a word or phrase, especially a noun or adjective, that follows a verb and gives information about the subject, as in *He became **a famous*** *writer* or *That smells good*. See COPULA, and OBJECT and SUBJECT COMPLEMENT.

composition

1 an essay produced as an educational exercise.
2 any literary work.
3 the parts that make up a literary work including settings, episodes and characters.

compound

a word formed by joining two or more other words, e.g. *airmail, ice-cream, head teacher, one-upmanship, never-ending*.

Notice that compounds can be written as one word with or without a hyphen, or as two separate words. There is still no agreement about which style is correct but one word without a hyphen is becoming popular. Whatever style you adopt, be consistent.

compound sentence

a sentence with two or more clauses, e.g. *I lifted the sheet and looked at her face*. See SIMPLE SENTENCE.

compressed simile   See METAPHOR.

compromiser

an adverb or adverbial phrase (an *intensifier*) that affects the meaning of a sentence by reducing the force of part of it but only slightly, e.g. *quite, mildly*, as in *I **quite** enjoyed it but I wouldn't go again* or *I'm **mildly** interested but not really*. See APPROXIMATOR, DIMINISHER, MINIMIZER.

conceit

an elaborate image or comparison that holds our attention because it is so unusual. It depends on the fact that the two things being compared are very different from each other.

The **Petrarchan conceit**, borrowed from the Italian poet Petrarch, was much used in Elizabethan love poetry. It was satirized by Shakespeare in his famous sonnet beginning:

> My mistress' eyes are nothing like the sun,
> Coral is far more red than her lips' red.

The conceit was frequently used by the metaphysical poets, who strived for originality. John Donne (1572–1631), one of the best known of the metaphysical poets, used many conceits in his verse. A famous example is from his *A Valediction Forbidding Mourning* (1633) where he compares the nature of his love with a pair of compasses:

> If they be two, they are two so
> As stiffe twin compasses are two,
> Thy soule the fixt foot, makes no show
> To move, but doth, if th'other doe.

Another of Donne's conceits can be found in his *The Second Anniversarie* (1612):

> Or as sometimes in a beheaded man,
> Though at those two Red seas, which freely ranne,
> One from the Trunke, another from the Head,
> His soule be sail'd, to her eternall bed.

Dr Johnson (1709–1784) disapproved of this kind of poetry and made a damning judgement of it. Of conceits he said, 'The most heterogeneous ideas are yoked by violence together'. In this he was probably echoing 18th century attitudes because by then the conceit had fallen out of fashion. It has been revived in the 20th century, most notably by T S Eliot in his *The Love Song of J Alfred Prufrock* (1917) with its famous example:

> When the evening is spread out against the sky
> Like a patient etherised upon a table.

conclusion

the final part of a lecture, essay or speech, or of a plot. This can include a summary of the main objectives and evaluation of its qualities; it can be simply a statement that concludes the argument, or that describes the effects of an incident or the whole action of a plot; it may be a summary of the writer's impressions of a character, of the potential results, good or bad, of a situation or a suggested course of action. See FREYTAG'S PYRAMID.

concord = AGREEMENT.

concordance

an alphabetical list of all the words used in a literary work or in the works of a particular writer. Included with the list is information such as frequency of use, references to particular works or passages, identification of interesting or frequent meanings etc.

An examination of concordances can help to establish the authorship of disputed works. It has been used, for example, to assess whether plays attributed to Shakespeare were written by him.

concrete noun

any noun that refers to something that can be seen, touched, heard, smelled or tasted, e.g. *box, cloud, animal, flower, scent*. See ABSTRACT NOUN.

conditional

the form of a sentence, clause, verb etc used to talk about the conditions for something happening, being possible, likely, allowed etc. See IF-CLAUSE.

A **conditional clause** is one that begins with *if, unless, when, whenever* etc, as in *If I pay, will you come with me? She won't come **unless** he apologizes, **When she cries**, she looks so ugly!* or *I throw up **whenever I travel in a boat**.*

A **conditional verb** is the verb form using *would* or *should* in conditional sentences, as in *If they asked me to lie, I would refuse. Should* can be used instead of *would* with *I* and *we* but *would* is becoming much more usual. See PERFECT and PRESENT CONDITIONAL TENSE.

confidant or confidante (female)

a character in a literary work who knows the private and personal thoughts, experiences, intentions and desires of another character. Horatio is Hamlet's confidant in Shakespeare's *Hamlet* and Emma is Harriet Smith's confidante in Jane Austen's *Emma* (1815).

conflate

to combine two versions of a text in order to produce a complete and comprehensive one. **conflation** noun.

conflict

the struggle between opposing forces in a literary work.

This struggle can be between two or more characters (Shakespeare's *King Lear* is full of this kind of conflict, e.g. between Lear and two of his daughters), the wills of two or more characters (as in Jane Austen's *Pride and Prejudice* (1813)) or between a character and her or his environment (in Flaubert's *Madame Bovary* (1857) the heroine finds her bourgeois society stifling) – these are described as *external conflicts*.

Or, the conflict can be within the character, e.g. between her or his conscience and personality (Shakespeare's *Hamlet* is mainly concerned with this personal struggle and Emily Brontë's novel *Wuthering Heights* (1847) concerns Heathcliff's struggle with his self-image, his great love for Catherine and his cruel temper) – this is described as *internal conflict*.

conjugation

the act or process of stating all the forms of a verb used to show person, tense etc. See DECLENSION. **conjugate** verb.

conjunct

an adverb or adverbial phrase that links what is being said with what has already been said, e.g. *Finally, ..., Nevertheless, ...* or *I often wonder, **though**, whether....* It can be left out without making the sentence ungrammatical.

A conjunct is less integrated in the structure than an adjunct (it is separated by a comma when it is in the initial position) and it cannot be contrasted with an alternative adverb in a question (e.g. you cannot say *Did she make the point finally or firstly?*). See ADJUNCT, DISJUNCT.

conjunction

a word used to join clauses in a sentence, e.g. *and, but, so,* as in *I ate it **and** I was sick, I like him **but** I don't trust him* or *We were late **so** we missed the bus.* See COORDINATING, CORRELATING and SUBORDINATING CONJUNCTION. **conjunctive** adjective.

connotation

the thoughts and ideas suggested by particular words and phrases. This is distinct from the literal meaning. For example, *greatness* has the connotation of 'importance' or 'fame' but *largeness* does not. Many words for animals have connotations, e.g. *snake* (a deceitful person) or *donkey* (a stupid or stubborn person). See DENOTATION. **connote** verb.

consciousness, stream of

a phrase taken from William James' *Principles of Psychology* (1890) that has become common in literary terminology where it refers to the attempt by novelists to reproduce the thoughts, impressions and ideas of a character's mind as they occur. James Joyce used this technique throughout his novel *Ulysses* (1922) whose narrative consists of the hero, Bloom's, thoughts, impressions and ideas. Almost any page shows an example:

> As they turned into Berkeley Street a street organ near the Basin sent over and after them a rollicking rattling song of the halls. Has anybody here seen Kelly? Kay ee double ll wy. Dead march from *Saul.* He's as bad as old Antonio. He left me on my ownio. Pirouette! The *Mater Misericordiae.* Eccles Street. My house down there. Big place. Ward for incurables there. Very encouraging. Our Lady's Hospice for the dying. Deadhouse handy underneath. Where old Mrs Riordan died.

This takes us inside the mind of Bloom, the main character. This stream of consciousness technique radically altered the nature of the novel by removing the novelist as a barrier between the reader and the characters.

One of the earliest experimenters with this technique was Dorothy Richardson in her 13-volume *Pilgrimage* (1915–1938), although as early as 1888 the French novelist Edouard Dujardin had used it, admittedly in an unpolished way, in a novel called *Les Lauriers sont coupés* and it proved very influential. Another well-known example of the use of stream of consciousness is in Virginia Woolf's *To the Lighthouse* (1927). It is now an established device in writing fiction. See INTERIOR MONOLOGUE.

consonance

1 harmony between sounds created by the choice of individual words or the chosen arrangement of words. See DISSONANCE.

2 similarity between, or repetition of, consonants but not vowels, as in 'tell-tale' or in this line from Dylan Thomas' *Refusal to mourn the death, by fire, of a child in London* (1946):

Deep with the first dead lies London's daughter

consonant

any letter, or its speech sound, that is not a vowel. See DOUBLING OF CONSONANTS.

construction

1 the way a group of words is put together to form a phrase, clause or sentence.

2 the meaning of a word, phrase or sentence, especially in its particular context.

contents

1 the parts, e.g. introduction, chapters, appendices etc, that make up a literary work. It is often produced as a list at the beginning of a book together with page numbers.

2 (also **content**) the meaning of a literary work, especially a poem, rather than its structure or style.

content word

a word with a meaning that is independent of any phrase or sentence it is used in, e.g. *baby, idea, swim*. See FUNCTION WORD.

contextualize

1 to put an event or incident in its setting, e.g. its historical context or in the context of the author's life.

2 to put a word in a typical context in order to illustrate its meaning, usage or grammatical function.

continuous tense

a verb form used to express an action or condition that continues or continued during a period of time. It is made up of a form of *be* and *-ing*, as in *am reading, were laughing, had been sleeping*. See FUTURE, PAST, PRESENT and FUTURE PERFECT CONTINUOUS TENSE; STATIVE VERB.

contract

a document that describes and confirms a formal agreement between people and organizations.

contraction

a short form of a word or group of words, e.g. *can't* for *cannot*, *he'll* for *he will*, *ne'er* for *never*.

contrast

the comparison of two or more different ideas, characters, styles etc in order to show or emphasize their respective qualities. Here is an example from W B Yeats' *Sailing to Byzantium* (1928) where youth and old age sit side by side (uneasily, in Yeats' view):

> That is no country for old men. The young
> In one another's arms, birds in the trees
> – Those dying generations – at their song.

conundrum

a riddle that includes a pun, e.g. '*When is a door not a door?*' '*When it's ajar*'. See PARAGRAM.

convention

1 a rule, usage, style etc that has been accepted by most people and is in general use. In Shakespeare's time it was a convention that only men acted on stage and so men played the female parts.
2 a device or method often used by a writer for a particular purpose. For example, a spoken description of a scene was a necessary convention in Shakespeare's time because there was very little scenery on the stage.
3 the generally accepted form of behaviour and manners, especially on formal occasions. It was a convention to wear brown shoes during the day but not the evening.
   conventional adjective.

conversational = COLLOQUIAL.

coordinate clause or independent clause

a clause that can be used by itself as a sentence and has the same status as another clause in a complex sentence, as in *He works well and he'll easily pass the exam.* See SUBORDINATE and MAIN CLAUSE.

coordinating conjunction or coordinator

a conjunction that joins coordinate clauses, e.g. *or, and, yet,* as in *I'll be in the library or I'll be in my room, I live in Paris and I stayed near the city centre or I tried many times yet it would not open.* See SUBORDINATING CONJUNCTION.

copula

a verb used to link a subject and a complement, e.g. *be, seem, taste,* as in *She is a good writer, It seems difficult* and *That tastes horrible.* **copulative** adjective.

copy

text that is ready to be printed, especially in a newspaper or advertising leaflet.

copybook

a book with exercises for learning how to write or do calligraphy.

copy edit = EDIT.

copyright

the legal right held exclusively by an author, publisher etc to produce a literary or artistic work. The symbol © is used to show who holds the copyright.

copywriter

a person whose job is to write text for advertising material. **copywriting** noun.

corn

sentimental and trite written or spoken language.

correlating conjunction or correlative

a conjunction used with other words to express a link between two or more ideas, e.g. *either ... or ...*, *neither ... nor ...*, *not only ... but ...* or *both ... and ....*

corrigendum = ERRATUM. /ko-ri-**dgen**-dəm/

(two *corrigenda*)

costume piece

a drama, film etc in which the characters wear clothes from an earlier period of history.

counterplot = SUBPLOT.

counterword

a word with a usage that is now much wider than its original meaning, e.g. *incredibly* (originally 'unbelievably' but now 'very').

count noun or countable noun

a noun that can be used with *a*, *an* or numbers and has a plural form, e.g. *girl*, *grade*, *problem*. These nouns can refer to a separate object or living thing such as *a book* or *a tree* or to a particular abstract concept such as *an idea* or *a thought*. See UNCOUNTABLE NOUN.

coup de théâtre   /**koo** da tay-aa-tra/

an unexpected event in a play that alters the plot. J B Priestley's *An Inspector Calls* (1946) ends with a coup de théâtre when a phone call reveals to the stunned characters that a tragic event which they believed was a hoax might be real after all.

couplet

a pair of lines in verse that rhyme. Whole poems have been written in couplets including many of Chaucer's *The Canterbury Tales* (c. 1387) in heroic couplets. Here is a modern example from T S Eliot's delightful *Macavity: The Mystery Cat* (1939):

> Macavity's a Mystery Cat: he's called the Hidden Paw –
> For he's the master criminal who can defy the Law.
> He's the bafflement of Scotland Yard, the Flying Squad's despair,
> For when they reach the scene of crime – *Macavity's not there!*

See OPEN, CLOSED, HEROIC and ELEGIAC COUPLET.

court circular

a daily publication of the official engagements of the monarch and senior members of the royal family.

courtly love

a system of courting and expressing love that is common in medieval literature, probably stemming from the lyric poetry of the troubadours in southern France in the 12th and 13th centuries.

It describes the love a man feels for a woman; this love causes great emotional pain together with physical symptoms such as aches, loss of appetite, paleness and sleeplessness. The man is inspired to perform heroic deeds and undergo suffering to prove the depth of his love. The expressions of their love, often between a man and a married woman, are made in secret and he will remain faithful whatever the obstacles or liabilities. The classic example is the Arthurian legend concerning Sir Lancelot's love for Queen Guinevere, King Arthur's wife.

All this is very different from the reality of medieval marriage in which the wife had to obey her husband in all things. However, it does suit the feudal aspect of medieval society in which a man serves his master or lord. He could also be influenced by the conventional adoration given at that time to the Virgin Mary.

Courtly love was treated in great detail in the French allegory *Roman de la Rose* (c. 1240–1280) which was partly translated by Chaucer. The conventions of courtly love are evident in Chaucer's own *Troylus and Cryseyde* (c. 1385). Two centuries later, Elizabethan love poetry continued to show the influences of courtly love.

cradle book = INCUNABULA.

Creole /kree-ohl/

1 the English dialect, both oral and written, used in parts of the Caribbean, southern United States, Sierra Leone etc by people of African descent. See PIDGIN ENGLISH.

2 the French dialect used by people of French descent in the south of the United States, especially Louisiana.

crime fiction = DETECTIVE FICTION.

crisis

(two *crises*)

the point in the conflict in a story or drama when there is the greatest struggle between opposing forces and after which there will be a resolution; a literary work can contain several crises. The crisis is an episode or event that is a critical point in the plot and the situation will either improve or deteriorate. A decision or action by a character will influence the timing as well as the type of climax. See FREYTAG'S PYRAMID.

critic

a person whose profession is literary criticism, who examines and judges the qualities of a literary work. In Britain, theatre critics are very influential in determining the success or otherwise of a play or theatrical performance; their views of current productions are widely read in newspapers and magazines, or discussed on television or the radio.

Some literary critics have become almost as famous as creative writers, e.g. William Empson (1906–1984) and his well-known text *Seven Types of Ambiguity* (1930), and F R Leavis (1895–1978) who taught at Cambridge University. He edited a well-known critical quarterly, *Scrutiny*, from 1932–1953 and published many books on literary criticism. He was extremely influential in establishing and re-establishing authors' reputations. Critics can affect the literary fashion and tastes of a period which in turn influences the work of contemporary writers.

criticism

the science of examining the good and poor qualities in order to judge a literary or artistic work. Criticism is an academic study; studying literature for examinations involves making critical judgements. Lecturers often publish their own works of criticism which introduce new ideas and approaches.

There are many possible ways to interpret and judge any literary work, even classic novels and drama. Often, a particular method is used because it suits the contemporary social attitudes, for example the objection to anything considered too emotional or sexually explicit during a period when society is generally rigid and conventional. At the present time, the emphasis has been on 'practical criticism' which analyses individual texts. See APPRECIATION.

critique

an essay or article that criticizes a literary work. This includes the good as well as the poor qualities.

crown of sonnets

a poem that contains seven sonnets with the last line of each sonnet repeated as the first line of the next one. The last line of the seventh sonnet is the opening line of the first one. A well-known example is John Donne's *La Corona* (1636).

cruelty, theatre of

drama based on ideas put forward in the French dramatist Antonin Artaud's series of essays *The Theatre and Its Double* (1938). Artaud hated the industrial society he lived in because it crushed creativity and natural artistic instinct. He argues that theatre must shock so that it can release a person's private emotions and inborn qualities, in this way acting as a sort of exorcism and creating 'an outlet for repression'. To this end, he maintained that scenery, lighting, music, movement and gesture are far more important than the text.

Artaud's theories had a particular influence on French dramatists such as Jean Genet and Albert Camus, but his effect on British theatre was far less obvious. The best-known example of a play influenced by Artaud is the German dramatist Peter Weiss' *Marat/Sade* (1964).

cryptic

describes a short expression, comment or description that is not easy to understand and needs careful thought.

cryptogram

a secret symbol, or set of symbols, used to write a code.

curiosa

literature about unusual topics, e.g. sexual deviation (and especially when treated erotically).

cursive

describes handwriting in the form of joined letters.

cursus

the rhythmic pattern of prose. See CADENCE.

curtain raiser

a short, separate piece at the beginning of a theatrical performance. It was performed to entertain the audience while waiting for latecomers and was often a one-act play. Curtain raisers are now rare, but the term is sometimes used of the first act in a variety show.

curtal sonnet

a shortened version of a sonnet, invented by Gerard Manley Hopkins (1844–1889). Instead of fourteen lines, he used ten and a half, the first verse being six lines long and the second four lines with a 'half line tailpiece'. In his *Poems (1876–1889)* there are two curtal sonnets, *Peace* and *Pied Beauty.*

cycle

a set of stories, poems or plays with the same theme, especially a significant character or event. Early examples are the Arthurian legends, or the mystery plays which are dramatizations of biblical events.

cyclic poets

a group of very early classical Greek poets whose works (called the *epic cycle*) form a history of the ancient world up to that time.

Though some of these epic poems were at first attributed to Homer, a closer study of the texts shows qualities that contrast with Homer's style and content. Significant poems in the series included those on *The Trojan War* (?8th and 7th centuries BC) and *The Argonauts* (?6th century BC).

cyclopaedia

(two *cyclopaedias* or *cyclopaediae*)
a rare alternative for *encyclopaedia*. **cyclopaedic** adjective.

cyclorama

a curtain or wall used as the background on a stage. It is usually designed to represent the sky and lit in a way that gives the stage extra depth and height.

cynical

describes any writer or piece of writing that expresses strong doubt about goodness in people.

cypher = CIPHER.

D

dactyl

a metrical foot with a stressed syllable followed by two unstressed syllables ($\bar{}\ \smile\ \smile$). See ANAPAEST, ELEGIAC COUPLET, METRE. **dactylic** adjective.

dangler

a word or phrase that is separated from the rest of the sentence (often as a modifier), e.g. **Suddenly**, *I heard a child scream.* Danglers (see HANGING PARTICIPLE) can produce humour, intended or not, because of their separation and the possibility of ambiguity, e.g. **Crossing the desert**, *the palm trees grewer smaller and smaller.*

danse macabre or dance of death

a dramatic scene in which living people, in order of social rank, are led in a procession or dance to their graves by a figure or figures representing 'Death'.

It probably emerged from medieval France where it was first performed as a mimed sermon about the inevitability of death and the necessity for repentance; it also illustrated that a person is equal to any other person in death.

The danse macabre is used in verse, song, book illustration, painting, carving, embroidery etc, and was very popular up to the 16th century. It was adapted by Chaucer for his *The Pardoner's Tale* (c. 1387).

Dark Ages, the

the period of European history from about 500 AD (the collapse of the Roman Empire) to about 1300 AD (the early beginnings of the Renaissance). It had been described as a period of little academic achievement or writing of value, but modern scholars do not consider this period to be a time of intellectual or creative poverty and therefore no longer use the description 'dark'.

dark comedy   See BLACK COMEDY.

dash

the punctuation mark – or — used

a at either end of a phrase or clause that is a separate or extra comment, piece of information etc, as in *We tried — in spite of all the difficulties — to get the injured driver out of the car.*

b to separate an explanation, conclusion, example etc from the first part of the sentence, as in *Three countries abstained — Britain, Denmark and Greece.*

c to show a clear break in thought, as in *She refused to sign — what an extraordinary decision!*

d to show a deliberate omission, as in *I don't give a d—!*

e to show a sudden and unexpected end to a speech, as in *'I give all my wealth to —' and she died.*

In formal writing, parentheses or commas are preferred for **a**, a colon or semicolon for **b** and a full stop or semicolon for **c**.

dead metaphor   See METAPHOR.

decadent

describes the deterioration in standards that often marks the closing of a period of literary, artistic or historical greatness. An example is the period after Elizabethan drama when less importance was given to critical standards, when there was less commitment to accepted poetic and dramatic forms and no respect for the texts of earlier great works. At that time, Shakespeare's plays were rewritten and produced as spectacular melodramas that were unrecognizable versions of his original plays. One highly successful version of his *King Lear* created a romance between Cordelia and Edgar and even restored Lear to the throne!

The last years of the 19th century in England are sometimes described as decadent because of the relaxing of strict Victorian morality shown by the pursuit of romance, excitement, humour and the exotic, and the freedom of individual expression from academic tradition. Oscar Wilde (1854–1900) wrote his plays and poems during this time. See YELLOW BOOK.

But **Decadent** is used principally of the literary movement in France during this same period when poets such as Baudelaire (1821–1867) and Verlaine (1844–1896) sought the freedom of the arts from the strict bourgeois values that dominated French society at that time. These writers aimed to prove that freedom of artistic expression and the free expression of personal feelings do not produce a decline in literary standards.

decasyllabic

describes a line of verse with ten syllables, as in the opening lines of Wordsworth's sonnet XXXIII *The World is Too Much With Us* (1807):

> The world is too much with us; late and soon,
> Getting and spending, we lay waste our powers.

declarative

a sentence that states a fact. Some sentences either begin by stating a fact (*declarative*) and end by asking a question (*interrogative*), as in *I wanted to go, but was it a good idea?* or begin by asking a question and end by stating a fact, as in *Isn't it odd how rain makes you miserable, that's what happens to me.* Note that a question mark is not used here.

A **declarative question** has the same grammatical form as a statement but has a question mark so that it is read or spoken as a question, e.g. *So you think it's my fault?*

declension

the act or process of changing the endings of nouns or pronouns for case, gender and number in some inflected languages such as German and Latin. Declension can also refer to the complete set of possible forms for any noun or pronoun. See CONJUGATION. **decline** verb.

deconstruction or **poststructuralism**

the method for studying literature that develops the principles of structuralism and shows their limitations. It is agreed that language is a system of signs that only have meaning in relation to each other. However, this cannot be applied to texts since it assumes a strict logical approach to language that is not possible.

Structuralism, when considering texts in terms of opposites and contrasts, assumes logical certainties when there are none. By identifying elements in a text that do not fit a logical structure, it is shown that the text 'deconstructs' under this kind of critical examination. This is not necessarily destructive; on the contrary, it illustrates the endless possible interpretation of the text.

Like structuralism, deconstruction is a difficult subject. The important books to read are Jacques Derrida's *Grammatology* (1967), *Writing and Difference* (1967) and *Speech and Phenomena* (1967). See STRUCTURALISM.

deep structure

the presentation of words in a sentence to show grammatical and syntactic relationships in order to explain the general rules and limitations of grammatical choice. See SURFACE STRUCTURE.

defective verb

a verb that does not have the usual range of forms. For example, modal auxiliary verbs (*can, might, should* etc) have no infinitive or participles, and *must* has no infinitive, participles or past forms.

defining relative clause = RESTRICTIVE RELATIVE CLAUSE.

definite article

the word *the* (see DETERMINER). It is pronounced /thee/ before a vowel or a silent *h*, as in *the arts*, or *the honourable speaker*.

The is used

a to refer to a particular person or thing, as in *the clever one* or *the worst performance*.

b when a listener or reader knows which person or thing is being referred to, as in *Did you enjoy the book?* If a person or thing is referred to for the first time and is not yet known, *a* or *an* is used, but when he, she or it is mentioned again *the* is used, as in *A year later she wrote a play ... The play has been a big success*.

c to refer to a unique person or thing, e.g. *the sun, the Globe theatre, the Elizabethan period, the works of Shakespeare* or *the poet laureate*.

d to refer to a part of the body as in *functions of the liver* or *a diagram of the brain*.

e to refer to people in a definite group (using a plural form of the verb), as in *The rich are getting richer* or *The British are reserved*.

f to refer to a whole class or group (using a singular form of the verb), as in *The elephant is in danger of extinction* or *The oak is an attractive tree*.

g to refer to an abstract as in *the good in people* or *the joy in her heart*.

h to refer to seasons, as in *during (the) winter* (where 'the' can be left

out) or to a period of time, as in *in the afternoon*, and position or direction, as in *at the centre, on the edge, from the beginning* and *towards the south* (where *the* cannot be left out).
i as part of a placename, e.g. *the Alps, the Mediterranean, the Sahara, the British Isles, the Danube* or *the Far East*, but not with towns, cities, continents and most countries (an exception is *the USA*).
j with *learn, play* etc and a musical instrument, as in *learn the guitar* or *play the piano*.
k in many fixed phrases, e.g. *make the bed, listen to the radio* or *be paid by the hour*.
   Never use *the* when giving an opinion about something general, as in *A good education is essential* or *Man is mortal* (but *the* can be used about a particular thing or condition, as in *The economy is in a mess*).

definite noun

a noun that is always used with *the*, e.g. *the moon* or *the north*. These nouns are used with a singular verb. Those that use a plural verb, e.g. *the blind*, are referred to as *definite plurals*. See ZERO PLURAL.

definite plural

a noun that is always used with *the* and a plural verb, e.g. *the poor, the Chinese*. See ZERO PLURAL.

degree

any of the forms of an adjective used to show different grades or amounts of intensity; the three degrees in English are:
positive, as in *big, bad, good*.
comparative, as in *bigger, worse, better* and also *more . . . .*
superlative, as in *biggest, worst, best* and also *most . . . .*
   An **adverb of degree**, e.g. *very, rather, well, scarcely* or *too*, is an intensifier that modifies other adverbs, as in ***very** quietly*, adjectives, as in ***rather** cold*, and sometimes particles in multi-word verbs, as in *hammer it **well** in* or similar fixed verbal expressions, as in *be **well** off*. See ADVERB.

deictic   /diek-tik/

describes a word used to indicate a person or thing in a context, e.g. ***That** is the cause of the leak* or ***Here** is the one you chose*.

deism   /day-izm/

belief in God based on what can be learned from the natural world; God is responsible for the existence of the universe and its natural laws, but there has been no Christian revelation or divine Bible. **deist** adjective and noun.

The **Deists** were a group of writers who lived from the end of the 17th to the late 18th centuries led by Lord Herbert of Cherbury (1583–1648). Their writing influenced poets and essayists; a love of nature and interest in man's perfection, characteristic of the Romantics, owes much to the philosophy of the Deists.

demonstrative or demonstrative adjective/pronoun

this or *that*, and their plural forms *these* or *those* (as adjectives or pronouns) used to point out particular ones, as in ***This*** *is easier to cook than* ***that***, ***This*** *is my mother*, ***That*** *sounds like the postman*, ***Those*** *students who have paid can collect their tickets.*

demotic

describes language or script used by ordinary people, not in special contexts such as diplomacy, the church etc, especially *demotic Greek* (not classical Greek) and *demotic Egyptian hieroglyphics.*

denotation

the specific meaning of a word or phrase as given in a dictionary. See CONNOTATION.

denouement or dénouement   /day-**noo**-mon/

the final unwinding of the plot of a play or novel, usually after the climax. It includes the outcome together with explanations of any mysteries or problems, especially in detective fiction. Dénouement means 'unknotting' in French. The last act of Shakespeare's *Measure for Measure* is a particularly action-packed denouement. See FREYTAG'S PYRAMID.

dependent clause = SUBORDINATE CLAUSE.

derivative

1 describes a style, plot, idea for a literary work etc that is based on an existing work and is copied without any attempt at originality.
2 a word derived from another word, e.g. *descriptive* from *description*. **derivation** noun.

derogative

(of) a word or phrase used to criticize or express an unfavourable opinion of a person or thing, e.g. *native* used to label a nonwhite person. **derogatory** adjective.

description

the part of a literary work that describes the characters, settings or events. It is an essential feature, used to obtain and hold the reader's attention.

Charles Dickens provided powerful and imaginative descriptions of characters, linking physical characteristics with their personalities. For example, Mrs Joe Gargery, Pip's stepmother in *Great Expectations* (1860–1861) is physically unattractive which is wholly appropriate for her harsh and unloving personality. **descriptive** adjective.

descriptive linguistics

the study of the grammatical and semantic features of a language without reference to its origins or development. See HISTORICAL LINGUISTICS.

detective fiction

novels, stories or plays in which the plot involves committing a crime, the mystery surrounding the event, and the solution to the crime by a detective. A common characteristic of such literature is a reversal of the familiar plot sequence – the catastrophe occurs at the beginning.

There are recognized elements in judging detective fiction:

a the facts or qualities that make the crime interesting or exciting.

b the logic of the plot with the unravelling of clues and the rejection of red herrings (false pieces of information given to take attention away from the correct clues) so that the reader or audience can solve the crime 'in competition with' the author's detective.

c the strong and clear personality of the detective who is often eccentric or extraordinary.

d the interest in the general setting of the story or play, and the desire to have the crime solved.

Edgar Allan Poe produced the first recognized detective story with his *Murders in the rue Morgue* (1841), and Wilkie Collins' *The Moonstone* (1868) was the first English detective novel. At this time Émile Gaboriau introduced detective fiction into France with his *L'Affaire Lerouge* (1866) and *Monsieur Lecoq* (1869) among a string of successful novels. Sir Arthur Conan Doyle's creation of the enormously popular amateur detective Sherlock Holmes who appeared in many tales at the end of the 19th century, encouraged an abundant flow of detective fiction that remains extremely popular today.

There are many 20th century authors of international renown including Agatha Christie (and her detective Hercule Poirot), Georges Simenon (and his detective Maigret) and the American Raymond Chandler (and his detective Philip Marlowe). P D James (and her detective Adam Dalgliesh) and Ruth Rendell (and her detective Inspector Wexford) are two very popular and successful current authors.

determiner

a word used before a noun or noun phrase to refer to a particular example, kind, group, quantity etc. Determiners can be:
articles, *a*, *an*, *the*.
demonstratives, *this*, *that*, *these*, *those*.
possessives, e.g. *my*, *its*.
None of these determiners can be used together.

Another set of determiners includes *some*, *each*, *every*, *many*, *few*, *another*, *enough*, *several* and numbers. These determiners can also be used as pronouns, and as pronouns they are often followed by 'of', as in **some** *of them*, **enough** *of it*, **seven** *of the questions*.

The determiners *all*, *both* and *half* can be used as pronouns with 'of' but 'of' can be omitted, as in **all** *(of) this group*, **both** *(of) the wheels*, **half** *(of) its length* except when using personal pronouns, as in **all** *of us*, **both** *of them*, **half** *of it*. See PREDETERMINER.

deverbal or deverbal noun

describes a noun that ends in *-ing* and could be replaced by any noun with a similar meaning, e.g. *writing* in *the writings of Shakespeare* where *writings* could be replaced by *works*, *plays* etc. See VERBAL.

diacritic

a mark put above or below a letter to show that it has a particular sound value, e.g. ⎺ or ˘ used above letters in lines of verse to show stressed and unstressed syllables.

diaeresis   /die-e-ra-sis/

(two *diaereses*)
the mark ¨ placed above the second of a pair of vowels to show that each is pronounced separately, as in *naïve*. Today, most writers no longer use a diaeresis. See UMLAUT.

dialectic

a method of logical debate in order to arrive at true facts using rules of question and answer. It can be the method of the ancient Greek philosopher Socrates (c. 469–399 BC) who asked particular questions in order to obtain from his pupils the basic truths he considered that everyone should know implicitly. Or, it can be that used by the German philosopher Hegel who established a logical method of argument in his *Logic* (1812–1816).

Dialectic is also used to describe the logical thought and ideas contained in any literary work, e.g. the dialectic in S T Coleridge's *Biographia Literaria* (1817).

dialogue

1 a conversation in a drama, novel or story. It can be judged by considering whether it

a offers new or alternative methods for judging character or understanding events;

b is suitable for the personalities, social background and interests of the participants;

c is suitable for the historical period it is set in;

d makes a positive contribution towards the play or novel;

e contains enough variety in vocabulary, structure and rhythm to be interesting;

f is not a distraction from the action of the plot or subplots.

Remember that dialogues are often used as a means of creating a pause during more condensed or profound passages.

2 a formal or serious discussion or 'debate with oneself' on a particular topic. The ancient Greek philosopher Plato's *Dialogues* (4th century BC) are philosophical debates (see DIALECTIC) and the device was adapted by later philosophers such as David Hume in his *Dialogues Concerning Natural Religion* (1779) and also by playwrights such as G B Shaw in his *The Apple Cart* (1929).

diatribe

a long abusive attack during an argument.

diction

1 the selection and use of vocabulary in discourse. See POETIC DICTION. Diction can be judged according to whether

a the selected words and phrases are suitable for the characters and the setting;

b these words and phrases are successful in creating or reflecting a particular atmosphere, and are clearly understood;

c these words and phrases are generally considered to be good English and, if not, this is because the character or situation makes it necessary to include nonstandard usages or vulgarities.

2 the way each person pronounces words and sounds.

dictum

a serious and true statement based on experience of life, e.g. *History repeats itself, first as a tragedy and then as a farce.*

digest

1 a book, magazine etc that is a set of abridged books, essays etc.

2 a single article that is a summary or abridgement and contains the main or important facts.

digression

any incident or period during the action of a literary work of turning away from the main plot, subject, tone of speech etc.

dimeter

a line of verse with two metrical feet, as in the third and fourth lines of a limerick. See METRE.

diminisher

an adverb or adverbial phrase (an *intensifier*) that affects the meaning of a sentence by reducing the force of part of it, e.g. *partly* or *to some extent* as in *He **partly** understands* or *It's your fault **to some extent***. Diminishers are not as strong as minimizers. See DOWNTONER.

diminishing metaphor

a figure of speech when imagery is used in a context that appears to be illogical or unsuitable because it seems banal but results in a clever and effective metaphor. A highly original example is in Stevie Smith's poem *The Bereaved Swan* (1937):

> Wan
> Swan
> On the lake
> Like a cake
> Of soap.

diminutive

a word, or ending of a word, used to indicate a small size, a young age, a low level of importance etc, e.g. *flatlet, baby talk*. Diminutives are often used as expressions of affection or to refer to qualities that may seem negative but are permissible, endearing or familiar.

diphthong

a vowel sound made by moving the position of your tongue and lips so that there is a change in the vowel quality as it is uttered, e.g. the vowel sounds in *page, home, dive, cow, joint, here, pair* and *cure*.

A diphthong is often similar to uttering two vowel sounds one after the other very quickly. For example, the *e* sound of *egg* followed quickly by the *e* sound of *the* makes the diphthong in *there*.

dipody

a unit of verse that contains a pair of metrical feet. Dipody also refers to verse in which pairs of metrical feet are considered as the basic units.

It is very common in nursery rhymes and ballads, as in this traditional nursery rhyme:

> The Queen of Hearts, | she made some tarts
> All on a summer's day;
> The Knave of Hearts, | he stole the tarts
> And took them quite away.

direct object

a noun, pronoun or noun phrase to which the action of the verb in a sentence is directly related, as in *He kicked **the ball*** or *She gave it **a good shake***. See INDIRECT OBJECT.

directory

a publication that contains an organized list of names, addresses etc, e.g. *a telephone directory*.

direct question

any question used in direct speech, e.g. *Where did you put it?* See INDIRECT SPEECH.

direct speech

a style of writing in which a person's exact words are stated, e.g. *'I refuse to come,' she said* or *'I agree with you,' I wrote*. See INDIRECT SPEECH.

dirge

a solemn song or chant at a funeral. Its earliest recorded use is at ancient Greek and Roman funeral processions, but the dirge later developed as a short lyrical poem and can also be found in plays such as Shakespeare's *The Tempest*. See ELEGY, LAMENT, MONODY, THRENODY.

disclaimer

a deliberate written or spoken denial, especially one expressing a company's denial of responsibility, used to protect against legal claims.

discourse

a formal and intellectual exchange or discussion such as Izaak Walton's discourse on fishing *The Compleat Angler* (1653) in the form of a dialogue between a fisherman and hunters. It can also be a serious and formal treatise such as Descartes' *Discourse on Method* (1637).

Modern linguists also use discourse to refer to any set of sentences in speech or writing.

discourse marker

a word or phrase that links what is being stated with other factors about the discourse but is not essential to the meaning.

A discourse marker can have many purposes:

a Some link what was said before with what will be stated, e.g. *Nevertheless...* and *All the same ....*

b Some identify the attitude of the speaker or writer, e.g. *Frankly,...* and *I'm afraid that ....*

c Some show a logic arrangement or sequence, e.g. *Therefore...* and *First of all ....*

d Some signal a contrast in opinion or action, e.g. *However,...* and *But at the same time ....*

e Some identify a general statement, e.g. *In most instances ....*

f Some show that what was stated before will be repeated in a different way, e.g. *In other words, ...*

g Some show a complete change of topic, e.g. *Incidentally,...* and *That reminds me, ...*

h Some show that expectations were met, as in *Actually, I enjoyed it very much*, or not met, as in *To tell the truth, it was boring*.

These discourse markers are an essential element in natural, idiomatic use of language.

disjunct

an adverb or adverbial phrase that expresses an opinion of how something was done or an opinion of its context, e.g. **Luckily,...** or *I cleverly changed the subject*. It can be left out without making the sentence ungrammatical. A disjunct is often used in the initial position.

It is less integrated in the structure than an adjunct (it is separated by a comma when it is in the initial position). See ADJUNCT, CONJUNCT.

disjunctive

describes a word, especially a conjunction, used to show contrast or opposition, as in *She was clever **but** lazy*.

dissertation

a detailed and formal account of a piece of academic research; it is prepared for the award of an academic qualification. See ESSAY.

dissonance

a harsh and unpleasant sound or pattern created by the choice of individual words or the chosen arrangement of words. See CONSONANCE (1).

Dissonance is sometimes used deliberately in poetry to create a particular effect, as in these opening lines from one of Gerard Manley

Hopkins' so-called 'terrible' sonnets (number 42) (c. 1885) in which the harshness of the sounds reflects his mood of despair:

> No worst, there is none. Pitched past pitch of grief,
> More pages will, schooled at forepangs, wilder wring.

distich   /dis-tik/

a pair of rhyming lines used to express a truth, rule of behaviour or principle, e.g. this translation of the ancient poet Callimachus' *Nicoteles* (3rd century BC):

> Philip's Nicoteles, a twelve-year lad
> Lies buried here: the hope his father had.

D-notice

a British government notice to journalists that prohibits the publication of information that could threaten national security.

do.

an abbreviation from Italian *detto* for the Latin *dictus* meaning 'the same as the above', used in lists to avoid repeating a word, phrase etc.

The symbol ʺ (called **ditto marks**) is put under the word or words that are repeated.

doctrinaire

describes a speech or piece of writing that is theoretical and insists on strict attachment to a philosophical political or religious doctrine. Because of this, the idea or argument is often impractical and narrow and therefore unsuitable.

document

1 an official paper, booklet etc that contains information, a report etc, e.g. a contract.
2 to provide references, proof etc to support a theory or idea in a book, essay, film etc, e.g. *a thesis that is documented clearly*.
3 to report the details of an item of news in the media, as in *The famine was well documented on television*.

documentary

a factual account of an event, person's life, organization etc with no, or very little, fictional content. It is usually a television programme. Documentaries often use evidence provided by investigative journalists, official reports, statistics and personal diaries to examine social, political and environmental issues, influential personalities, large government and commercial institutions and particular careers and professions.

More recently, a documentary can be a play, film or novel that presents factual evidence in a setting that has sufficient fictional elements to create a good dramatic or literary piece. This kind of writing (often called *documentary drama*) can result in powerful television programmes that bring an issue to the attention of a much wider audience. See FACTION.

doggerel

verse that expresses trivial sentiment in the context of a weak subject-matter. Such verse usually has an awkward or monotonous rhyme and rhythm. A few have been accepted as comic verse. A well-known example of intentional doggerel is in Samuel Butler's satirical poem, *Hudibras* (1663–1678). But here is a delightful lighthearted example by Hattie Jacques in *Milligan's Ark* (1971):

> When porcupines are
> a little bit sickerly
> They are not
> so blooming prickerly.

Domesday Book, or Doomsday Book, the

the survey carried out in 1086 by order of King William I of England. It included information about the population, livestock and buildings in England and was used to assess taxation.

domestic drama

drama that concerns the everyday lives of people, especially in familiar situations. Earliest examples have upper and middle-class settings, as in Goldsmith's *She Stoops to Conquer* (1773), and such settings were still popular much later, for example in some of Noel Coward's plays written in the 1930s and 1940s.

More recent examples concern the lives of ordinary people. These include the work of Tennessee Williams and Arthur Miller in the USA, Jean Anouilh in France, and Terence Rattigan and John Osborne in Britain. See DRAWING-ROOM COMEDY, KITCHEN-SINK DRAMA.

Domestic tragedy involves tragedy within families or the personal affairs of ordinary people rather than within countries, grand events, royalty or the nobility. It was popular from the end of the 16th century in England, e.g. Thomas Heywood's *A Woman Killed with Kindness* (1607).

Domestic tragedy is still used to describe the work of Henrik Ibsen, Eugene O'Neill, John Osborne, Arthur Miller and others.

double entendre   /**doo**-bl*a* aan-**taan**-dr*a*/

a word or phrase with more than one interpretation of which one is usually indecent. It is often the result of careless choice of vocabulary but it is sometimes used deliberately for comic effect. Shakespeare's *Romeo and Juliet* is full of double entendres, particularly during the first half of the play when Mercutio is alive. Here is a well-known example from a conversation between Peter, a servant, and Juliet's nurse. Peter says:

> I saw no man use you at his pleasure. If I had, my weapon should quickly have been out.

Although Peter is referring to fighting, his words have a sexual undertone.

double negative

a grammatical construction using two negatives to express a negative idea when in fact the negatives cancel each other out, e.g. *I won't have none of your rudeness, You can't come, under no circumstances* or *I won't tell you nothing!* Such usages are errors but may be used for dramatic effect or to show speech from a particular social, usually lower, class.

double rhyme = FEMININE RHYME.

doubling of consonants

the repetition of the final letter (a consonant) of some words when forming a present participle (before -*ing* as in *shopping, swimming*), the past tense (before -*ed* as in *grabbed, signalled*), and the comparative and superlative forms of some adjectives (*bigger, fattest*).

The basic rule is, double the consonant only if
a the word is short and the vowel sound is spelled with one letter, as in *betting* but not *beating*.
b the word has a stressed final vowel sound that is also spelled with one letter, as in *preferred* but not *developed*.

The common exception is words ending in -*el* when British users double the final *l*, as in *travelled*, but North Americans do not, as in *traveled*.

Finally, verbs ending in -*ic* form the present participle and past tense by changing -*ic* to -*ick*-, as in *panicking, picnicked*.

downtoner

an adverb or adverbial phrase (an *intensifier*) that affects the meaning of a sentence by decreasing the force of part of it. See APPROXIMATOR, COMPROMISER, DIMINISHER, MINIMIZER. The opposite of a downtoner is an *amplifier*.

draft

an outline or trial copy of a speech or piece of writing.

drama

literature written to be performed on a stage.

Drama has a very long history dating from the ancient Greek writers who were themselves influenced by performances during even older religious and cult festivals. Medieval drama also finds its origins in earlier religious ceremonies.

There was a revival of classical influences during the Renaissance and this period of great cultural interest and activity produced the outstanding dramas of the Elizabethan Age in England. The next flowering of English drama occurred during the Restoration period, when Charles II who came to the throne in 1660 reopened the theatres after their closure by the Puritans. Plays at this time tended to be witty and stylish comedies. Heroic drama also enjoyed a brief popularity at this time. The neoclassical period saw a return to classical values.

The 19th century experienced little of dramatic importance until towards the end of the century when a relaxation in rigid Victorian morality provided the opportunity for amusing and romantic plays using real life situations. Modern drama continues to reflect everyday life in both tragedy and comedy, and is particularly noted for experimental dramatic works.

See ABSURD, COMEDY, CRUELTY, KABUKI, MASQUE, MUMMERY, NŌ, PANTOMIME, TRAGEDY and TRAGI-COMEDY; CLOSET, DOMESTIC, FOLK, HEROIC, KITCHEN-SINK, LITURGICAL and MEDIEVAL DRAMA; CHRONICLE, MIRACLE, MORALITY, MYSTERY, ONE-ACT and PASSION PLAY.

dramatic irony

a device used in drama when the audience is aware of the true significance of what a character is saying, or of the true circumstances at the time, but one or more of the characters on stage is not.

The whole of the ancient Greek playwright Sophocles' *Oedipus the King* (5th century BC) is based on dramatic irony. The audience knows from the beginning that Oedipus is doomed and when he sets in motion the search for a murderer, the audience knows that it is he who has committed the murder. Dramatic irony of this kind increases considerably the tension in the theatre.

In Shakespeare's *Macbeth*, after the murdered body of Duncan has been found, Macbeth, who is the murderer, makes a speech to the assembled company with the intention of hiding his guilt and trying to show sorrow. The speech, however, is full of dramatic irony; unknown to Macbeth, he is speaking the truth:

> Had I but died an hour before this chance,
> I had liv'd a blessed time; for, from this instant,
> There's nothing serious in mortality;
> All is but toys; renown, and grace, is dead;
> The wine of life is drawn, and the mere lees
> Is left this vault to brag of.

There is also a delightful moment of dramatic irony in Shakespeare's comedy *Twelfth Night* when everyone except the pompous and unpopular Malvolio knows that the happiness he is expecting is based on a fake letter.

Dramatic irony can, of course, be applied to prose. Evelyn Waugh's *A Handful of Dust* (1934) contains many examples, particularly concerning the unexpected death of the child John Andrew who has been allowed to follow the hunt. One of the best examples is:

> (John Andrew) 'If I'm in at the death I expect Colonel Inch will blood me.' 'You won't see any death' said Nanny.

dramatic monologue

a poem that consists of a speaker (not the poet) who is at a significant point in her or his life and is addressing an audience about the situation. Although there may be references to others, there is no other speaker. The type of audience is not known to the reader.

The main purpose of a dramatic monologue is to allow the speaker to reveal, often without realizing it, a great deal about her or his personality. Although we are made to see everything through the speaker's perspective, we do not have to accept her or his point of view.

Robert Browning perfected the dramatic monologue; one of his most famous and successful is *My Last Duchess* (1842) in which the speaker is a particularly unpleasant Renaissance duke.

dramatic unities   See UNITIES.

dramatis personae   /draa-m*a*-tis p*a*-**soh**-nie/

a list of all the names of the characters in a play. It includes the names of the actors when it is produced as part of a theatre programme or publicity for a performance.

dramatist = PLAYWRIGHT.

dramatize

to create a play or screenplay using a story or novel. See DOCUMENTARY. **dramatization** noun.

drawing-room comedy

a kind of comedy in which the setting is the home, usually the living-room. It concerns everyday lives of middle-class people. Noel Coward's *Hay Fever* (1925) and Tom Stoppard's *The Real Inspector Hound* (1968) are good examples. See DOMESTIC DRAMA.

dream allegory or dream vision

a kind of narrative in which the writer falls asleep and dreams a story. It was very popular in medieval England, and William Langland's *Piers Plowman* (c. 1360–1399) is the best-known early example. John Bunyan's *The Pilgrim's Progress* (1678) and Lewis Carroll's *Alice's Adventures in Wonderland* (1865) are also well known. This kind of narrative continues to be very popular, especially in children's fiction, and has been used successfully in films such as *The Wizard of Oz* (1939).

duologue

a conversation between two characters, especially when the conversation is a major part, or all, of a drama.

durative

an adverb or adverbial phrase (an *adjunct*) that expresses or measures duration, e.g. *We've slept **a long time*** or ***How long** can you wait?* A durative may also be an *intensifier*, as in *Last night, I danced **a lot***, or a *booster* as in ***a lot of** dancing*.

dust jacket

a paper cover used round a hardback. Although it originally consisted of plain paper used to protect the binding, it has quickly developed as an important means of attracting the reader and buyer by including highly decorative lettering and design. Many dust jackets support the well-known saying 'Don't judge a book by its cover'.

dynamic verb

a verb used to express activity including actions, processes and sensations as in *I **washed** the car*, ***Stand up!***, *The tree **grew***, and *My head **aches***. Dynamic verbs can be used in the continuous tenses, e.g. *I'm **washing** the car*, and those expressing action can have an imperative form, e.g. ***Wash** it!* See STATIVE VERB.

dyslexia

serious difficulty in reading and spelling (also called *word blindness*) caused by a brain disorder. See ALEXIA.

E

echo verse

a poem made up of lines with the final word or syllable repeated as if it is an echo; the repeated sound produces a change in meaning. Here is a well-known example from Swift's *A Gentle Echo on Woman*:

> Shepherd:
>   Echo, I ween, will in the woods reply,
>   And quaintly answer questions: shall I try?
>   Echo: Try
>   What must we do our passion to express?
>   Press
>   How shall I please her, who ne'er loved before?
>   Be Fore
>   What most moves women when we them address?
>   A dress
>   Say, what can keep her chaste whom I adore?
>   A door

eclectic

describes a piece of writing (as well as other art forms) that uses a careful selection and combination of various styles, ideas etc.

It is a notable feature of T S Eliot's poetry, as in *The Waste Land* (1922) where he uses metre in all kinds of ways, includes German, French and Italian vocabulary (see COLLAGE), and provides his own notes in which he talks about the many books which influenced the writing and adds an explanatory commentary. **eclecticism** noun.

eclipsis = ELLIPSIS (1).

eclogue

a formal verse on pastoral themes, often as a dialogue or soliloquy. Eclogue was used originally to describe the pastoral themes of the ancient Roman poet Virgil. Virgil had imitated the techniques of an even earlier Greek poet, Theocritus (3rd century BC), who was the first to compose pastoral idylls.

Eclogue is now used of any pastoral idyll in this conventional style. It can be a singing contest between two shepherds, a dialogue between two farmworkers, a love song to a shepherd's sweetheart, a funeral lament in praise of a dead shepherd etc. Dante, Boccaccio and others revived the eclogue in the 13th and 14th centuries. The Italian writer Sannazaro wrote his extremely popular *Arcadia* (1504) as eclogues linked by prose narratives. Edmund Spenser's equally popular *The Shepheard's Calendar* (1579) consists of twelve eclogues influenced by Mantuan's Latin eclogues produced a century earlier. The later eclogues in the *Calendar* deal with themes unrelated to shepherds and this break with convention was to influence later poets. An eclogue is also used at the end of each book in Sir Philip Sidney's *Arcadia* (1590).

Pope and Swift wrote eclogues, and Louis MacNeice's *Eclogue from Iceland* (1937) and W H Auden's *The Age of Anxiety* (1948) are modern examples.

ed.

an abbreviation meaning 'edited', 'edition' or 'editor', often used on title pages of books and in footnotes and references.

edit

to prepare a piece of writing for publication by checking grammar, spelling, dates and references, and recommending improvements to style and presentation.

edition

1 the total number of copies of a book, magazine etc printed from one set of film or plates without any changes to the text or illustrations. See IMPRESSION. If minor corrections are made, the next set of copies may be called *a revised edition*, and if major changes are made or the text is rewritten and reset, it may be called *a second* (or *third* etc) *edition* or *a new edition*.
2 a book about a classic author's work produced by a particular editor, e.g. *W B Yeats: Selected Poetry*, edited by A Norman Jeffares (1962).
3 the form in which a book is published, as in *a paperback edition* or *a deluxe edition*.
4 a version of a newspaper printed from a set of type or film, e.g. *the early morning edition*.

editor

1 a person who edits manuscripts or selects written material for publication.
2 a person responsible for selecting and ordering pieces of writing from one author or on one theme, e.g. the editor of a collection of short stories. Two famous editors of Shakespeare's plays were Nicholas Rowe in 1709 (see ACT (1)) and Edward Capell who produced his scholarly edition in 1768.

3 the person who manages the contents of a newspaper, magazine, journal, television programme etc.
4 the person who selects and arranges sequences of shots for a film.

editorial

a major article in a newspaper or magazine. It refers in particular to the main article prepared by the newspaper's editor that is usually a commentary on major national or international events.

Edwardian

describes the period in British history when Edward VII was on the throne from 1901 (Queen Victoria's death) until 1910. Many people consider it to be a serene golden period before the tragic events of the First World War (1914–1918) which produced fundamental changes in British society.

But the Edwardian period was also a period of change in which many Victorian values were questioned. It was a lively time for literature; Joseph Conrad, H G Wells and Henry James were publishing their novels, J M Synge and G B Shaw were writing for the theatre and Thomas Hardy and W B Yeats were the major poets, although Yeats' most innovative work was published after 1910.

Eisteddfod   /ie-**sted**-fad/

one of several annual festivals held in Wales with competitions in Welsh poetry, drama, music, painting etc. There is one major national Eisteddfod held each year. See BARD.

elaborate

describes a complex and decorative literary style.

elegiac   /el-i-**dgie**-ak/

describes characteristics in a piece of writing that are suitable for an elegy; it often describes a sorrowful or gloomy style or content.

elegiac couplet

a couplet with a metrical line of six feet (a dactylic hexameter) followed by a metrical line of five feet (a dactylic pentameter). It is rare in English poetry. See DACTYL.

elegiac stanza

a stanza with four lines, each an iambic pentameter, with the rhyme scheme *a b a b*. It is named after the stanzas used in Thomas Gray's

Elegy Written in a Country Churchyard (1750), for example:

> Full many a gem of purest ray serene
> The dark unfathom'd caves of ocean bear,
> Full many a flower is born to blush unseen,
> And waste its sweetness on the desert air.

elegy

a sorrowful and thoughtful lyric poem, usually the poet's thoughts about death, or a lament for a person or tragic event. See DIRGE, LAMENT, MONODY and THRENODY.

Elegy can also refer to a poem written in elegiac couplets or elegiac stanzas. In classical literature, elegy was used of any serious personal theme such as love or war, but was characterized more by its elegiac structure (see ELEGIAC STANZA) than by its subject-matter.

Many fine elegies have been produced in England from medieval times. These include Milton's pastoral elegy *Lycidas* (1637), Gray's *Elegy Written in a Country Churchyard* (1750) and Keats' ode *On Melancholy* (1819). Elegies for particular people or events include Thomas Carew's elegy on John Donne, Lord Tennyson's *On the Death of the Duke of Wellington* (1852) and W H Auden's *In Memory of W B Yeats* (1939).

elision

the omission of a syllable or vowel when composing verse or dialogue in order to have the correct number of syllables for the metre or make the phrase or line easier to say. It usually involves the omission of an unstressed vowel sound that comes before a stressed one, as in *th' impossible*. See SYNCOPE. **elide** verb.

Elizabethan

describes the period when Elizabeth I ruled England (1558–1603).

In its narrow usage, it covers the latter part of her reign (and a few years afterwards), a period of great English literature, especially drama, from writers such as Shakespeare, Marlowe, Bacon and Jonson.

In its wider usage, it covers every aspect of Renaissance influence and productivity in England from the mid 16th to the mid 17th centuries. See JACOBEAN.

ellipsis or eclipsis

(two *ellipses* or *eclipses*)

a figure of speech in which one or more words are omitted in order to emphasize the idea or theme. The omitted word may be considered necessary for strict grammatical structure but it does not contribute to meaning; the reader can easily identify and supply it. Ellipsis is often used in modern verse as in this excerpt from T S Eliot's *The Waste Land* (1922) where *are* is omitted before *humble*:

> On Margate Sands
> I can connect
> Nothing with nothing.
> The broken fingernails of dirty hands.
> My people humble people who expect
> Nothing.

ellipsis

the mark ... used to show that part of the text has been omitted, as in ... *The Queen was in a furious passion ... shouting 'Off with his head!'* ...

emblem

a saying or motto that expresses a moral idea that is produced with a symbolic illustration, usually a woodcut or engraving, and an explanation or commentary in the form of a short poem.

Published collections are called **emblem books**. These books appeared in England in the 15th century when the skill of engraving was established. Geoffrey Witney's *A Choice of Emblems* (1585) is the earliest English example, but Francis Quarles' *Emblems* (1635) is the better-known collection.

emotive

describes language used to express feelings or arouse an emotional response. The opening lines to John Keats' ode *To a Nightingale* (1819) are emotive; he uses language which expresses vividly his sense of despair and his desire to escape from the troubles in the world:

> My heart aches, and a drowsy numbness pains
> My sense, as though of hemlock I had drunk,
> Or emptied some dull opiate to the drains
> One minute past, and Lethe-wards had sunk.

empathy

an emotional or intellectual feeling of identification with a theme, idea, person, work of art etc that is so close you almost become the person or thing. In literature, particularly vivid descriptive passages can make the reader empathize with the subject or theme.

In this extract from Keats' *The Eve of St Agnes* (1820), an old servant who is walking through the family chapel on a bitterly cold winter's night is so cold that he even feels sorry for the statues. So successful is Keats in describing the cold that we empathize with the servant's feelings and his concern for the statues:

> The sculptur'd dead, on each side, seem to freeze,
> Emprison'd in black, purgatorial rails:
> Knights, ladies, praying in dumb orat'ries,
> He passeth by; and his weak spirit fails
> To think how they may ache in icy hoods and mails.

emphasizer

an adverb or adverbial phrase (an *intensifier*) that affects the meaning of a sentence by increasing the strength of the verb to emphasize that something is true, e.g. *definitely*, *really* or *obviously*, or to state that the speaker or writer is telling the truth, e.g. *frankly*, *honestly* or *sincerely*. See AMPLIFIER, DOWNTONER.

emphatic pronoun

a pronoun used to emphasize a noun or pronoun in a sentence, as in *The artist had framed the painting **himself*** or *I kept the letter **itself** and gave him a photocopy*. See REFLEXIVE PRONOUN.

empyrean /em-**pie**-ri-an/

describes a theme or subject-matter in verse about the heavens.

en clair /on klair/

a French phrase meaning 'in ordinary language', in other words not in coded text such as used by soldiers or spies.

encyclopaedia

a book, often a set of volumes, that contains an organized group of articles on particular topics. These topics can cover a broad range of general knowledge or they can be concerned with one subject, e.g. butterflies, or one area of study, e.g. sport. **encyclopaedic** adjective.

Encyclopaedia Britannica appeared between 1768 and 1771; the edition produced between 1777 and 1784 was the first attempt in English to cover the whole spectrum of human knowledge.

ending

any final part of a word that is a grammatical suffix, e.g. *-ing*, *-ed*, *-est*, *-ly*.

end-matter

all the parts of a book, e.g. appendices, an index, glossary or set of notes, that are printed after the main text.

endpaper

either of the folded pieces of paper that are glued to the inside front cover or inside back cover of a book and to the edges of the first and last pages; they fix the cover to the pages.

end position

the position of a word or phrase at the end of a sentence or clause, e.g. *too* in *He wants one too*. End position is significant when describing the structure of sentences and noting that some words cannot be used in a certain position or are only used in that position. See INITIAL and MID POSITION.

end rhyme

the most common form of rhyme in English verse in which the words or syllables at the end of a line rhyme with the words or syllables at the end of another line, as in these opening lines from Thomas Hardy's *The Sigh* (1909):

> Little head against my shoulder
> Shy at first, then somewhat bolder.

end-stopped rhyme

a line of verse in which both the sense and the grammatical structure are completed at the end of the line as either a sentence or clause. See ENJAMBEMENT. Here is an example taken from the opening lines of Gavin Ewart's *Xmas for the boys* (1968):

> A clockwork skating Wordsworth on the ice,
> An automatic sermonizing Donne,
> A brawling Marlowe shaking out the dice,
> A male but metaphysical Thom Gunn.

English

the official language of Great Britain, the United States of America and many other countries.

English developed from dialects spoken by Angles, Saxons and others who crossed Europe and occupied parts of England, especially the northern and eastern parts, in the 5th and 6th centuries. *Anglo-Saxon* is the earlier term for *Old English*. See OLD, MIDDLE and MODERN ENGLISH.

enjambement   /in-**dgam**-mant/

a device used in verse when both the sense and the grammatical structure are carried over to the next line. It is therefore the opposite of *end-stopped rhyme*. Enjambement is very common in all kinds of verse. It can be seen in this modern poem, Vernon Scannell's *Gunpowder Plot* (1957):

> Now in the garden's darkness they begin
> To flower: the frenzied whizz of Catherine-wheel
> Puts forth its fiery petals and the thin
> Rocket soars to burst upon the steel
> Bulwark of a cloud.

Enlightenment, the or the Age of Reason

the period in Europe from the last part of the 17th to the end of the 18th centuries, characterized by the importance given to logical thought, mathematical and scientific truth, politics and ethics.

This period witnessed the growing belief among many intellectuals that using reasoned thought mankind would be able to conquer attitudes such as superstition and prejudice which cause only unhappiness. It was an age of great scientific discovery and of great philosophical thinkers such as Kant, Voltaire, Berkeley, Locke and Hume.

Alexander Pope's epitaph for the scientist Sir Isaac Newton who died in 1727 is an example of Enlightened thinking:

> Nature and Nature's Laws lay hid in Night.
> God said, *Let Newton be!* and All was *Light*.

en passant   /on pa-**saan**/

a French phrase meaning 'in passing' or 'incidentally', used to indicate the inclusion of related or connected information.

En passant referred originally to the capture of a pawn in chess that has been moved foward two squares as if it had been moved forward only one square.

entr'acte   /on-**trakt**/

an interval between two acts of a play or opera. In earlier times, light musical entertainment was performed during this period. See INTERLUDE.

envoi or envoy

a short stanza at the end of a poem, especially a ballade. It repeats the refrain given in the poem and is usually explanatory. Henry Austen Dobson wrote several popular ballades each with its envoi, such as this envoi from his *Ballad of the Thrush* (1897):

> Bird, though they come we know
> The empty cage, the hush,
> Still, ere the brief day go
> Sing on, sing on, O Thrush.

epic

a long narrative poem about heroic deeds and adventures. The earlier ones concern the history and legends of a country or region and include stories and information from many anonymous sources. These were **oral** or **folk epics** of which some were later written down.

The epics of the ancient Greek poet Homer, the *Iliad* and *Odyssey* (although scholars question his authorship), are the most notable examples and tell the adventures of Achilles and Odysseus. *Beowulf*, written in Old English and found in the late 10th century, tells of the heroic exploits of Beowulf, king of a tribe living in a region that is now southern Sweden.

Such epics had typical characteristics; a central hero, detailed descriptions of battles and daring adventures, the influence of the supernatural, formal speech and a general dignified tone.

Later epics were deliberately composed by one author and written down; these are referred to as **literary, art** or **secondary epics.**

The ancient Roman Virgil is regarded as the first composer of such epics; he influenced the style of all later examples. His *Aeneid* (1st century BC) tells the exploits of Aeneas who founded Rome. There were other great Roman epics.

The European chansons of the 12th and 13th centuries are often epics. This was a period when oral and literary epics became difficult to distinguish although oral epics remained, and still remain, an important literary feature of many societies and communities. Dante's *Divina Commedia* (?1314–1321), Spenser's *The Faerie Queene* (1589–1596) and Milton's *Paradise Lost* (1667) with *Paradise Regained* (1671) are all fine literary epics. See EPIC SIMILE, MOCK-EPIC.

In modern times, the novel and the cinema have become the popular vehicles for epics. **Epic novels** include Tolstoy's *War and Peace* (1863–1869), James Joyce's *Finnegans Wake* (1939) and John Steinbeck's *The Grapes of Wrath* (1940). **Epic cinema** has produced *Quo Vadis, Spartacus, Ben Hur* and *Gandhi*.

Epic theatre refers to the narrative dramas produced in Germany in the 1920s of which Bertolt Brecht was the finest exponent, especially his *The Threepenny Opera* (1928) and *Mother Courage* (1941) in which he rejected the restrictions of classical epic characteristics and preferred a series of connected scenes.

epic cycle   See CYCLIC POETS.

epicene   /e-pi-seen/

describes any noun that can refer to a male or female, e.g. *worker, doctor, clerk* (but not *confidante, chairman, blonde*).

Some people argue that epicene nouns do not give equal weight to male and female. The American feminist author Sarah Lucia Hoagland illustrates this point using a riddle:

> A father and his son were driving when they had a bad accident. They were rushed to the nearest hospital and the surgeon on duty was called. The surgeon entered the boy's cubicle and exclaimed 'O my god, that's my son!'

How can this be?

(The surgeon is the boy's mother.)

epic simile or Homeric simile

a long simile used in epics that often extends to several lines of verse. It is a complex and elaborate comparison with a great deal of detail, and it is a deliberate imitation of the similes used by the ancient Greek epic poet Homer in his *Iliad* and *Odyssey*. Milton's *Paradise Lost* (1667) contains notable examples, including this one from *Book I* where Satan's shield is compared to the moon seen through a telescope by Galileo, the Italian astronomer and mathematician:

> his ponderous shield
> Ethereal temper, massy, large, and round,
> Behind him cast; the broad circumference
> Hung on his shoulders like the moon, whose orb
> Through optic glass the Tuscan artist views
> At evening, from the top of Fesole.

epigram

a concise and witty comment that expresses a personal opinion about a general principle, such as this one from William Blake's *The Marriage of Heaven and Hell* (1790):

> Truth can never be told so as to be understood and not be believed.

In ancient Greece, epigram referred to an inscription in stone, usually an epitaph, that was a carefully phrased comment; this was copied by ancient Roman poets including Catullus and Martial who provided examples for Ben Jonson to use 1500 years later. **epigrammatic** adjective.

In the early part of the 19th century, the English poet Walter Savage Landor composed memorable epigrams, such as:

> Goodness does not more certainly make men happy than happiness makes them good.

A **verse epigram** is a short satirical poem that expresses a particular thought. Landor is a very well-known exponent, and Hilaire Belloc,

Walter de la Mare, Oscar Wilde and G B Shaw also contributed notable examples. The American poet e e cummings has provided these well-known verse epigrams in *Selected poems 1923–1958* (1960):

> a politician is an arse upon
> which everyone has sat except a man.

> sam was a man
> grinned his grin
> done his chores
> laid him down.

> Sleep well.

epigraph

1 an inscription in stone on a monument or building, or an inscription on a coin.

2 a quotation at the beginning of a book or chapter that suggests the theme. **epigraphic** adjective.

epilogue

a statement that concludes a piece of writing. This includes the closing speech of a play; in Elizabethan drama, this usually took the form of asking the good will of the audience and approval of the critics. Shakespeare's last play, *The Tempest*, finishes with an epilogue spoken by the main character, Prospero, in which he asks the audience to allow him to leave the island on which he has been living for twelve years and return home.

An epilogue can also be found in a fable in which the moral point is expressed, often using witty and precise language.

Used more generally, epilogue can be a postscript to any article, speech etc. See PROLOGUE.

episode

1 an event that is a continuous sequence of incidents. One episode is interlinked with others to form a plot.

2 a distinct part that is not related to the action of the plot but is used to describe a character, provide background, produce a pause in the action (see COMIC RELIEF), allow the author to demonstrate skills in descriptive writing etc.

3 one section of a serialized play or novel.

4 in ancient Greek tragedy, an episode was a section of the drama between two Choruses. See CHORUS.

episodic adjective.

epistle

a literary work in the form of a formal letter, especially a poem with an ethical theme dedicated to a particular person or group.

This kind of epistle was first composed by the ancient Roman poet Horace; his *Epistles* (1st century BC) influenced poets such as Petrarch, Jonson and Pope, and even later W H Auden.

The familiar association of Epistle is some of the books of the New Testament attributed to St Paul, St Peter and others. **epistolary** adjective.

epistolary novel

a novel that is a series of letters written by one or more characters. It was popular in the 18th century, especially Samuel Richardson's *Clarissa Harlowe* (1747 and 1748) and the French writer Laclos' *Les Liaisons Dangereuses* (1782).

This form of novel has not been used much since, although Lytton Strachey wrote his satire on Victorian sexual repression during adolescence, *Ermyntrude and Esmeralda* (1913), as an exchange of letters. Saul Bellow has revived this genre with *Hertzog* (1964) and Alice Walker wrote her popular *The Color Purple* (1982) as an epistolary novel.

epitaph

an inscription on a gravestone or tomb; it can be of any variety, such as a short phrase or a complimentary, pious or satirical verse. Here is Shakespeare's epitaph over his grave in the chancel of the parish church in Stratford-on-Avon:

> Good friend for Jesus' sake forbeare
> To digg the dust enclosed heare:
> Bleste be ye man yt speares thes stones
> And curst be he yt moves my bones.

An epitaph can also be a commemorative comment, either referring to another person or to oneself, that is not produced as an inscription. A well-known example is Thomas Gray's comment on himself at the end of his *Elegy Written in a Country Churchyard* (1750). Here is the second of the three stanzas:

> Large was his bounty, and his soul sincere,
> Heav'n did a recompence as larg'ly send:
> He gave to Mis'ry all he had, a tear,
> He gain'd from Heav'n ('twas all he wish'd) a friend.

epithet

a word or phrase used to describe a notable characteristic of a person or thing, e.g. *Catherine **the Great**, the **all-powerful** gods*. See HOMERIC EPITHET.

epitome
/i-**pit**-*a*-mee/

a condensed version of a longer work such as a single volume that represents the key facts dealt with in a set of books.

epode
/e-pohd/

the third of three sections of a Pindaric ode (see ODE) based on the movement and chant of the Chorus in classical Greek tragedy. Only during the epode did the Chorus stand still. In Pindaric odes, the epode has a different metrical pattern from the earlier two sections. See ANTISTROPHE, STROPHE.

eponym
/e-p*a*-nim/

the name of a real or imagined person from whom a place, period, country etc has, or is thought to have, derived its name, e.g. *Romulus* the eponym of Rome, *Elizabeth I* the eponym of Elizabethan drama. **eponymous** adjective.

eponymous hero or heroine
/i-**pon**-i-m*a*s/

the name of a hero or heroine used as the title of a literary work, e.g. *Othello*, *Jane Eyre*, *Oliver Twist* and *Voss*.

erotica

literature with deliberate attention to sexual activities, especially that arouses sexual desire. See EXOTICA.

erratum

(two *errata*)
an error when writing or typing, especially when setting text for printing a book. If it is noticed after the pages have been printed, the publisher may include *an erratum slip* giving details of the necessary correction.

esprit d'escalier
/e-**spree** de-**skal**-i-ay/

a suitable and witty reply when it is too late because you have left the person or he or she has gone (a French expression roughly translated as a witty saying on the stairs).

essay

a piece of writing, usually in prose, on a particular subject; it often concerns a point of view that the author wants the reader to adopt. The essay is usually aimed at a general audience; it therefore differs from a thesis, treatise or dissertation, all of which are aimed at a specialist reader.

Essays can be serious and logically argued, or informal with humour, wit and personal examples to illustrate a point. The ancient Greeks and Romans wrote essays, but the word *essai* (meaning 'attempt') was first used by the French writer Montaigne in 1580 as a title for a collection of some of his prose discussions. He chose the title because he wanted to show that these pieces were informal. In England, Francis Bacon used *essay* in 1597 for some of his prose discussions and the term was established.

Essays were an extremely popular literary form in England in the 18th and 19th centuries when many magazines and periodicals were established, including Addison and Steele's *The Tatler* and its successor *The Spectator*. Famous essays of that period include those written by William Hazlitt, Charles Lamb and Thomas de Quincey.

The essay was equally popular in North America; R W Emerson and Mark Twain are particularly well-known authors. In modern times, periodicals provide a rich source of essays.

essayist

a person who writes literary or important essays. William Hazlitt was a popular and respected essayist in England at the beginning of the 19th century.

et al.

an abbreviation of the Latin phrase *et alibi* meaning 'and elsewhere' or *et alii* meaning 'and others'.

etymology

the study of the origin and history of vocabulary, or a brief account of the origin of a particular word as given in some dictionaries. **etymological** adjective.

eulogy

a piece of writing, or a speech, that praises the life and character of a particular person. In Shakespeare's *Julius Caesar*, Mark Antony gives a brief eulogy for Caesar:

> O, pardon me, thou bleeding piece of earth,
> That I am meek and gentle with these butchers!
> Thou art the ruins of the noblest man
> That ever lived in the tide of times.

euphemism

a figure of speech in which an indirect and more sensitive word or phrase is used instead of a direct and precise one, e.g. *to put an animal down* instead of *to kill an animal*, or *conventional* for *nonnuclear* weapons. Shakespeare regularly uses *Zounds* for *God's wounds* because the latter would have been condemned as blasphemous. **euphemistic** adjective. **euphemistically** adverb.

In Robert Browning's dramatic monologue *My Last Duchess* (1842) the Duke, unwilling to admit that he had the Duchess killed, speaks euphemistically so that he hardly seems to be referring to death at all, let alone murder:

> Oh sir, she smiled, no doubt,
> Whene'er I passed her; but who passed without
> Much the same smile? This grew; I gave commands;
> Then all smiles stopped together.

euphony

a gentle and pleasant rhythm and sound; it usually relies on longer and softer vowels and consonants, e.g. -*ar*-, -*ee*-, -*ay*- and -*s*-, -*sh*-, -*m*-. See CACOPHONY.

John Keats' ode *To Autumn* (1819) contains many lines that illustrate the effective uses of euphony. In this example, the personification of Autumn on a drowsy sunny afternoon is made extremely vivid by using vocabulary that produces euphony:

> Thy hair soft-lifted by the winnowing wind;
> Or on a half-reap'd furrow sound asleep,
> Drows'd with the fume of poppies, while thy hook
> Spares the next swath and all its twined flowers.

euphuism

a complex, extravagant and imaginative style of prose that combines elements such as alliteration, similes, decorative description and classical or mythological references.

The term comes from John Lyly's *Euphues* (1578 and 1580); this attempt by Lyly to establish standards and characteristics was to influence writers throughout the following century. In his earlier plays, Shakespeare was influenced by Lyly's style as shown in this extravagant speech by Hotspur from *Henry IV Part I*:

> By heaven, methinks it were an easy leap
> To pluck bright honour from the pale-fac'd moon,
> Or dive into the bottom of the deep,
> Where fathom-line could never touch the ground,
> And pluck up drowned honour by the locks,
> So he that doth redeem her thence might wear
> Without corrival all her dignities.

The same play also includes some parodies of Lyly's style.

ex cathedra

a Latin phrase meaning 'from the chair', used to indicate that a statement, e.g. a papal declaration, is from the highest authority and therefore must be obeyed.

exclamation

a word or sentence that expresses surprise, anger, pain etc, e.g. *My goodness, it's you!*, *I refuse to pay!*, *Damn!*, *Ouch!* or one that is a command, e.g. *Go away!* and *Beware of the dog!*

exclamation mark

the punctuation mark ! used at the end of an exclamation, as in *That's incredible!*, *How generous you are!*, *Isn't she amazing!*, *Be careful!*, *Blast!* and *'Go away!' he shouted.*

exclusive

an adverb or adverbial phrase (an *adjunct*) used to show that what is being stated is restricted to a particular example or group, e.g. *only*, *simply*, *alone* as in *I can come on Wednesdays **only***, *I did it **simply** to please you* or *He **alone** knows her true identity*.

Notice that the position of the adjunct, such as *only*, and the way the sentence is spoken can determine meaning. Consider the differences between *Only Helen asked for more coffee*, *Helen only asked for more coffee* and *Helen asked for more coffee only*. Or, consider the different spoken forms, *Helen only asked for more coffee*, *Helen only asked for more coffee* and *Helen only asked for more coffee*. See PARTICULARIZER.

exegesis   /ek-si-**dgee**-sis/

(two *exegeses*)

a critical interpretation or explanation of a piece of writing, often one produced in order to explain a difficult passage.

Existentialism or existentialism

a set of philosophical beliefs about life which originated with the Danish philosopher Kierkegaard (1813–1855) but which we associate in the 20th century with writers such as Jean-Paul Sartre (1905–1980), Simone de Beauvoir (1908–1986), Albert Camus (1913–1960) and Samuel Beckett (1906–1989).

Existentialism is concerned with a person's existence in very general terms; a person is born with the freedom to give some meaning to her or his existence and to do this a person must make choices about how to live. If not, a person will experience a passive, meaningless existence (although for Christian existentialists there is comfort to be found in God). Sartre's novel *Nausea* (1938) deals through fiction with Existentialist ideas, as does Camus' novel *The Outsider* (1942). In drama, the theatre of the absurd shows the influence of existentialism. Beckett's *Waiting for Godot* (1956), in which two tramps are waiting to meet Godot who may not even exist, is the finest example.

ex libris

a Latin phrase meaning 'from the collection of books belonging to . . .', often used on a bookplate.

exotica

literary works, a collection of pieces, with a cultural setting that is very different from a British, North American or European one. Such subject-matter, usually from tropical regions or the Far East, is often considered strange and mysterious and therefore exciting and seductive. See EROTICA.

expletive

1 a word or phrase, or even a syllable, included in a line of verse in order to obtain a particular rhythm but without adding anything to the meaning. In the following extract from Chaucer's *The Nun's Priest's Tale* (c. 1387), the expletive *pardee*, meaning 'by God' has been added to the end of the third line:

> Certes this dreem, which ye han met tonight
> Cometh of the grete superfluitee
> Of youre rede colera, pardee,
> Which causeth folk to dreden in hir dremes . . .

In a modern rendering, *pardee* could be left out.
2 a swearword or any word or sound used to express a curse, oath etc.

exposé   /ek-**spoh**-zay/

a piece of writing that makes known a scandal, crime, bad reputation etc to the general public.

exposition

an element in the first part of a play in which the author provides information necessary for understanding the action, for example about the setting or events that have already happened.

This need not be separated from the flow of the plot but can be carefully integrated into the introductory section. In Shakespeare's *Richard II*, the exposition comes in an introductory soliloquy delivered by Richard himself. See FREYTAG'S PYRAMID.

expression

a group of words with a particular meaning, e.g. *make the bed*, *come into view*, *be all ears* and *by heart*. See FIXED EXPRESSION.

expressionism

a movement begun in Germany in about 1900 that emphasized the expression of emotions rather than realism of subject-matter. This emotional vision was often intense, exaggerated and pessimistic. The movement was in decline by 1925 and was finally put down by the Nazis in the late 1930s. See IMPRESSIONISM. **expressionist** adjective and noun.

Expressionist artists rejected realistic imitation of shape and colour, as is noticeable in some of the paintings of Vincent van Gogh (1853–1890), a forerunner of the expressionist movement. Expressionist writers rejected conventional approaches to plot, characterization and time sequences. For example, Franz Kafka's characters were trapped in an apparently endless nightmare in his novels *The Trial* (1925) and *The Castle* (1926). Drama was a popular expressionist form; the Swedish playwright August Strindberg (1849–1912) is an early example and the German writer Bertolt Brecht (1898–1956) is a later one.

Expressionism has also influenced the cinema with the director Robert Weine's *The Cabinet of Dr Caligari* (1919) as a notable example.

Although expressionism was a loose and fairly shortlived movement, it continued to influence the arts, including literature. The theatre of the absurd, for example, owes various of its elements to the earlier expressionist period.

expurgated

describes a text that has had obscene or offensive elements removed.

extravaganza

a kind of light dramatic composition using extravagant speeches, music, costumes and dance, and a fantasy theme. The term was first used for similar dramatic productions created in the 19th century; these were based mainly on fairy tales and were lighthearted and humorous. The best-known author of these plays was J R Planché (1796–1880).

Similar modern musical entertainment is often referred to as an extravaganza, although this form of entertainment is becoming far too expensive to produce unless it is created for television or film. See REVUE.

eye-rhyme

written words that look as if they rhyme but do not, especially when used in verse. Here is an example from Keats' *Old Meg* (1818); the eye-rhyme is at the end of the second and fourth lines:

> And with her fingers, old and brown,
> She plaited Mats o' Rushes
> And gave them to the Cottagers,
> She met among the Bushes.

F

fable

1 a narrative poem or story with a moral and usually with animals as characters. The best-known fables and certainly the earliest known to us are those attributed to the ancient Greek slave Aesop, who lived in the 6th century BC. These fables have become part of the English literary tradition. See BEAST EPIC.

The French poet Jean de La Fontaine (1621–1695) wrote a collection of fables in the late 17th century based on ancient Greek, Roman and Oriental tales. His choice of themes, his obvious love of the natural world and his refreshing simplicity as a storyteller have given his fables the justified reputation as the finest written collection in the world. See PARABLE.

2 any narrative that involves supernatural characters and events, such as Huxley's *Brave New World* (1932).

3 a story, explanation or description that was once believed but is now known to be untrue.

fabliau   /fab-li-oh/

(two *fabliaux*)

a poem that tells a comic or satirical tale, often about clergymen. Such verse was written in simple language that everyone could understand and was popular in medieval France. There are a few examples in English such as Chaucer's *The Miller's Tale* (c. 1387). See LAY.

fabulist

a person who invents and writes fables.

facsimile edition

a copy of a book, newspaper etc produced as an exact photocopied version of the original.

faction

a play, novel or film about events that really happened and characters who actually existed. In other words, it is a mixture of fact and fiction, e.g. a dramatized documentary.

factitive

describes a verb that takes a direct object together with a noun that modifies its meaning, e.g. *elect* in *We elected him chairperson.*

fair comment

the legal right of a journalist to report something of public interest as a comment. It must be reported fairly and can be written in an entertaining style but must not be libellous; it must be shown to be comment and not necessarily fact.

fair copy

a set of proofs of a book, contract etc that includes all the corrections and amendments.

fairy tale

a story about the adventures of fairies and similar supernatural beings, especially one for children.

Fairy tales have their origin in oral tradition but became particularly popular at the end of the 18th century. The German brothers Jacob and Wilhelm Grimm published a classic collection of popular tales between 1812 and 1815; the Danish writer Hans Christian Anderson also wrote a splendid series of fairy tales twenty years later. The works of these authors were quickly translated into many languages and continue to be popular with children worldwide.

falling action

the events in a literary work, especially a drama, that follow the climax. They usually include the collapse in the fortunes and happiness of the main characters, and lead to the catastrophe. See FREYTAG'S PYRAMID.

false friend

a word or phrase whose relationship to another is based on mistaken facts or irrelevant information, especially in two different languages, e.g. *actually* (meaning 'in reality') is not the same as the French *actuellement* (meaning 'now, at present'). It is also known as a **faux ami** (French).

fancy   See IMAGINATION.

fantasy

any piece of writing that extends the imagination beyond what seems possible, often by inventing imaginary worlds set in the past or future. Such writing is often interesting and clever, and is usually written in an elaborate or extravagant style. See IMAGINATION.

J R R Tolkien's trilogy *The Lord of the Rings* (1954–1955) is a powerful and popular example of literature that is fantasy. Fantasy has enjoyed a recent increase in popularity and interest; one very successful author is Terry Pratchett with his *Discworld* series. Others include Stephen Donaldson and David Eddings. See SCIENCE FICTION.

farce

a kind of light comedy that uses unlikely and exaggerated situations to make the audience laugh. Farce often includes bawdy or coarse humour, practical jokes and rough or lively fun. It can also include impossible coincidences, mistaken identity, sudden appearances and caricatures as characters.

There are these ridiculous elements in early classical literature, but the term was first used in the 14th and 15th centuries in France to describe comic interludes in the religious plays of that time. These mocked common bad habits such as marital infidelity or unethical commercial activity. Later, such interludes were developed into full-length dramas.

French farce influenced drama in England, Germany and Italy during the 15th and 16th centuries. Elizabethan dramatists included comic episodes, and Shakespeare's plays contain many examples, such as the scene in *Twelfth Night* when Malvolio wears yellow, cross-gartered stockings. Jonson's *Bartholomew Fair* (1614) is a notable farce. But the French playwright Molière is the acknowledged genius of farce with plays that ridicule the prejudices and stupidity of 17th century French society.

By the 19th century farce had become an established dramatic form and enjoyed a popularity that continues to the present day. Georges Feydeau (1862–1921) wrote several popular farces in France, and A W Pinero (1855–1934) wrote three highly successful farces in England towards the end of the 19th century, including *Dandy Dick* (1887), before he gave his attention to his more serious plays. Brandon Thomas' *Charley's Aunt* (1892) is a classic English farce that is still regularly performed.

Farce continues to be written and produced and is highly popular, particularly with plots containing amorous adventures and sexual jokes, known as **bedroom farce**. **farcical** adjective.

fascicule

a section of a printed work that is produced and issued as an instalment.

faux ami   See FALSE FRIEND.   /fohz a-**mee**/

(two *faux amis*)

feature

1 any distinctive element or characteristic such as a particular structure, style or theme.
2 (also **feature film**) the main film shown at a cinema, or on television, that is usually a full-length drama.

3 (also **feature article**) a long article in a newspaper or magazine on a particular topic; it is often one of a series or set of articles and concerns a topic of contemporary interest rather than news.

feminine caesura

a caesura that follows an unstressed syllable (˘), as in this line from Keats' *Endymion* (1818):

> Its loveliness increasĕs: || it will never

See MASCULINE CAESURA.

feminine ending

an unstressed syllable (˘) at the end of a line of verse; it is common in blank verse, as in this line from Wordsworth's sonnet *Surprised by Joy* (1815):

> Bŭt hōw | cŏuld Ī | fŏrgēt | thĕe? Thrōugh | whăt pōw|ĕr

See MASCULINE ENDING.

feminine rhyme

a kind of rhyme in verse when a stressed syllable (¯) is followed by an unstressed syllable (˘), as in these two lines from Tennyson's *The Lady of Shalott* (1832):

> Willows whiten, aspens quīvĕr,
> Little breezes dusk and shīvĕr.

See MASCULINE RHYME.

feudal

describes the social and political structure of medieval Europe with each person as the tenant of a higher landlord: the king followed by the barons, knights and the clergy, and finally the serfs. This structure was based on each group giving his superior a service in the form of military aid, labour, food etc. Chivalry developed out of such obligation and became a common element in medieval literature.

ff.

1 an abbreviation meaning 'folios'.
2 a symbol meaning 'and the following', used after references to particular pages or lines.

fiche = MICROFICHE. /feesh/

fiction

any literary work that uses the author's imagination to invent characters, events, places and situations. Fiction is usually associated with novels or stories and not with drama or poetry except for narrative poems. See FACTION. **fictional** adjective.

figurative

describes the meaning and usage of a word or phrase that is, or includes, a figure of speech. See LITERAL (1).

figure of speech

(two *figures of speech*)
an expression used in writing that does not have its literal meaning. Common examples are metaphor, simile, hyperbole and personification. Figures of speech are used to add imaginative or creative qualities, to emphasize humour, emotions and opinions, or to display a writer's skill at inventive phrasing.

Many figures of speech have lost their appeal because they are overused so that they no longer have creative, witty or surprising qualities. But well-known expressions can be adapted to regain an imaginative freshness, e.g. *put all its nuclear eggs in one atomic basket*.

See ANTIPHRASIS, ELLIPSIS, EPIC SIMILE, EUPHEMISM, HYPERBOLE, LITOTES, METAPHOR, METONYMY, ONOMATOPOEIA, PERSONIFICATION, PUN, SIMILE.

filler

a short article, photograph, cartoon or illustration used to fill space when creating a page of a newspaper or magazine.

fin de siècle   /fan da see-ek-la/

describes the last years of the 19th century in Europe, a period of social change during which writers were experimenting with liberal ideas and techniques. See DECADENT.

finite

describes a form of a verb or verb phrase that shows grammatical features such as person, number, tense, voice or mood, e.g. *I laugh*, *We are reading*, *They will cry*, *It was grown* and *You're a fool*.

A **finite clause** contains a finite, as in *I refuse to go **until he apologizes to me***. See NONFINITE CLAUSE.

finite verb

a verb in any of its finite forms

first conditional

the structure of a conditional sentence used to state that the possibility expressed in the *if*-clause may have a particular result:

if-clause PRESENT TENSE	**main clause** FUTURE TENSE
If I see your brother,	*I'll give him your message.*
If I finish early,	*I'll come to the sports centre.*

The first conditional is also used to express:

a a warning, as in *If you don't hurry, you'll miss the bus.*
b a threat, as in *If they don't stop that noise, I'll take away their radio.*
c an offer, as in *If you can't pay, I will.*

Note that in some cases you can use other verb forms in the *if*-clause, e.g. *If I've finished by 8 o'clock* (PAST TENSE), *I'll come to the sports centre* or *If I am still working at 6 o'clock* (PRESENT CONTINUOUS TENSE), *I'll join you after the game.*

In some cases *unless* can replace *if* but the structure changes, as in *I'll come to the sports centre unless I finish late.* An example of the first conditional using *in case* is *I'll take some money in case I need it.*

See SECOND, THIRD and ZERO CONDITIONAL.

first language = MOTHER TONGUE.

first person

a form of a pronoun or verb used by the speaker to refer to herself or himself. The **first person singular** is used to refer to the speaker alone, as in *I am sorry*, and the **first person plural** is used to refer to the speaker together with others, as in *We are sorry*. See SECOND and THIRD PERSON.

fixed expression

an expression that cannot be changed (no word can be left out or replaced and the word order cannot be changed, as in *fight tooth and nail* (not *fight nail and tooth*)).

Other expressions are not fixed; *work day and night*, *work night and day*, *labour night and day* etc are all possible.

flannel

insincere praise or flattery, especially when given in a polite and sophisticated style.

flashback

a part of a drama, film or novel that shows or describes events which happened earlier in time than the main story.

flat

describes either style that lacks interest, variation or excitement, or a character who is described in a dull way and who does not develop or change during the course of the action. The term was coined by E M Forster in his *Some Aspects of the Novel* (1927) in which he gives Mrs Micawber in Charles Dickens' *David Copperfield* as an example of a flat character.

fleshly school, the   See PRE-RAPHAELITES.

flyleaf

the inner leaf of an endpaper of a book, used to protect the opening or closing pages of the text.

foil

a character in a drama or novel whose behaviour or personality is contrasted with a main character in order to emphasize particular qualities of the main character. Jane Bennet in Jane Austen's *Pride and Prejudice* (1813) is a foil for her livelier and more interesting sister, Elizabeth.

folio

1 a sheet of paper folded once to make two leaves or four pages.
2 a large, tall book made up of printer's sheets folded once. Early published versions of Shakespeare's plays are called *Folios* because they were produced in this way. The editions are known as the *First*, *Second*, *Third* and *Fourth Folios*, and were produced between 1623 and 1685. The First Folio was edited by Heminge and Condell, Shakespeare's friends and fellow actors. It was not an easy task since the plays had often been adapted and restructured to suit individual performers and particular audiences. The Second Folio of 1632 was a reprint of the First Folio, but the Third Folio of 1663 included *Pericles* and other plays of doubtful authorship. The Fourth Folio appeared twenty years later. See QUARTO (2).
3 a page number in a manuscript or book, or a page printed on one side only.

folk drama

drama that originated in oral tradition among ordinary people, particularly the plays connected with local custom and festivals. It may include early mystery plays, morality plays or the drama performed by mummers. See MORALITY PLAY, MUMMERY.

folklore

the contents or legends of spoken folktales, folksongs, fairy tales, riddles etc that form oral tradition. Folklore often relates to a particular place or group of people. **folkloric** adjective.

folksong

a song that originated in oral tradition among ordinary people and that has been handed down from one generation to the next. It may be a ballad, sea shanty, carol, spiritual, lullaby etc.

folktale

a story that originated in oral tradition among ordinary people and that has been handed down from one generation to the next. It may be a legend, fable, fairy story, myth etc.

Fool, the

a professional jester in a medieval royal household; he often appeared as a character in drama up to and including the Elizabethan period. See JESTER, TOM (THE) FOOL.

foot or metrical foot

a basic unit of rhythm in verse made up of a group of stressed ($\overline{}$) and unstressed ($\breve{}$) syllables. In scansion, the symbol | or / marks a foot. See METRE.

footnote

a note printed at the bottom of a page (or at the end of a chapter of a book) with a reference mark, e.g. †, * or [2], that matches one next to a word in the main text. Footnotes add information, give sources for quotations, suggest further reading etc.

foreshadowing

any device used in a literary work to indicate events that will occur later. These hints of future episodes, or even the outcome of the plot, can give structural unity or completeness.

foreword

a statement produced as an introduction to a book. Unlike a preface, it is not usually written by the author.

form

the structure or pattern of a literary work as opposed to its content. For example, the sonnet, ode and ballad are all verse forms. The form of a novel will depend on how the author organizes the plot and characters. In a slightly broader sense, form can be used to mean 'genre'. For example, detective fiction and science fiction are both literary forms or genres.

Form is a word commonly used in literary criticism. Most critics consider it much too rigid to separate form from content too completely when judging the merits of a literary work. In the Romantic period, Samuel Taylor Coleridge (1772–1834) wrote that the ideas and emotions contained in a piece of writing must help to shape the product so that form and content can fuse together in a successful whole. See FORMALISM.

formal

describes a style of language, behaviour etc that is suitable for showing respect to strangers and for business and other official occasions, conventional ceremonies or educational purposes. See INFORMAL.

formalism

the literary movement in Russia after the Revolution of 1917 when literary works were critically analysed for structure and style rather than content. Writers were valued in the same way as other workers or craftspeople, not as intellectuals or as creative interpreters of social values or human character. **formalistic** adjective.

formalist

a person who is in favour of formalism.

format

1 the size of a book, magazine or newspaper determined by the size of the original printer's sheet and how many times this sheet has been folded.
2 the physical appearance of a book, including its shape, thickness, paper, binding etc.

four-letter word

an obscene swearword, especially one with sexual references that contains four letters, e.g. *fuck*.

four levels of interpretation

literal, allegorical, moral and spiritual (or mystical) criteria used to interpret literature, especially those works that included these elements, e.g. Orwell's *Animal Farm* (1945).

four meanings

sense, feeling, tone and intention used as criteria to interpret a poem. They were first listed by I A Richards in his *Practical Criticism* (1929).

fourteener

a rare form of a line of verse with fourteen syllables arranged in seven iambic feet. The term was first used by Elizabethans but the form had already been used in earlier classical verse. It has rarely been used since.

fourth estate, the

the press or journalism as a rank or class in society. The first estate is the senior clergy, the second is the nobility and the third is the middle classes together with ordinary people.

frame story

a story (or series of stories) within a narrative frame so that it is a story (or stories) within a story. There are many well-known examples including Chaucer's *The Canterbury Tales* (c. 1387).

free association

a term used to describe the situation in which a word or thought suggests other words or thoughts as a subconscious chain reaction.

It is mainly used by psychoanalysts but has also become useful to literary critics when describing elements such as stream of consciousness in the works of writers such as James Joyce. See CONSCIOUSNESS, STREAM OF.

freelance(r)

a self-employed writer, editor, journalist, illustrator etc who is paid a fee to work on a particular assignment.

free translation   See TRANSLATION.

free verse

verse that does not conform to conventional forms of structure and organization such as metrical feet, rhyme and stress patterns. Instead, it has lines of varying length and uses the more natural cadences of everyday speech to gain its rhythm. It is wrong to consider that free verse has no structure; the structure given is the result of free choice by the poet on matters such as vocabulary selection and order, arrangement of lines and the use of devices such as rhyme and alliteration.

Poets began experimenting with free verse in the early 19th century because they wanted more freedom of structure. Well-known examples are the French symbolists such as Charles Baudelaire (1821–1867) or the American Walt Whitman (1819–1892) whose *Leaves of Grass* (1855) made an enormous impact when it was published.

Free verse has been, and continues to be, widely used in the present century; T S Eliot (1888–1965) has produced outstanding examples as shown in this passage from his *Four Quartets: Burnt Norton* (1943):

At the still point of the turning world. Neither flesh nor
  fleshless;
Neither from nor towards; at the still point, there the dance
  is,
But neither arrest nor movement. And do not call it fixity,
Where past and future are gathered. Neither movement
  from nor towards,
Neither ascent nor decline. Except for the point, the still
  point,
There would be no dance, and there is only the dance.

A more modern example is *Liverpool Poems* (1967) by Adrian Henri.
Here are the first four verses:

1

GO TO WORK ON A BRAQUE!

2

Youths disguised as stockbrokers
Sitting on the grass eating the Sacred Mushroom.

3

Liverpool I love your horny-handed tons of soil.

4

PRAYER FROM A PAINTER TO ALL CAPITALISTS:
Open your wallets and repeat after me
        'HELP YOURSELF!'

frequentative

an adverb or adverbial phrase (an *adjunct*) that expresses frequency in
time, in other words how often, as in *I visit them **often**, I don't go out
much* or *She phoned **twice***. A frequentative may also be an intensifier,
as in *I **scarcely** see her nowadays* (in which *scarcely* is a minimizer
(superficial contact) and also a frequentative (not at all often)).

Freudian slip

an error in speech or writing when one word is used instead of
another; it is considered to reveal a subconscious attitude, desire, fear
or motive.

Freytag's pyramid   /frie-taak/

Gustav Freytag, the German critic, argued in his *Techniques of the
Drama* (1863) that the structure of a typical five-act play (and that
would include the works of Shakespeare) is like a pyramid in shape; it

consists of the introduction, rising action, climax, falling action and catastrophe. His own diagram illustrates this:

1	introduction
2	rising action
3	climax
4	falling action
5	catastrophe or denouement

Although this structure has been popular with many playwrights and has produced classic successes, it does not apply to all drama. The terms 1–5 are often used by critics in relation to prose as well as drama.

frontispiece

an illustration opposite the title page of a book.

full-length

1 describes a published version of a novel that is its original length and has not been abridged.
2 describes a film or literary work that is not shorter than the usual or expected length.

full stop or full point

the punctuation mark **.** used
a at the end of a sentence that is not a question or an exclamation;
b in abbreviations, especially when the abbreviation does not end with the final letter of the original word, e.g. *approx.*

function shift

a change in the syntactical purpose of a word so that it is a different part of speech, e.g. there is a function shift from *early* as an adjective in *an early reply* to the use of *early* as an adverb in *arrive early*.

function word

a word, such as a particle or conjunction, that has a grammatical function in a sentence but has very little meaning when it is not in a context, e.g. *of* and *but* as in *a matter of life and death* and *not blue but red*. See CONTENT WORD.

fustian

describes a pompous style of writing.

future continuous tense

the verb form used to talk about an action or situation that will be happening or continuing during a future period. It is formed by using *will be* and a present participle (-*ing*), as in *I'll be smiling all day tomorrow*.

You can also use *was/were going to* with a verb to talk about a future action that was planned (especially when the action did not happen), as in *He **was going to come** but he didn't have any money for a ticket*.

future perfect continuous tense

the verb form used to talk about an action or situation that will continue for a particular period and be completed later. It is formed by using *will have been* and a present participle (-*ing*), as in *I'll **have been studying** English for ten years next October*.

future perfect tense

the verb form used to talk about an action or situation that will be completed by a particular time in the future. It is formed by using *will have* and a past participle, as in *I'll **have read** it by next weekend*.

future progressive tense = FUTURE CONTINUOUS TENSE.

future simple tense = FUTURE TENSE.

future tense

the verb form used to talk about an action or situation that will happen in the future. It is formed by using *will* and a bare infinitive (the verb without *to*), as in *I'll **go** tomorrow*.

The future can also be formed by using a form of the verb *be* and *going to* with a verb, as in *What **are you going to wear** next Saturday?* or *It's **going to rain***. Use *will* and a verb to talk about something you know or believe will happen, e.g. *You'll be ill if you eat that*, or to state something you decide to do at the moment you speak, e.g. *I'll **wait** here for you*. Use *be* and *going to* with a verb to talk about something that will definitely happen because of a present situation, e.g. *I'm **going to faint***, or to state something you have already planned, e.g. *I'm **going to phone** him tomorrow*. See PRESENT CONTINUOUS TENSE.

Futurism

a movement begun in Italy in 1909 by Emilio Fillipo Marinetti (1876–1944) that favoured completely new forms, styles and subject-matter. It preferred to concentrate on industry and machines rather than aesthetic values. **Futurist** adjective and noun.

The Futurists reacted against Symbolism, particularly in Russia where the movement continued until the mid 1920s. Elsewhere it had very little influence.

G

Gaelic   /gay-lik/

the language of the Celtic people of Ireland and, in a different form, of the Celtic people of Scotland. See CELTIC.

At the end of the 19th century, there was a movement to encourage and preserve Gaelic in Ireland but it was soon eclipsed by the Celtic revival which encouraged Anglo-Irish literature. See CELTIC REVIVAL.

galley or galley proof

a printer's proof of text that has been set and produced on a long strip of paper. It is sent to the publisher and author for corrections and emendments.

Galley refers to the long tray used to hold type that was once set from hot metal. Modern typesetting is usually computerized and galleys are now ordinary sheets of paper.

Gallicism

a word or phrase adopted from French that is now part of normal English usage, e.g. *chef d'oeuvre* or *genre*.

gallows humour

any form of sinister humour, especially ironic humour used as a desperate gesture in a setting of impending disaster.

gather

to collect together printed signatures so that they can be sewn or glued together to make a book.

gazette

an official record of government business including official appointments, public notices etc.

The first English newspaper was the *Oxford Gazette* produced in November 1665 by the Court which had moved from London to Oxford because of the plague. It later became the *London Gazette* which still survives as a gazette, not a newspaper. See NEWSLETTER.

gazetteer

a section of a book that lists and describes places.

gender

the set of grammatical groups into which some words are divided in order to show masculine, feminine or neuter, e.g. *cow*, *bull* etc, or between personal or impersonal, e.g. *he*, *she*, *it* and *who*, *that* or *which*.

general conditional = ZERO CONDITIONAL.

generalization

a word, statement, principle etc used to cover a wide range of concepts, examples or details, especially when this implies oversimplification. **generalize** verb.

generative grammar

a grammatical description of a language that sets out the rules which provide criteria for every possible sentence structure. For modern linguists, these rules govern semantic, lexical and phonological considerations as well as syntax. See SYSTEMIC and TRANSFORMATIONAL GRAMMAR.

genitive

the form of a noun used to express 'possession' as well as other closely related uses, as in *His **brother's** bike* (possessive), *a **girls'** school* (descriptive), *The **earth's** magnetic field* (shows origin), *my **husband's** attempt* (subjective (my husband tried)) and *the **building's** support* (objective (. . . is supporting the building)). Some grammarians restrict genitive to the use of -'s or -s', but others include the *of*-genitive, as in *the bike **of my brother***. See POSSESSIVE.

genre   /zhaan-ra/

a category into which a literary work can be put according to type and purpose, and also to whether the work conforms to a particular set of techniques. Comedy, tragedy, tragi-comedy, ballad, epic, one-act play, documentary drama, short story and novel are all genres. See FORM.

Georgian

describes the period in Britain when the kings were called George (1714–1830). Poets who wrote during this period are often referred to as Georgian.

Five anthologies called *Georgian Poetry*, produced between 1912 and 1922 during the reign of George V, included poems by Rupert Brooke, Walter de la Mare, John Masefield, A E Housman, D H Lawrence, Siegfried Sassoon, Wilfred Owen, Robert Graves and others. See VICTORIANS.

gerund

a noun formed from a verb by adding -*ing* and used as the subject of a sentence, as in ***Smoking*** *is dangerous*, as an object, as in *He loves* ***reading***, after a preposition, as in *I get exercise by* ***swimming*** etc.

Some grammarians prefer to refer to a gerund as a *verbal noun* (and a *deverbal noun* would be any other word ending in -*ing* that can be replaced by another noun with the same meaning, for example *the writings of Shakespeare* could be *the works* . . . , *the plays* . . . etc).

A **gerund phrase** is a gerund together with any modifiers and its subject or object; the phrase is used as a noun, as in ***Having a good imagination*** *is necessary for a good writer.*

ghostwriter

a person who writes a book, article etc on behalf of another person who is then credited as the author.

It is particularly common today for ghostwriters to produce the autobiography or memoirs of a famous personality, such as an athlete, who does not have writing skills. **ghostwrite** verb.

Globe, the

a theatre erected in 1599 on the south bank of the river Thames in central London. It was assembled by Richard Burbage who was a friend and fellow actor of Shakespeare and Jonson.

It was a circular open-air theatre made of wood, with a thatched roof over the galleries that provided seating round the sides. The stage projected into the central open area where the audience stood about drinking, eating and laughing throughout the performances.

Many of Shakespeare's plays were performed here, including *Hamlet, King Lear, Macbeth, A Midsummer Night's Dream* and *Twelfth Night.* The Globe was destroyed by fire in 1613 but rebuilt within a year. All public theatres were closed by the government in 1642. See BLACKFRIARS and THEATRE, THE.

gloss

a comment on a word, phrase etc given as a short note, usually an explanation or definition; it is often put in the margin.

glossary

an alphabetical list of special vocabulary used for a particular subject.

glossy

a magazine that contains colour pictures and is printed on expensive shiny paper.

gnomic   /noh-mik/

describes writing that includes many aphorisms, or a writer of such material. Oscar Wilde is described as gnomic because of the many witty remarks in his plays. See JEU D'ESPRIT.

Golden Age, the

the most creative and productive period in the history of a country or region. It is often used of the period of Latin literature during the 1st century BC (the period of Virgil) and also of the period of Elizabethan drama. See AUGUSTAN AGE, GRAND SIÈCLE, LE.

Gothic

describes a novel, film etc that includes ghosts, mystery, villainy and the supernatural to create a general atmosphere of terror. It was popular in the late 18th and early 19th centuries.

An early example is Horace Walpole's *The Castle of Otranto* (1764) with its medieval setting and written in Walpole's home which was a Gothic castle; applied to architecture, Gothic describes dark, cold and gloomy buildings with tall stained-glass windows, detailed stonework, tall ribbed vaults, flying buttresses – the ideal setting for mystery and ghosts. The popularity of Walpole's novel led to many others: Ann Radcliffe's *The Mysteries of Udolpho* (1794) is a well-known example. The term had been extended to cover novels which, while not necessarily medieval in setting, have frightening or gloomy themes. Mary Shelley's *Frankenstein* (1818) is an obvious example.

The influence of the Gothic novel has lasted in the 20th century; the American writer William Faulkner's *Sanctuary* (1931) and Mervyn Peake's extraordinary Gothic trilogy *Gormenghast* (1946–1959) are two examples. But the development of the horror film during the same period has provided many more examples.

Grail   See HOLY GRAIL.

grammar

1 the study of the ways words are formed (see MORPHOLOGY) and how words join together to form sentences (see SYNTAX); this is often presented as a set of rules. See GENERATIVE, SYSTEMIC, TRANSFORMATIONAL and UNIVERSAL GRAMMAR.
2 a book that describes and explains the grammatical facts of a language.
grammatical adjective.

grammarian

a person who studies or teaches grammar.

grammatical subject

the word *it* in sentences such as *It is raining*. See PREPARATORY SUBJECT, IMPERSONAL VERB.

grand opera

opera with a serious plot that has no spoken dialogue. See COMIC OPERA, OPERETTA.

grand siècle, le   /*la* graan see-**ek**-l*a*/

the 17th century as a period of great French literature and art during which lived writers such as Molière, Racine, Corneille and La Fontaine. See GOLDEN AGE.

grand tour, the

a long trip round Europe, especially in the 18th century, to visit the major cities and places of particular artistic and academic interest. It was undertaken by rich families to complete a young person's education.

Many writers completed the grand tour, e.g. Thomas Gray and Hugh Walpole travelled round Europe together for three years. Episodes such as the French Revolution, and factors such as the development of railway networks and tarred roads, combined to take away the popularity this tour had enjoyed.

grave accent   /graav/

the mark ` placed above a vowel, usually 'e', to show how the vowel should be spoken, as in *Molière*.

great chain of being

a belief that goes back to the ancient Greek philosopher Plato's time (c. 429–347 BC) and which was strongly held during the Renaissance many centuries later. It was more fully developed early in the 18th century by the German philosopher Gottfried Leibniz (1646–1716) and was important to several thinkers of the Enlightenment, and also to neoclassical writers in England.

Very briefly, God was considered to be excellent in having created every possible variety of life; life was made up of a great chain or ladder of existence with the humblest creature at the bottom and God at the top. Mankind occupies a position somewhere near the middle, above the animals because we are capable of rational thought but below the angels or spiritual beings.

The two best-known references to this great chain of being are Ulysses' speech in Act I of Shakespeare's *Troilus and Cressida* and

Alexander Pope's *Essay on Man* (1733–1734). Two 20th century studies are Arthur O Lovejoy's *The Great Chain of Being* (1936) and E M W Tillyard's *The Elizabethan World Picture* (1943).

Greek tragedy   See TRAGEDY.

Grub Street

a former street near Moorfields in the City of London that was the home of many poor writers, and is referred to by Dr Johnson in his *Dictionary* (1755).

Grub Street is now used as a pejorative to describe hack writers and hack writing.

guidebook or **guide**

a small book that contains general information for visitors to a place.

gutter press, the

newspapers and magazines that contain articles, stories and photographs about disgraceful or shameful acts. They sensationalize people's lives and often pay little attention to accuracy or truth; they have been responsible for destroying reputations of ordinary people as well as celebrities. See CHARACTER ASSASSINATION.

H

hack

1 a writer or journalist who is paid for work on uninteresting or difficult topics and who usually produces mediocre material.
2 describes mediocre writers or writing. See GRUB STREET.

hackneyed

describes a phrase that has become dull and stale because it has been used too often.

hagiographer

a writer who produces material on the lives of the saints.

haiku /hie-koo/

(two *haiku*)

a form of simple but imaginative Japanese verse that has seventeen syllables in three lines – five syllables in the first, seven in the second and five in the third. See TANKA.

Because haiku are so short and cannot therefore include a lot of detail, a careful choice of words is crucial. But, in spite of being short, they can encompass much; on the surface they create a picture of one particular object or scene, but the description is often suggestive of a mood or emotion. Here is an example by Kikaku:

> *Full moon*
>
> Bright the full moon shines:
> on the matting on the floor,
> shadows of the pines.

Basho was a famous haiku poet. Here is *Crow* (the number of syllables has changed in translation):

> *Crow*
>
> On a withered branch
> a crow has settled –
> autumn nightfall.

half-rhyme

a rhyme in which the vowel sounds are not the same but the consonants are. See ASSONANCE. Wilfred Owen (1893–1918) is well known for experimenting with half-rhyme. Here is an extract from his poem *Strange Meeting* (1920):

> With a thousand pains that vision's face was grained;
> Yet no blood reached there from the upper ground,
> And no guns thumped, or down the flue made moan.
> 'Strange friend,' I said, 'here is no cause to mourn.'

half-title

a righthand page at the front of a book with only the title printed on it. It is positioned in front of the title page.

halftone

a photograph illustrated in a book by reproducing it as a composition of many very tiny dots using a fine screen.

hamartia See TRAGIC FLAW.

handbill

a small leaflet giving information and distributed by hand.

handbook

a small guidebook or manual that contains basic facts and information.

handout

a publicity leaflet that is distributed by hand.

hanging participle

a participle or participial phrase with a subject that is not the same as the subject of the sentence, e.g. *Turning the last page of my book, I heard a knock on the door.* Such sentences should be avoided because of ambiguity and the likelihood of being misunderstood.

Hansard

the official complete report of proceedings of the Houses of Parliament in Britain. The name comes from that of the original compiler Luke Hansard (1752–1828) although *Hansard* was removed from the title page from 1892.

hard

describes *c* or *g* pronounced from the back of the tongue, as *k* as in *came* or *g* as in *get*. See SOFT.

hardback, hardbound or **casebound**

a book published in a cover made of thick card covered in cloth, paper or leather. See CASE (2), PAPERBACK.

heading

a title for a chapter, section, newspaper article etc. See RUNNING HEAD, SUBHEADING.

heavy-duty verb

a verb that can combine with many different adverbial particles, prepositions or nouns to make a wide variety of multi-word verbs and idiomatic expressions, e.g. *be, come, do, get, give, go, have, keep, let, make, pull, put, run, set, take* and *turn*, as in *be off, come in, do up, get by, give way, go back on one's own* etc.

helping verb = AUXILIARY VERB.

heptameter

a line of verse with seven metrical feet. It can be broken down into ballad metre of alternating three or four stress lines as in the opening lines of this traditional ballad *Sir Patrick Spens*:

> The King | sits in | Dunferm|line town |
> Drinking | the blood | red wine |

Otherwise, it is very rare in English poetry.

hero

the main male character in a novel, drama etc who provides the most interest. He may be good or evil. See ANTIHERO, HEROINE.

heroic couplet

a form of verse with lines of iambic pentameters that are rhymed in pairs.

It was used by Chaucer (most of his *The Canterbury Tales* (c. 1387) is written in heroic couplets) but the form did not become popular until the mid 17th century particularly through poems by Dryden. Alexander Pope perfected this verse form at the beginning of the next century and his poems established the heroic couplet as the most preferred verse form for English poetry well into the 19th century. However, it has been rarely used during the present century. Here is an example from Keats' *Lamia* (1820):

> I saw thee sitting, on a throne of gold,
> Among the Gods, upon Olympus old,
> The only sad one; for thou didst not hear
> The soft, lute-finger'd Muses chaunting clear.

heroic drama

a tragedy concerning honour, romance and spectacular action; the style was extravagant and elaborate and the stage settings were grand and exotic. The plays were written in heroic couplets.

This drama was popular at the start of the Restoration period in England with Dryden considered as the best exponent, for example his *The Indian Emperor* (1665) or the better-known *All For Love* (1678).

At its worst, heroic drama became pompous and farfetched; it laid itself open to ridicule and by about 1700 was falling out of fashion.

heroic verse

epic poetry composed in heroic couplets. Earlier poetry, such as Milton's *Paradise Lost* (1667), is written in unrhymed pentameters but is still described as heroic verse, a reference more to its subject-matter than to its form.

heroine

the main female character in a novel, drama or story who provides the most interest. She may be good or evil. See HERO.

heterographic

describes different groups of letters used to represent the same sound, as in 'we*igh*t', 'w*ai*t' and 'l*ate*'. See HOMOPHONE.

hexameter   /hek-**sam**-i-t*a*/

a line of verse with six metrical feet.

The **dactylic hexameter** was widely used in classical verse, particularly for epic verse; for example in the ancient Greek poet Homer's *Iliad* and *Odyssey*. It has not been widely used in English verse, although Spenser used the **iambic hexameter** for the last line of his stanzas in *The Faerie Queene* (1589–1596):

But short|ly was | likewise | seene ly|ing on | the plaine. |

Some 19th century poets experimented with hexameters. Here is Shelley in his *To a Skylark* (1820):

Like an | unbod|ied joy | whose race | is just | begun. |

hexastich   /hek-s*a*-stik/

a stanza with six lines that is used frequently in English poetry, especially as the second division of one of the sonnet forms. Here is an example from *Woods*, part of W H Auden's *Bucolics* (1955):

Sylvan meant savage in those primal woods
Piero di Cosimo so loved to draw,
Where nudes, bears, lions, sows with women's heads,
Mounted and murdered and ate each other raw,
Nor thought the lightning-kindled bush to tame
But, flabbergasted, fled the useful flame.

hiatus

1 a pause between vowel sounds in the pronunciation of a word so that the vowels are spoken carefully as in *cooperative*, *hiatus*, *iamb*, *liaison*, *naive*.
2 a gap in a manuscript where there is missing copy.

highbrow

describes a person with superior intellectual, literary or artistic taste, or literature, music, painting etc produced to appeal to such a person. See LOWBROW, MIDDLEBROW.

high comedy

a kind of comedy with characters who are educated and cultured, with a witty and sophisticated dialogue. Such comedies require an intellectual effort from the audience; they attempt to satirize the absurdities of human nature, social manners and customs, and political or social institutions.

George Meredith coined the terms *high comedy* and *low comedy* in his essay *The Idea of Comedy* (1897). He used high comedy to refer to clever, witty comedy where the audience is made to laugh because of the action on the stage but does not become emotionally involved. According to Meredith, high comedy was best seen in the comedies of manners where intellectual wit and wordplay were much in evidence.

Plays such as Shakespeare's *As You Like It* or G B Shaw's *Pygmalion* (1912) can be described as high comedies. See LOW COMEDY.

historical linguistics

the study of the grammatical and semantic features of a language through the development and changes in order to identify principles for the changes or to classify a particular language. See DESCRIPTIVE LINGUISTICS.

historical novel

a novel about historical events and characters using recorded evidence but in a fictional framework. Such novels first appeared in the middle of the 18th century and Sir Walter Scott is acknowledged as the finest author with novels such as *Waverley* (1814). Manzoni's *The Betrothed* (1825–1827) is the classic historical novel in Italian. The poet and critic Robert Graves also wrote excellent historical novels, including *I, Claudius* (1934) and *Claudius the God* (1934). Historical novels continue to enjoy enormous popularity through works by T H White, Mary Renault, Georgette Heyer and Antonia Fraser.

The historical elements in such novels must be researched thoroughly not only to ensure historical accuracy for the actual events and episodes but to give the work a quality of realism and authenticity, for example by using appropriate language in the dialogues or accurate detail in settings, materials, names etc for the period.

historical present tense

the use of the present tense to give details about the actions and events in a novel or drama. The present tense is used because the actions and events do not change, e.g. the hero always dies or lives happily ever after.

The historical present tense is often used in informal conversation to tell a story about a recent incident, e.g. *I'm standing at the bus-stop when this man comes up to me and he says* ....

historiographer

a historian who writes about the works of other historians, or about the history of a particular institution or society.

history play = CHRONICLE PLAY.

hokku = HAIKU.

holograph

a published book that has been handwritten by the author. Wainwright's very popular *Guides* to walking in the Lake District of England are fine examples.

Holy Grail, the

the bowl, according to medieval legend, that was used by Jesus Christ during the Last Supper and by Joseph of Arimathea to collect Jesus's blood during the Crucifixion.

After journeys through Europe, Joseph left the Grail with guardians and was imprisoned in Britain. Many knights undertook to find the Holy Grail in order to prove their chivalry, purity and holiness.

There are several famous legends about these quests, particularly in Sir Thomas Malory's *Le Morte Darthur* (1469–1470). According to this book, the Grail is finally received by Galahad, Percival and Bors from Jesus but after Galahad's death a year later, it is taken up to heaven.

Homeric epithet

any compound adjective formed by joining adjectives or nouns. It was first created by the ancient Greek poet Homer, as in *rosy-fingered dawn, the **wine-dark** sea, **god-like** Odysseus* or *the **all-powerful** gods*.

Homeric simile = EPIC SIMILE.

homily

a serious speech or piece of writing on a moral or religious subject.

homograph

a word with the same spelling as another but with different meaning and pronunciation, for example *tear* (to split) and *tear* (from crying). **homographic** adjective.

homonym

a word with the same spelling or pronunciation as another but with different meaning, for example *row* (to move a boat) and *row* (a line of seats etc). **homonymic** adjective.

homophone

a word with the same pronunciation as another but with different spelling and often different meaning, for example *higher* and *hire*. See HETEROGRAPHIC. It also includes different letters or syllables with the same pronunciation, for example *k* and *c* (in *kill* and *cup*) or *s* and *c* (in *sigh* and *cypher*). **homophonic** adjective.

Hope theatre, the

the theatre owned by Philip Henslowe and opened in 1613. It was by the river Thames in Southwark, London and was used mainly as a bear garden, but it had a moveable stage for the performance of plays such as Ben Jonson's *Bartholomew Fair* in 1614. See ROSE.

hornbook

a sheet of paper with text printed on it including the alphabet, vowels and consonants used to form syllables, the Lord's Prayer and Roman numerals. This sheet was inside a frame with a thin layer of cattle horn over it as protection.

It was used from the 16th to 18th centuries to teach children to read but was then replaced by the primer. See PRIMER.

howler

an obvious mistake in spelling, grammar or the choice of vocabulary.

hubris

in tragedy, the fault of having too much pride and over-confidence causing errors of judgement and eventual disaster. See TRAGIC FLAW.

Hubris is an important aspect of the hero in classical Greek drama such as Sophocles' *Antigone* (5th century BC) but also in later drama such as Marlowe's *Dr Faustus* (c. 1601) and Shakespeare's *Macbeth*.

humanism

the belief in the dignity, morality and creative potential of a person and in progress and achievement because of human effort rather than faith or religion. This meaning was first used in the 19th century, a period when great importance was given to the human intellect. **humanist** adjective and noun.

Humanism can be traced back to those scholars of the Renaissance period who studied subjects such as poetry and history rather than, say, mathematics; they revived many Greek and Latin texts and in doing so revived the classical beliefs in human potential. Although most of these scholars held on to their Christian faith, by placing mankind at the heart of the universe they opposed the beliefs carried down to them from medieval scholars who had emphasized sinfulness and had viewed life on earth as only a preparation for life after death. The Dutch priest and scholar Erasmus (1466–1536) and Castiglione (1478–1529) in Italy, among others, spread humanist belief throughout Europe. In England, Sir Philip Sidney (1554–1586) and Sir Francis Bacon (1561–1626) were influenced by humanism.

Humanism gained new strength in the 19th century when the growth of scientific thought and industry led some writers and philosophers to fear that these would become too dominant; in Britain, Matthew Arnold (1822–1888), the poet and critic, is well known for his argument that education must give equal value to the arts and humanities. This was reflected in the **New Humanism** in the United States of America during the first half of the 20th century, led by the teacher and critic Irving Bubbit (1865–1933). The term humanism is still used but many modern humanists have rejected religion.

humours, the

In medieval Europe it was believed that our bodies contain four liquids, or *humours* as these were known. These four liquids released vapours which affected the brain and were therefore responsible for an individual's personality. Each humour was a combination of two of the four basic elements (hot, dry, cold or wet). The humours were:

blood (hot and wet) which made you lively, cheerful and lighthearted.
black bile (cold and dry) which made you sad and pessimistic.
yellow bile (hot and dry) which made you irritable and unfriendly or bilious.
phlegm (cold and wet) which made you weak, inactive and unenthusiastic.

Each humour was also associated with a natural element; blood with air, black bile with earth, yellow bile with fire and phlegm with water. It was considered that an ideal personality had a balance of all four humours; an excess of one, blood for example, led to an imbalanced personality, such as being reckless. See VAPOURS.

Belief in the humours lasted until the 17th century and influenced dramatists when creating personalities for the characters of their plays. See HUMOURS, COMEDY OF.

humours, comedy of

drama written at the end of the 16th and beginning of the 17th centuries which was influenced by the theory of the humours as a basis for creating characters, and particularly the idea of imbalance in the humours affecting personality. See HUMOURS. Ben Jonson's *Every Man in his Humour* (1598) is probably the first such play. He followed it with *Every Man out of his Humour* (1599). In these plays, Jonson's characters are dominated by a particular personality trait.

Later, humour was used for a person's general frame of mind or mood. By the 18th century, it was associated with manners intended to impress people which often caused amusement in others so that humour came to mean laughter.

hybrid

a word formed by joining together parts from more than one language, for example *television* (Greek *tele* meaning 'far' and Latin *visio* meaning 'sight' from *videre* meaning 'to see').

hymn

a Christian song of praise to God or a saint and usually intended for a group of voices.

Hymn was first used to refer to a song of praise to any god or hero, for example the ancient Greek poet Homer's *Hymn to Demeter*. Latin Christian hymns were developed from the 12th and 13th centuries but most popular hymns sung nowadays date from the 17th century onwards.

Many poets have composed hymns including Blake, Longfellow and Tennyson but the better-known writers are Isaac Watts, John Wesley, John Newton and William Cowper. Julia Ward Howe's *Battle Hymn of the Republic* (1862), a patriotic poem composed to be sung as a march, is a fine and popular hymn in the United States of America.

hymnal

a book of hymns, especially a collection chosen to be used in church services.

hype

the extravagant style used by advertisers to promote a product or by other writers with a similar intention.

hyperbole   /hie-**per**-b*a*-lee/

a figure of speech that deliberately uses exaggeration in order to give emphasis, increase a particular poetic effect etc. See LITOTES.

There are numerous examples from poetry and drama including the one from Shakespeare's *King Lear* in which Lear's daughters, Goneril and Regan, deliberately exaggerate their love for their father in order to gain his lands. Goneril says:

> Sir, I love you more than word can wield the matter;
> Dearer than eye-sight, space and liberty;
> Beyond what can be valued rich or rare;
> No less than life, with grace, health, beauty, honour;
> As much as child e'er lov'd, or father found;
> A love that makes breath poor and speech unable;
> Beyond all manner of so much I love you.

Hyperbole is very common in ordinary conversation, as in *have a million things to do*. **hyperbolic** adjective.

hyphen

the punctuation mark - used to form a word by
a joining other words, e.g. *ice-cream, mother-in-law*
b joining a common prefix (*anti-, co-, pre-, post-* etc) to a word, e.g. *anti-nuclear*, especially when the second part begins with a vowel, e.g. *pre-eminent* or a capital letter, e.g. *pre-Raphaelite*.

hyphenate

to spell a word by using a hyphen, e.g. *pre-eminent*. Many writers do not hyphenate but write the word as a single word, e.g. *cooperate*.

A word is also hyphenated if it is divided at the end of a line of typing or printing so that some letters begin the next line. The hyphen is always placed at the end of the first part. See WORD DIVISION and COMPOUND. **hyphenation** noun.

hypocorism   /hie-**pok**-*a*-rizm/

a friendly petname or diminutive, e.g. *Bob* for *Robert*.

hypothetical past tense

the past tense used in conditional clauses, as in *If I had wanted to, I'd have come*, or constructions that produce a similar negative inference, as in *You act as if you **owned** this place*. See SECOND CONDITIONAL.

I

iamb, iambus or iambic foot /ie-amb/

a metrical foot with one unstressed syllable followed by a stressed syllable (˘ ‾). See CHORIAMB, TROCHEE, METRE. **iambic** adjective.

iambic pentameter

a line of verse with five iambic feet. It is very common, especially because of its association with blank verse. See the example at BLANK VERSE.

ibid. or ib.

an abbreviation of the Latin *ibidem* meaning 'in the same place', used to show that a quotation or reference is associated with the author, book, chapter, poem etc mentioned previously. See ID., LOC. CIT.

iconomatic /ie-kon-*a*-**mat**-ik/

describes a type of writing using pictures to illustrate the sounds of the names of objects rather than the object itself.

id.

an abbreviation of the Latin *idem* meaning 'the same', used to refer to the same word, name, article etc mentioned previously. See IBID., LOC. CIT.

idealism

1 belief in ideas and principles you consider to be perfect and make every effort to achieve. It includes the representation of people and ideas about life as the best possible, not perhaps as they really are. Dr Pangloss in Voltaire's *Candide* (1759) is a well-known example of an idealist.
2 a philosophical theory that the external world does not exist outside our own minds but is a product of our ideas and thought.
idealistic adjective, **idealist** noun.

idée fixe /i-day **fiks**/

(two *idées fixes*)
an obsession, especially one that dominates the content or style of a writer's work, or the actions and judgements of a character in a novel or drama.

idem See ID.

identifying relative clause = RESTRICTIVE RELATIVE CLAUSE.

ideogram or ideograph

a type of writing using pictures of things to represent them, as in written Chinese and Japanese.

idiolect

the variety of words, phrases, expressions and structures understood and used by a particular person.

idiom

1 an expression with a meaning that is different from the meanings of the individual words. The meaning of an idiom has to be learned as a set of words, e.g. *eat one's hat*, *on the other hand*, *set to*, *have a change of heart*, and *tell tales*.
2 the usage of a language that is correct and natural to people who speak it as their first language.
3 the set of characteristics that identifies the usage of a language by a particular person, religion, historical period, class etc.
idiomatic adjective.

idyll

any poem or part of one that describes peaceful and innocent rural life and scenery in an idealistic way. See BUCOLIC.

The first idyll was written by the ancient Greek poet Theocritus in the 3rd century BC. A later well-known example is Marlowe's *The Passionate Shepherd to his Love* (1599). Later, idyll was used of any descriptive piece written in a calm and simple style. In Tennyson's series of poems, *The Idylls of the King* (1842–1885), each poem is a descriptive narrative of an incident in the Arthurian legends. **idyllic** adjective.

idyllic

1 describes any peaceful and pleasant situation or condition, especially an ideal one.
2 See IDYLL.

if-clause

a clause that begins with *if*, used to express the conditional in English, as in **If I need to**, *I'll ask you*, *She must hate him if she said that*, *We'll come now if you like*, *You can go in if you've paid*, *If you're hungry*, *eat something*, **If I had the money**, *I'd buy a sports car* and *I'd have bought it if you'd asked me*. The tenses of the *if*-clause and of the main clause determine the meanings of the sentences. See FIRST, SECOND, THIRD and ZERO CONDITIONAL.

illiterate

describes a person or people who cannot read or write and, less often, a person who is not educated. See LITERATE.

image

in literature, image can have several meanings and uses:
a at its simplest, it is a mental picture or idea produced by reading a piece of writing, especially a poem. See IMAGERY.
b the actual description in the writing which appeals to our senses and produces a mental picture or idea.
c a figure of speech, such as a metaphor or simile, in which the mental picture is conveyed by using comparison.
d a symbol used in the writing to stand for something else, especially an abstract idea. Images can appeal to any or all of our senses, or they can be imagined through our intellect.

imagery

the use of particular vocabulary in a piece of writing to represent thoughts, emotions and sensory experiences and produce a mental picture or idea. This usually involves imaginative and figurative language. Skilful imagery can add greatly to our enjoyment of a literary work.

Here is a brief but clear 'word picture' of sharpening a pencil in a contemporary poem *Sharpener* by Rose Bennet:

> The sharpener peels a conical fan,
> A paint-trimmed petticoat of scented curls.

John Keats' ode *To Autumn* (1819) is rich in imagery. In this extract from the first verse, Keats appeals to all of our senses and gives us a vivid mental picture of the richness of autumn:

> To swell the gourd and plump the hazel shells
> With a sweet kernel; to set budding more,
> And still more, later flowers for the bees,
> Until they think warm days will never cease,
> For Summer has o'er-brimm'd their clammy cells.

Equally successful in his appeal to our senses using imagery, but with a completely different objective, is Wilfred Owen, a poet who wrote about the First World War in Europe. Here is his horrifying description of a dying man from his *Dulce et Decorum Est* (1920):

> If you could hear, at every jolt, the blood
> Come gargling from the froth-corrupted lungs,
> Obscene as cancer, bitter as the cud
> Of vile, incurable sores on innocent tongues –

An interesting use of imagery can be found in the religious poet George Herbert's *The Church-Floore* (1633). Here the stones of the church floor are symbols for some of the Christian virtues:

> Mark you the floore? that square and speckled stone,
> Which looks so firm and strong, is *Patience*!
> And th'other, black and grave, wherewith each one
> Is checker'd all along, *Humilitie*.

As an example of imagery that shows an abstract idea, we can turn to Shakespeare's *Macbeth* where Macbeth's uneasiness of mind is summed up in his cry:

> O! full of scorpions is my mind, dear wife!

In some of Shakespeare's plays, recurring images are used to highlight the theme. For example, there are many references to blood in *Macbeth*, and in *Hamlet* disease and sickness are often referred to.

A famous example where one image is followed immediately by another, very different one is in Ezra Pound's *In A Station of the Metro* (1916):

> The apparition of these faces in the crowd:
> Petals on a wet, black bough.

But it is apparent in another short poem of his:

> Fan-Piece, for her Imperial Lord
> O fan of white silk,
> Clear as frost on the grass-blade,
> You also are laid aside.

See FIGURE OF SPEECH.

imagination

The role of the imagination in the creative process has been a topic of debate for writers and thinkers over many centuries, but until the 19th century fancy and imagination were considered to have the same meaning and usage.

It was S T Coleridge in his *Biographia Literaria* (1817) who distinguished between them. He maintained that fancy is the lesser of the two faculties because it acted in a mechanical way to sort and reorganize images in the mind. Imagination was held to be superior because it was the creative faculty, in his own words a 'synthetic' and 'magical' power. Coleridge's beliefs were influential and in critical theory the distinction between the two has become accepted.

In general usage, fancy is used when referring to our ability to be imaginative and creative. Imagination includes the activity of creating images as well as our ability to do so. Fantasy is used for extravagant mental pictures and ideas which extend the imagination beyond what seems possible.

Imagists or imagists

a group of leading American poets before the start of the First World War in 1914. They wrote poems according to their own rigid rules such as

a the words and structures should be from ordinary language;
b there must be clear imagery but clichés are to be avoided;
c there must be complete freedom in the choice of subject-matter;
d poetic rhythm can be used as a means of expressing mood.

Among Imagist poets were Ezra Pound, Amy Lowell and H.D. (Hilda Doolittle). *The Egoist* (1914–1919) was an influential periodical that became an important voice for Imagists because of Ezra Pound's association with it. The English critic and poet T E Hulme's stress on precise imagery and structure rather than sentimental and unrealistic description also influenced the Imagists. Amy Lowell set down the objective of Imagists in her book *Tendencies in Modern American Poetry* (1917). **Imagism** noun.

imitation

1 the act of deliberately copying the style of another literary work or writer. See PLAGIARISM.
2 the representation in literature or art of what already exists.

imperative or imperative mood

the form of a verb used to give an order or to make a suggestion; it is the infinitive without *to*, as in *Stop!*, *Stand up!*, *Wait until the others get here, Everyone, stop talking!, Let me see that!, Do let her come*. See INDICATIVE, SUBJUNCTIVE.

imperfect tense = PAST CONTINUOUS TENSE.

impersonal subject = GRAMMATICAL SUBJECT.

impersonal verb

a verb in a sentence such as *It rained all day* that has no logical subject. *It* is the grammatical subject.

impression

one book out of the copies printed from one set of film or plates at a particular time. Impression can also refer to all the copies printed at a particular time and *first impression, second impression* etc is used for the original printing and reprints. See EDITION (1).

Impressionism

a movement in the later part of the 19th century that encouraged writers to portray characters and settings as their personal impression of them rather than as they exist independently.

The term originally referred to the Impressionist painters who included Monet and Pissarro with Cézanne and Renoir; these artists were not interested in art merely as imitation but painted their personal impression of a scene. Sometimes they painted the same scene several times to show how different it could look according to the time of day, the mood of the artist, the emotional atmosphere at the time etc. See EXPRESSIONISM. **Impressionist** adjective and noun.

Impressionist writers can be divided into two groups; the first group, e.g. French symbolists such as Arthur Rimbaud (1854–1891) and the English writers Oscar Wilde (1854–1900) and Arthur Symons (1865–1945), can be described as literary equivalents of Impressionist painters; the second group, for example James Joyce (1882–1941) in his novel *A Portrait of the Artist as a Young Man* (1916), and Virginia Woolf (1882–1941) in her novel *The Waves* (1931), dealt with the thoughts and impressions of their characters rather than objective descriptions, objects, settings and people. See INTERIOR MONOLOGUE.

Impressionist criticism

literary criticism that judges a work using the critic's own feelings produced by it rather than using objective literary theories or examining techniques. This approach was advocated by Walter Pater in his preface to *Studies in the History of the Renaissance* (1873); it is also evident in his critical essays in the same book. Other writers who used a similar approach are Arthur Symons (1865–1945) and Virginia Woolf (1882–1941). Here is a fragment of Virginia Woolf's criticism of Elizabeth Barrett Browning's *Aurora Leigh* (1857):

> Aurora Leigh, the novel-poem, is not, therefore, the master-piece that it might have been. Rather it is a master-piece in embryo; a work whose genius floats diffused and fluctuating in some pre-natal stage waiting the final stroke of creative power to bring it into being. Stimulating and boring, ungainly and eloquent, monstrous and exquisite, all by turns, it overwhelms and bewilders; but, nevertheless, it still commands our interest and inspires our respect.

imprimatur /im-pri-**may**-ta/

a Latin word meaning 'let it be printed', used to indicate that the Roman Catholic Church has given its authority for a book to be printed and published. Imprimatur is now used more broadly for any permission or approval for the publication of a book, report or article.

imprint

1 the publisher's name and date of publication in a book, usually at the bottom of the title page.

2 the printer's name and address in a book, magazine or newspaper.

incantation

a recitation of a set of words used to produce a magic spell. Perhaps the best-known is the witches' incantation in Shakespeare's *Macbeth* as they throw the ingredients into the cauldron:

> Fillet of a fenny snake,
> In the cauldron boil and bake;
> Eye of newt and toe of frog,
> Wool of bat and tongue of dog,
> Adder's fork, and blind-worm's sting,
> Lizard's leg, and howlet's wing,
> For a charm of powerful trouble,
> Like a hell-broth boil and bubble
>
> All: Double, double toil and trouble;
> Fire, burn; and cauldron bubble.

incident

one action or event in a plot. A set of incidents forms an episode. See EPISODE.

incunabula   /in-ky*a*-**nab**-y*a*-l*a*/

(one *incunabulum*)

books printed before 1500 when printing techniques were in their infancy. It is a Latin word meaning 'swaddling clothes' or 'within the period of the cradle' (and so these books are also called **cradle books**). Malory's *Le Morte Darthur* (1469–1470) is included in incunabula.

indefinite article

the word *a* or *an* (see DETERMINER). Usually *a* is used before words beginning with a consonant. However, if the consonant is not spoken, *an* is used, as in *half an hour* and *a* is used if the *u* at the beginning of a word is pronounced with a *y* sound, as in *a useless excuse*. With abbreviations *a* is used if the name of the first letter begins with a consonant, as in *a BA in history* and *an* is used if it begins with a vowel sound, as in *an MA in history*. *A* or *an* is used:

a to refer to a person or thing but not one particular example, as in *A baby needs love* or *You've got a spot on your nose*.

b to refer to a person or thing not yet named or known, as in *There's a man at the door* or *I read a good book last night*. See DEFINITE ARTICLE (b).

c to mean 'one', as in *a boy and two girls*.

d in expressions concerning quantity, as in *a great deal, a thousand times* or *a quarter past six.*
e to mean 'each', as in *four times a minute.*
f to explain meanings, as in *A metaphor is a figure of speech.*

indefinite pronoun

a pronoun that refers to a person or thing but not to a particular, named or known example.

Indefinite pronouns can present special difficulties; some are always used with a singular verb, e.g. *anybody, somebody, no-one*, some are always used with a plural verb, e.g. *both, many, several*, others can be either singular or plural depending on the context, e.g. *any* or *none.*

independent clause = COORDINATE CLAUSE or MAIN CLAUSE.

index

(two *indexes* or *indices*)
an alphabetical list at the back of a book. It contains all the topics, places, people etc mentioned in the text and page references to show where the reader can find the information.

indicative or indicative mood

the form of a verb used to make a statement; it is the most common verb form, as in *I stopped at the corner, He's standing up* or *We'll wait for you.* See IMPERATIVE, SUBJUNCTIVE.

indirect object

a noun, pronoun or noun phrase to which the action of the verb in the sentence is indirectly related. It is usually one referring to the person or thing affected by the verb, as in *I gave her the money* or *She gave it a good shake.* The indirect object almost always comes before the direct object. See DIRECT OBJECT.

indirect question   See INDIRECT SPEECH.

indirect speech or reported speech

a style of writing or speaking in which what a person said is reported, e.g. *She said that she refused to come* or *I wrote that I was willing to help.* See DIRECT SPEECH.

In indirect speech, an indirect statement includes a *that*-clause, e.g. *He explained that he's made a mistake*, an indirect question includes a clause beginning *whether, when, why* etc, e.g. *I asked why he disagreed*, an indirect command includes a clause (without a subject) beginning with *to* + infinitive, e.g. *They ordered us to wait by the door*, and an indirect exclamation includes a clause beginning with *what, how* etc, e.g. *I told her what a beautiful house she had.*

infinitive

the base form of a verb, not any of its forms used to show person, number, tense etc. It is usually used with *to*, e.g. *to love, to exist* and is used as the subject or object, after another verb and after an adjective or noun, as in *To smoke* is dangerous, *I need to eat, It's painful to have an injection* and *A nicer way to travel is by sea.* Most auxiliary verbs (e.g. *can, must, will*) do not have an infinitive form. See BARE and SPLIT INFINITIVE.

An **infinitive clause** is a clause that contains an infinitive, its subject and its modifiers, e.g. *I want Peter to hear the details of the report.* An **infinitive phrase** is a phrase that contains an infinitive and its modifiers, e.g. *To get a better idea of her ability, read her latest novel.* See PERFECT INFINITIVE.

infinitive particle

the word *to* used as part of an infinitive, e.g. *to exist*.

inflection

1 a change in the form of a word to show its grammatical usage and setting such as person, tense, number, case, voice and gender.
2 an addition, e.g. *-ed* or *-s*, used to inflect a word.

informal

describes a style of language, behaviour etc that is suitable for everybody and used in ordinary conversation and everyday life. See FORMAL.

-ing-form

the form of a verb that ends in *-ing*. It has several uses:
a as a present participle, as in *I love **swimming*** or *a **laughing** policeman.*
b as a noun, as in ***Swimming** is fun.* See GERUND, VERBAL (3).
c as part of a present participial clause, as in *The woman **reading the news** is my mother.*
d See PASSIVE.

initial position

the position of a word or phrase at the beginning of a sentence or clause. For example, adverbs of time (e.g. *yesterday, this morning* and *next year*) can be put in the initial position, e.g. ***Yesterday**, I went for a walk*, or the end position, e.g. *I went for a walk **yesterday***, but not the mid position. See END and MID POSITION, INITIATOR.

initiating action

the event or series of events, that begins the action of a plot. This would be the early part of the introduction in Freytag's pyramid. See FREYTAG'S PYRAMID.

initiator

an exclamation or interjection used in the initial position of a statement, as in *Oh, I didn't realize you were there!*, *My, what big teeth you have!*, *Well, you can always try again*, *Ugh, that tastes horrible!* and *Hey, what are you doing?*

instalment

one part of a film, book, magazine, television drama etc that is produced as a serial or series. See FASCICULE.

intensifier

an adverb or adverbial phrase (an *adjunct*) that affects the meaning of a sentence by increasing or decreasing the force of part of it, as in *I'm **very** sorry*, *She sat **right** in the middle*, *I **partly** agree* and *It was **nearly** finished*. See AMPLIFIER, DOWNTONER, EMPHASIZER.

intensifying adjective

an adjective that makes the meaning of a noun more forceful or more exact, as in *a **thorough** search*, ***complete** destruction* or *a **slight** fault*. See INTENSIFIER.

intensive pronoun = EMPHATIC PRONOUN.

intentional fallacy

the mistake of judging a literary work from the point of view of the author's stated intentions rather than criticizing the qualities in the work itself.

interior monologue

the attempt to represent in writing all the thoughts and impressions of a character as they occur, without the author organizing them into a logical sequence. The term is often used interchangeably with *stream of consciousness*. See IMPRESSIONISM.

interjection

a word or phrase used to express surprise, emotion etc, as in *Ah, there it is!* *Well, don't come* and *My goodness, look at that!* See INITIATOR.

interlocutor

one of the people taking part in a conversation.

interlude

a short dramatic performance intended to be given between courses at a nobleman's feast, or between the acts of a longer play.

Interludes were very popular around the 14th century in France and in the 15th and 16th centuries in England. Some took the form of a farce; others were dramatizations to illustrate a moral and these may have developed out of the earlier morality plays.

Several still exist; John Heywood's *Play of the Wether* (1533) and *The Four P's* (c. 1545) are well-known examples. Interludes became increasingly humorous and were still performed at the time of Shakespeare. The actors were usually professionals but amateur performances were not uncommon, as is evident in the delightful performance of *Pyramus and Thisbe* by the villagers in Shakespeare's *A Midsummer Night's Dream*.

internal rhyme

rhyme between two or more words in a line of verse, as in these lines from S T Coleridge's *The Rime of the Ancient Mariner* (1798):

The Sun came up upon the left,
Out of the sea came he!
And he shone bright, and on the right
Went down into the sea.

International Phonetic Alphabet

the set of symbols, based on the Greek and Roman alphabets, that is used to represent human speech sound. It was revised in 1951 and is now widely used in dictionaries and textbooks. Some examples of words translated into IPA are

map /mæp/, take /teɪk/, mother /ˈmʌðə/, thing /θɪŋ/.

The abbreviation for International Phonetic Alphabet is **IPA**.

interpellate

to question a member of a committee, parliament etc about an issue related to government policy, especially as a request for an explanation. **interpellation** noun.

interpolate

to insert a comment, extra section etc into a piece of writing or conversation, especially into an older manuscript in order to corrupt the text by adding valueless material. **interpolation** noun.

interrogative

describes words, phrases and sentences used to form questions. See DECLARATIVE.

An **interrogative adverb** or **pronoun** is an adverb or pronoun used to form a direct or indirect question, e.g. ***Where*** *have you left your coat?* or *She asked him* ***what*** *he was reading.*

intonation

the pattern of sounds produced by changes in the pitch of the voice, especially to convey meaning. For example, questions are usually spoken with a rising intonation.

intransitive

describes a verb that cannot be used with a direct object, as in *I* ***exist***, *I* ***smiled*** *when I read it* and *When he* ***phones***, *ask him to contact me.* See TRANSITIVE.

introduction

1 an essay produced at the beginning of a book that gives important information about the work and the author.
2 the first section of a formal speech.
3 See FREYTAG'S PYRAMID.

invective

speech or writing that accuses or criticizes a person or thing, especially in an abusive or harsh manner. Here is an example taken from a speech by Coriolanus to the plebeians in Shakespeare's *Coriolanus*:

> You common cry of curs, whose breath I hate
> As reek o'th'rotten fens, whose loves I prize
> As the dead carcasses of unburied men
> That do corrupt my air – I banish you.
> And here remain with your uncertainty!
> Let every feeble rumour shake your hearts;
> Your enemies, with nodding of their plumes,
> Fan you into despair!

inversion

the reversal of the standard order of words in a sentence. This is often used in poetry to emphasize words or to obtain a particular rhythm. See ANASTROPHE.

Milton's *Paradise Lost* (1667) is full of inversions, as in this example from Book IX where the inversion is necessary for the rhythm:

> But if much converse perhaps
> thee satiate, to short absence I could yield

inverted commas = QUOTATION MARKS.

ionic

a metrical foot in classical verse with four syllables. The major ionic has two long and two short syllables (// ˘ ˘) and the minor ionic has two short and two long (˘ ˘ //). Ionics are rare in English poetry.

Irish Literary Movement = CELTIC REVIVAL.

irony

the use of words to state the opposite of what is meant; this usage is often sarcastic or humorous, as when Mark Antony in Shakespeare's *Julius Caesar* calls Caesar's murderers *honourable men*. **ironic** adjective. **ironically** adverb.

In ancient Greek tragedy, the character Eiron was a deceiver; he pretended to be less intelligent than he really was and therefore succeeded in outwitting the boaster. Irony, which comes from Eiron, still has the suggestion of deceiving or pretending. In practice, it is a complex and subtle device used widely in literature in a variety of ways. At its simplest, it can be a remark that the writer makes clear is the opposite of what he or she means. However, the reader must often work this out using clues such as the context of the statement. Sometimes irony is based on an awareness of the absurdity of life or the seeming incongruity between appearance and reality. In this instance, a complete literary work may be ironic. See DRAMATIC IRONY, LITOTES, TRAGIC IRONY.

At all times, irony depends for its success on the reader's awareness that the surface meaning is not the one intended; it can be so subtle that it is almost not perceived, as in some of the novels of Jane Austen (1775–1817) and Henry James (1843–1916).

A familiar example of irony is Jonathan Swift's *A Modest Proposal* (1729) which is an attack on the British government's policy on Ireland that led to widespread starvation among the Irish. Swift argues that the answer to this suffering lies in the poor selling their babies as food for the rich. It is written in the careful, reasonable tone of a government paper. The irony lies in the horror at what is being proposed.

In Shakespeare's *Macbeth*, King Duncan's inability to perceive the difference between appearance and reality gives rise to irony. His speech about the thane of Cawdor who has just been executed as a traitor:

> There's no art
> To find the mind's construction in the face:
> He was a gentleman on whom I built
> An absolute trust

can refer equally to Macbeth, to whom Duncan has just given the title of thane of Cawdor, and who is hiding murderous thoughts behind a loyal appearance.

irregular

describes a noun or verb with forms that do not follow the normal pattern or rules. The irregular plural *men* and the irregular verbs *go*, *leave* and *stand* are examples. See REGULAR.

irregular ode   See ODE.

ISBN

(International Standard Book Number) a number printed on every book that is unique to that title and edition; it is a code for the country, publisher and title of the book. It is used by booksellers to order copies and by librarians.

issue

1 an edition of a literary work that contains particular alterations to the text or illustrations, or one that has been printed in a different format or binding style.
2 one copy or instalment of a magazine etc.

Italian sonnet = PETRARCHAN SONNET.   See SONNET.

italic

describes a style of type with the letters sloping towards the right, e.g. *in italics*. See ROMAN.

J

jabberwocky

nonsense verse. The word was coined by Lewis Carroll in *Through the Looking Glass* (1872) as the title of a nonsense poem. Here are the opening lines:

> 'Twas brillig, and the slithy toves
> Did gyre and gimble in the wabe:
> All mimsy were the borogoves,
> And the mome raths outgrabe.

Jacobean   /dgak-*a*-**bee**-*a*n/

describes the period that followed the Elizabethan Age when King James I (1603–1625) ruled England and Ireland (as James VI he also ruled Scotland); Jacobean is from *Jacobus*, Latin for 'James'.

Shakespeare was still writing at the beginning of this period; his last play *The Tempest* was written in about 1611. Jacobean literature developed from Elizabethan characteristics and included the works of John Donne, Ben Jonson, Thomas Middleton and John Webster. Robert Burton wrote his *Anatomy of Melancholy* (1621) which was to have a profound influeence on the poet John Keats two centuries later. One major achievement of the Jacobean period is the 'Authorized Version' of the Bible, also known as the 'King James' Version', which first appeared in 1611. This version is still in use today. See CAROLINE.

jargon

1 the form of language used by a particular profession, subject, hobby etc. Some of the forms are unnecessarily complex or specialist in both vocabulary and syntax.
2 meaningless talk.

jeremiad or Jeremiad

a long sad complaint, usually against life, the world or the demands of God. The term comes from *Lamentations of Jeremiah* in the Old Testament of the Bible. Much of William Blake's prophetic writing, his *America, a Prophecy* (1793) for example, consists of jeremiads.

jester

a medieval official whose duty was to make fun of people or situations in order to amuse the Court.

Shakespeare made use of a jester in several of his plays; Feste in *Twelfth Night* is a well-known example. A certain detachment from the action enables the jester to mock the main characters and much of the play's humour comes from him.

jeu d'esprit   /zher des-**pree**/

(two *jeux d'esprit*)
a brief and witty pun or comment. Oscar Wilde was a master of them, as in this example from among many in his *The Importance of Being Earnest* (1895):

> *Cecily:*   When I see a spade I call it a spade.
> *Gwendolen:* I am glad to say I have never seen a spade. It is obvious that our social spheres have been widely different.

or this well-known example from Wilde's *A Woman of No Importance* (1893):

> The English country gentleman galloping after a fox – the unspeakable in full pursuit of the uneatable.

jingle

a short and simple verse or song that is easy to remember. Jingles are often used by advertisers and they are also common as children's nonsense verse or rhymes for group games, as in

> Queenie, Queenie Caroline,
> Dipped her hair in turpentine,
> Turpentine to make it shine,
> Queenie, Queenie Caroline.

jobbing printer

a printer who produces leaflets, labels and other commercial items, not books, newspapers or magazines.

journal

1 a book that contains a daily record of events, for example when travelling. The journals of James Boswell (1740–1795) are well known. **2** a publication that is similar to a magazine but has a serious or academic content. It is often a collection of articles from members of a learned society.

journalese

jargon used by journalists to write copy in newspapers. It is considered to contain words and phrases that quickly become clichés and gives a superficial impression to the reader.

juvenilia

literary works written during adolescence. These are necessarily immature but many contain elements that indicate the fine qualities of adult
work.

There are many that have been published, e.g. a handful of poems by
William Wordsworth written before he was twenty, Byron's *Hours of
Idleness* (1807) which was first called *Juvenilia* because he was only
nineteen in 1807. A recent publication, in which the upper age limit for
the contents is sixteen years of age, is *Seeds in the Wind: Juvenilia from
W B Yeats to Ted Hughes* (1991) edited by Neville Braybrooke.

K

kabuki
/ka-**boo**-kee/

a kind of Japanese popular drama that uses legends as themes. All the
actors are male, the costumes, make-up and scenery are very elaborate,
and the stage is usually a revolving one. The dramas contain a musical
element similar to operetta. Kabuki seems to have developed from the
more formal and conventional Nō drama. See NŌ DRAMA.

key novel

a novel with characters who are real people but with fictitious names,
such as Thomas Love Peacock's *Nightmare Abbey* (1818) that contains
Coleridge, Byron and Shelley. A modern example is Aldous Huxley's
Point Counter Point (1928) that includes D H Lawrence, Middleton
Murry and Henry Moseley.

The French for key novel is *roman à clef* and the French were
responsible for the earliest key novels such as those by Jean de La
Bruyère in the 17th century.

King's English, the or the Queen's English

the form of English used by educated people in the south of England.
Until recently, this was regarded as the only correct or standard form
but regional usages and accents are now accepted as valid.

kitchen-sink drama

drama that deals with the stresses and problems of ordinary people in
domestic situations. The plays aim at a realistic portrayal of events and
the emotional responses to them; the environment is usually shabby
and characters are often degraded more by the arguments among them-

selves rather than by the squalid atmosphere. Tennessee Williams' *A Streetcar Named Desire* (1947) can be described as a kitchen-sink drama.

It was particularly popular in the 1950s and 1960s. John Osborne's *Look Back in Anger* (1957) is the best known but other examples are those in Arnold Wesker's trilogy *Chicken Soup with Barley* (1957), *Roots* (1959) and *I'm talking about Jerusalem* (1960).

kitsch   /kich/

any vulgar or pretentious literature, art, design etc. It is often sentimental and appeals to popular taste.

knocking copy

advertising material written to attack the qualities of a competing product.

L

labial

describes a sound in speech that involves movement of the lips, e.g. *p* and *m* in English.

lacuna

(two *lacunae* or *lacunas*)
a space in a manuscript because something is missing. Lacuna can also mean by extension an omission, intended or not, in a piece of writing.

lai = LAY.

Lake Poets, the

The three poets, William Wordsworth (1770–1850), Robert Southey (1774–1843) and S T Coleridge (1772–1834), friends of each other, who lived much of their lives in the Lake District of northwest England. Wordsworth was born and brought up in the Lake District, and returned in 1799 to live there until his death. This is an area of outstanding natural beauty with numerous lakes among an assortment of hills and crags. This scenery provided inspiration for their poetry.

lament

a sad poem or song that is an expression of sorrow, usually about a death but also about the loss of a high position. It developed at the same time as epic verse and has always been popular as a subject for poetry. *Lamentations of Jeremiah* in the Old Testament of the Bible is a well-known early example. See COMPLAINT, MONODY, PLAINT.

A later example is Thomas Hardy's *Tess's Lament* (1902) in which she mourns her lost happiness and wishes herself dead. Here is the last stanza:

> It wears me out to think of it,
> > To think of it;
> I cannot bear my fate as writ,
> > I'd have my life unbe;
> Would turn my memory to a blot,
> Make every relic of me rot,
> My doings be as they were not,
> > And leave no trace of me.

lampoon

a satirical piece of writing in which a person is ridiculed mercilessly or maliciously. It can be prose or poetry.

Probably the best-known literary lampoon is that of Lord Hervey (1693–1743) by Alexander Pope in his poem *Epistle to Dr. Arbuthnot* (1735). Here is a very small fragment from what is a very lengthy attack:

> Or at the ear of *Eve*, familiar Toad!
> Half froth, half venom, spits himself abroad,
> In puns or politics, or tales, or lies,
> Or spite, or smut, or rhymes, or blasphemies.

Latinism

a word or phrase based on Latin. John Milton sometimes used words with their original Latin meaning. In these lines from Book I of his *Paradise Lost* (1667), *frequent* is used in its Latin meaning 'crowded' from Latin *frequens*:

> The great Seraphic Lords and Cherubim
> In close recess and secret conclave sat –
> A thousand demi-gods on golden seats,
> Frequent and full –

Sometimes Milton's constructions are Latin in form as in these lines from Book X of *Paradise Lost*:

> He, after Eve seduced, unminded slunk
> Into the wood fast by . . .

laureate   See POET LAUREATE.

lay or lai

The lai, or lay in its Anglicized version, probably originated in the songs of wandering Breton (from Brittany, an area in western France) minstrels in the Middle Ages. They were popularized in the late 12th century by Marie de France who wrote poems based on the minstrel songs that she had heard. Marie, living at the court of the English King Henry II (1133–1189) wrote her poems in French; they were short narrative poems of a romantic nature, based on Arthurian and other Celtic legends, and often involving magic.

Two of her lays, *Lay le Frayne* and *Sir Launfal*, were translated into English before the middle of the 14th century and these led to English versions such as *Sir Orfeo*. Chaucer, author of *The Canterbury Tales* (c. 1387), certainly knew of them, although by the latter half of the 14th century lays were no longer popular. The Franklin in Chaucer's *The Franklin's Tale* (c. 1387) says his tale is going to be a Breton lay and it is appropriate that Chaucer should associate this old-fashioned man with what was by then an old-fashioned genre. In fact, the tale bears only superficial resemblance to the lay but it may have led to a revival of interest in the lay because at least four more Middle English versions appeared.

Although lays were a fairly short-lived literary genre, the term was used in the 19th century to describe other short narrative poems, like Sir Walter Scott's *The Lay of the Last Minstrel* (1805).

leading article or leader

the main article in a newspaper or magazine, usually representing the views of the editor about a topic of great importance. See FEATURE (3).

leaf

a sheet of paper, particularly one used to make a page in a book or magazine.

leaflet

a small printed and folded piece of paper that is distributed by post or by hand and is free of charge.

legend

an anonymous tale about a famous and heroic man or woman that has been handed down as part of oral tradition. The truth behind the story is impossible to affirm and the stories would have changed according to the imagination and interest of the storyteller. As time progressed, these legends became exaggerated and farfetched. See MYTH. **legendary** adjective.

In England, King Arthur (and his Knights of the Round Table) is a well-known legendary character from early medieval times. He possibly did exist as a king in the 6th century who led the ancient Celts against the Saxon invaders, but the legends surrounding him cannot be verified. See CAMELOT.

Robin Hood is another legendary character who may have existed during the reign of King Richard I (1189–1199); the legends about his life in Sherwood Forest, Nottingham and his commitment to robbing the rich in order to give to the poor have never been proven.

Not all legends are set in the past. They can attach themselves to any well-known person, good or evil, even while that person is still alive.

leitmotif or leitmotiv   /**liet**-moh-teef/
a theme or image that recurs often in a literary work or in the works of a particular author, for example, the frequent references to blood, central to the play's theme, in Shakespeare's *Macbeth*. In Evelyn Waugh's novel *A Handful of Dust* (1934), references to pigs recur throughout the novel. The word is German and means 'leading motif'.

letters
correspondence, especially between friends, interesting people or institutions, that is published as a collection, for example *My Darling Pussy; the Letters of Lloyd George to Frances Stevenson 1913–1941* edited by A J P Taylor (1975). It is clear that many writers expected their letters to be published and therefore paid particular attention to their contents and style. See BELLES-LETTRES, EPISTLE, EPISTOLARY NOVEL.

lettre de cachet   /**let**-ra da **kash**-ay/
(two *lettres de cachet*)
a French phrase for an official document authorizing the detainment of a person without trial. These documents were used during the period of the French Revolution (1789).

lexeme
the smallest meaningful unit of language. It can be a word or a combination of words. For example, *at any rate* is a lexeme since it cannot be understood from the meaning of the individual words *at, any* or *rate*. See MORPHEME.

lexical
about or concerning vocabulary.

lexical meaning

a definition of what a word means that is independent of any particular context or grammatical forms. Dictionaries give lexical meanings.

lexicography

the process of compiling a dictionary. **lexicographical** adjective. **lexicographer** noun.

lexicology

the study of the history and structure of vocabulary. **lexicological** adjective. **lexicologist** noun.

lexicon

1 a dictionary, usually one for Greek, Latin, Arabic or Hebrew.
2 a dictionary that groups vocabulary in categories according to subjects or related meanings. See THESAURUS.
3 a complete set of morphemes for a language.

lexis

1 all the vocabulary items in a language.
2 vocabulary in general.

libel

a false published statement communicated to one or more persons that is defamatory because it involves one of the following:
a an accusation of a criminal act;
b injury to a person's public reputation as in a profession or business;
c an accusation that invites hostility, rejection or ridicule;
d an accusation of suffering from a socially unacceptable disease or mental illness.

Libel does not have to be intentional. Any person considered to be guilty of libel can be sued for damages. See SLANDER. **libellous** adjective.

librettist

an author of a libretto.

libretto

the words for an opera, operetta or similar large musical.

ligature

a printed character made up of two or more letters produced as one typed letter, especially ffi, fi, and fl.

light entertainment

entertainment in a theatre or on television that is meant as relaxation and amusement. It usually consists of a set of songs, dances and comedy acts or a performance by a popular singer or musician. See SERIOUS THEATRE.

light opera = OPERETTA.

light verse

verse that aims to be enjoyed and often adopts a relaxed, informal tone. Sometimes its subject-matter is familiar and ordinary, or perhaps it takes a lighthearted, even humorous, approach to a serious topic.

This kind of verse is often very witty and it may be satirical with an underlying serious purpose. Many poets have written light verse; Hilaire Belloc (1870–1953) has left us a splendid collection including his *The Microbe* (1897):

> The Microbe is so very small
> You cannot make him out at all,
> But many sanguine people hope
> To see him through a microscope.
> His jointed tongue that lies beneath
> A hundred curious rows of teeth;
> His seven tufted tails with lots
> Of lovely pink and purple spots,
> On each of which a pattern stands,
> Composed of forty separate bands;
> His eyebrows of a tender green;
> All these have never yet been seen –
> But Scientists, who ought to know,
> Assure us that they must be so. . . .
> Oh! let us never, never doubt
> What nobody is sure about!

limerick

a very popular kind of comic light verse or nonsense verse that contains five lines with the rhyme scheme *a a b b a*.

The origin and history of the limerick seems to be based on conjecture since evidence is incomplete or contradictory. The first-known limerick to be published is in *History of Sixteen Wonderful Old Women* (1820). The most famous limericks are those written by Edward Lear for his *The Book of Nonsense* (1846). Here is an example:

> There was an Old Lady of Chertsey
> Who made a remarkable curtsey:

She whirled round and round
Till she sank underground
Which distressed all the people of Chertsey.

In Edward Lear's limericks, the first and last lines usually ended with the same word. However, this feature is not essential, as shown in a modern limerick by Kenneth Williams:

This is a creature called SNIDE
Whose endless pursuit of a bride
Was done all in vain
'Cos his nose in the rain
Would always stick out at the side.

limp binding

a style of binding for a book, such as thin card for a paperback.

lingo

a foreign language, or the jargon used by a particular group or profession, not ordinary English. The word is informal and becoming slightly dated.

lingua franca   /ling-w*a* frang-k*a*/

(two *lingua francas* or *linguae francae*)
the language in a region used by people who speak several different first languages. English is the lingua franca in many countries for education and commerce.

linguistics

the study of a language and how it works. See APPLIED, DESCRIPTIVE, HISTORICAL and STRUCTURAL LINGUISTICS.

litany

a prayer that is a series of requests to God for forgiveness, help etc, especially when spoken by a priest with responses from the congregation during a church service.

literal

1 describes the meaning and usage of a word or phrase which is the usual one, not a figurative one. The literal meaning of *pig* is an animal, the figurative meaning is 'a greedy person'.
2 a misprint in a book, newspaper or magazine.

literary agent

a person who manages the professional affairs of an author.

literary award

an award, usually including money, given to acknowledge the value and pleasure gained from writers and their works.

Some literary awards are of international renown, e.g. the *Booker Prize for Fiction* (Britain), the *Pulitzer Prizes* (USA) and the *Nobel Prize for Literature* (International). Others are of national importance, e.g. the *Whitbread Book of the Year* (Britain), the *Australian Literary Society Gold Medal, Grand Prize of French Poets, Theodore Fontane Prize* (Germany), *National Book Awards* (USA), the *Cervantes Prize for Literature* (Spanish-speaking countries) and the *Gregory Medal* (Ireland).

These awards have three main purposes:

first as a financial award since only a handful of authors are well rewarded (the award may include money, but income from increased sales and personal opportunities as a result of being selected is normally far more beneficial);

second as a way of encouraging people to talk about, read and buy books;

third to allow a writer to be given public acclamation by other writers and publishers, to many winners the most important personal aspect of receiving the award.

literary ballad   See BALLAD.

literate

describes a person or people who can read and write and, less often, a person who has been educated to a high level in a particular subject. See ILLITERATE.

literati   /lit-*a*-**raa**-tee/

people who have been educated to a high level. It is now an old-fashioned word.

literatim

a word meaning 'letter for letter', used for example to describe how a handwritten copy of a manuscript was made. See VERBATIM.

literature

written works including novels, essays, drama, verse, biographies etc, especially those considered to be of a high standard. Literature can also refer to works from a particular area, or in a particular language or for a particular subject, e.g. *African literature, Spanish literature* or *medical literature.*

litotes   /**lie**-toh-teez/

a figure of speech that uses understatement ironically, especially by expressing something in the negative in order to emphasize the opposite, e.g. *We travelled no small distance* meaning 'We travelled a long way'. See HYPERBOLE.

litterateur   /lit-*a*-raa-**ter**/

a professional author, especially one who studies and writes about literature.

Litterateur can also be used as a pejorative to refer to an author who is not serious or careful.

little magazine

a magazine that contains experimental pieces of writing, especially one of interest to only a minority of readers.

liturgical drama

drama that formed part of a Christian church service during early medieval Europe. Both the clergy and ordinary people took part and these plays were extremely popular.

Liturgical plays provided original material for the mystery plays. See MEDIEVAL DRAMA, MYSTERY PLAY.

Liverpool poets

a group of working-class poets who grew up in Liverpool, England in the same period as the Beatles. They performed their poems in the 1960s and were noted for their frank portrayal of the lives of ordinary people as well as their witty but powerful political criticism. Their styles are individual and experimental. Adrian Henri (b. 1932), Roger McGough (b. 1937) and Brian Patten (b. 1946) are typical Liverpool poets. Here is Roger McGough's *40-Love* (1971):

40	Love
Middle	aged
couple	playing
ten	nis
when	the
game	ends
and	they
go	home
the	net
will	still
be	be
tween	them.

loan word

a word adopted from another language, e.g. *le weekend* used in French.

localism

a word, phrase or pronunciation that is only used in a particular area.

locative

a word or phrase used to express place or direction.

loc. cit.

an abbreviation of the Latin *loco citato* meaning 'in the place quoted', used to refer to a book, page etc already mentioned. See IBID., ID.

locution

a word or phrase, especially with reference to the manner or style of a speech or piece of writing.

Locution can refer particularly to a roundabout way of expressing a feeling or idea, a common characteristic in the works of James Joyce (1882–1941). See CIRCUMLOCUTION.

logogram

a symbol used to represent a word or phrase, e.g. ∴, c/o and &.

logorrhoea   /log-*a*-**ree**-*a*/

the condition of talking far too much and too often. Its vulgar equivalent is *verbal diarrhoea*.

long syllable

a syllable in classical verse that is long in duration. It is marked by the symbol /. See IONIC, SHORT SYLLABLE.

loq.

an abbreviation of the Latin *loquitur* meaning 'he or she speaks', used in former times as a stage direction.

lowbrow

describes a person with very little intellectual, literary or artistic taste, or literature, music, painting etc produced to appeal to such a person. See HIGHBROW.

low comedy

comedy that has no intellectual purpose and is not sophisticated. Low comedy gets laughter from an audience using practical jokes, coarse

humour, rough and simple behaviour, drunkenness and slapstick. See
HIGH COMEDY.

Low comedy is not a particular kind of play but is an element in
many dramas. It is the essential characteristic of scenes of comic relief
in many of Shakespeare's tragedies but is especially essential to farce.
Examples can easily be found in Shakespeare's *The Merry Wives of
Windsor*.

lower case

small letters in printed text, not capitals.

lyric

describes verse that is emotional and imaginative, often with the form
and rhythm of a song.

Lyric verse originated in ancient Greece where it meant songs
accompanied by a lyre (an ancient Greek stringed instrument like a
small U-shaped harp). When Terpander of Lesbos established a regular
scale for the seven-stringed lute in the 7th century BC, there was an
enormous growth of lyric verse, and lyric songs are one of the most
popular poetic forms even today.

Its meaning has become more specific over the centuries and lyric
verse now refers to a short poem, nonnarrative and nondramatic,
written in the first person (who is not necessarily the poet) which tells
of an individual's feelings and mood. Love is obviously a favourite
subject. Although many verse forms can be lyric, such as the ode,
sonnet, elegy, even the dramatic monologue, it is the expression of
personal feelings that gives the lyric its particular quality.

The Elizabethans wrote a great deal of lyric verse, some of which
was set to music, Thomas Campion's poetry for example. The metaphysical poets tended to drop music and compose lyric verse that is
less graceful but more realistic and direct. Here is the opening stanza of
John Donne's lyric poem *The Dreame* (1633) with its realistic imitation of speech:

> Deare love, for nothing less than thee
> Would I have broke this happy dreame,
>   It was a theme
> For reason, much too strong for phantasie,
> Therefore thou wakd'st me wisely; yet
> My Dreame thou brok'st not, but continued'st it,
> Thou art so truth, that thoughts of thee suffice,
> To make dreames truths; and fables histories;
> Enter these armes, for since thou thoughtst it best,
> Not to dreame all my dreame, let's act the rest.

The romantics at the end of the 18th century widened the scope of the lyric to include a more reflective type of poetry; William Wordsworth's *Lines written above Tintern Abbey* (1798) is a well-known example.

Many examples of modern verse are lyric. Here is a short poem by the American poet Amy Lowell (1874–1925) about lovers parting, called *The Taxi*:

> When I go away from you
> The world beats dead
> Like a slackened drum.
> I call out for you against the jutted stars
> And shout into the ridges of the wind.
> Streets coming fast,
> One after the other,
> Wedge you away from me,
> And the lamps of the city prick my eyes
> So that I can no longer see your face.
> Why should I leave you,
> To wound myself upon the sharp edges of the night?

lyrics

the words of a popular song or a song in a musical. See SONG.

M

macaronic verse

humorous verse, usually vulgar and bawdy, that mixes vocabulary from a poet's own language with that of another, usually Latin. The Italian poet Teofilo Folengo, whose pseudonym was Merlin Coccai, is the best-known exponent, describing his *Opus Macaronicum* (1517) as like macaroni *a gross rude and rustic mixture of flour, cheese and butter*.

Several examples exist in other European languages including English, especially in modern limericks where the writer uses modern French, Spanish or Italian colloquial expressions to good comic effect. Here is an example mixing English with French:

> There was a young lady of Nantes,
> *Très jolie et très élégante*,
> But her **** was so small

It was no good at all
Except for *la plume de ma tante*.

madrigal

a short lyric poem set to music using themes concerning love or pastoral life and meant to be sung by several voices.

Madrigals were first written in Italy in the 14th century and usually consisted of three stanzas each composed of three rhyming lines followed by a rhyming couplet. Later examples were of various lengths, some as short as six lines, but usually ending with a rhyming couplet.

Madrigals were popular in England during the later part of the 16th and early 17th centuries. There is a beautiful example in Shakespeare's *Measure for Measure* beginning 'Take, O take those lips away'.

Thomas Weelkes (c. 1575–1623) wrote the well-known madrigal *As Vesta was from Latmos Hill descending*, but perhaps the greatest composer of English madrigals was John Wilbye (1574–1638) who wrote the popular *Draw on Sweet Night*.

magazine

a publication that contains articles, pictures, stories, cartoons, puzzles etc produced as a set of pages without a hard cover.

magnum opus

a great work of literature, especially the best example of a writer's work. *Nostromo* (1904) is Joseph Conrad's magnum opus.

main clause

a clause used alone as a simple sentence, e.g. *He reads often*, or a clause in a complex sentence that can be used as a simple sentence, as in *Because he enjoys novels, **he reads often***. In the example *He enjoys novels and he reads often*, the sentence contains two clauses of equal status and function; neither can be described as 'main' in relation to the other. But, both can be 'main' in relation to any other subordinate clause, as in *Although he has poor eyesight, **he enjoys novels** and **he reads often***. See COORDINATE and SUBORDINATE CLAUSE.

main verb

the verb used in the main clause of a complex sentence, e.g. *We **laugh** so much when she tells jokes* or *The man who reads the news on television **wears** horrible shirts.*

majuscule   /madg-*a*-skyool/

a very large letter, usually a capital letter, used in printing or writing. Majuscule describes in particular the large rounded capitals used in

Greek and Roman manuscripts of the 4th to 8th centuries AD. See
MINUSCULE, UNCIAL.

malapropism

an unintentional incorrect use of one word instead of another that
sounds similar.

The term comes from Mrs Malaprop, a character in Sheridan's comedy *The Rivals* (1775) who frequently used words incorrectly, e.g.
'She's as headstrong as an allegory on the banks of the Nile'. However,
such forms of verbal humour were used long before Sheridan. Dog-
berry, in Shakespeare's *Much Ado About Nothing* often made such
mistakes: 'Comparisons are odorous' is a well-known example. See
SPOONERISM.

manifesto

a public written or spoken declaration of political, religious or philosophical belief including its principles, intentions and policies. The
best-known political example is Marx and Engel's *The Communist
Manifesto* (1848). Literary movements have also published manifestos,
such as André Breton's *Manifeste de Surréalisme* (1924).

manner, adverb of

an adverb or adverbial phrase that describes how something is or was
done, e.g. *well, very fast, like a fish, Chinese-style*, as in *He writes well,
They ran very fast, She swims like a fish* and *We like eating Chinese-
style*. See MEANS.

mannerism

a distinctive element of a writer's style, including the use of certain
words, sentence structures and conventional forms.

manners, comedy of

a comedy that mocks the conventions and social manners of upper-
class society. The characters represent familiar types rather than individual personalities, and the plot is less important than witty satirical
dialogue. See HIGH COMEDY.

Although two of Shakespeare's comedies, *Love's Labour's Lost* and
Much Ado About Nothing, are often called comedies of manners, this
type of comedy reached its height during the Restoration period.

The best-known writer in France of such comedies is Molière with
masterpieces such as *Le Bourgeois Gentilhomme* (1670). Comedies of
manners were revived in England by William Congreve (1670–1729)
with plays such as *The Way of the World* (1700), by Oliver Goldsmith

(c. 1730–1774) and Richard Sheridan (1751–1816); many of Oscar Wilde's plays are also excellent examples, including *The Importance of Being Earnest* (1895). Modern plays such as Noel Coward's *Private Lives* (1930) are also comedies of manners.

mantra

1 any part of the Hindu literature of Veda that is a psalm of praise.
2 a sacred word with spiritual power used as a chant in Buddhist meditation.

manual

a book that contains instructions, information and diagrams about how to do something, especially how to build, mend or use machinery, e.g. *a car manual* or *a computer manual*.

manuscript

a document written by hand, especially the original handwritten version of a book or article. Manuscript is now also used to refer to a typed script, or one produced by computer, that is prepared for a publisher.

Before the use of printing in Europe (from about the 15th century), books were produced as handwritten manuscripts, usually in monasteries. Professional scribes made copies of classical and medieval literature; many were richly decorated with elaborate, colourful lettering and ornamentation.

The abbreviation of *manuscript* is **MS** or **ms** and of *manuscripts* it is **MSS** or **mss**.

marginalia

notes written in the margin of a book, either by the author as comments on the text, or by a reader who is studying the text.

masculine caesura

a caesura that follows a stressed syllable (⌒), as in Kathleen Raine's *The Silver Stag* (1943):

> On the horizon of the dawn he stood,
> The target of my eager sight; || that shone
> Oh from the sun or from my kindled heart
> Outlined in the sky, shaped on the infinite.

See FEMININE CAESURA.

masculine ending

a stressed syllable at the end of a line of verse, as in this excerpt from *The Scholar Gypsy* (1853) by Matthew Arnold:

> Go, for they call you, shepherd from the hill;
> Go, shepherd, and untie the wattled cotes

See FEMININE ENDING.

masculine rhyme

a single monosyllabic rhyme in a poem, as in the last words of the alternate lines in the opening verse of Anthony Thwaite's *The Pond* (1967):

> With nets and kitchen sieves they raid the pond,
> Chasing the minnows into bursts of mud
> Scooping and chopping, raking up frond after frond
> Of swollen weed after a week of flood.

This is the most common form of rhyme in English verse but French poets often alternate it with feminine rhyme. See FEMININE RHYME.

masque or mask

a dramatic entertainment using pantomime, dialogue, dancing and singing. During medieval times in Europe, processions of masked figures would dance in the streets and enter buildings to perform silent dances (see MUMMERY). These entertainments developed into elaborate spectacles and by the 16th and 17th centuries were large popular entertainments performed in front of royalty, the nobility and official foreign visitors. They became known as *masques* with gorgeous costumes and elaborate scenery; the plot, which was usually allegorical or mythological, was usually negligible. All the actors wore masks and the entertainment ended with a dance in which the audience joined.

The playwright and poet Ben Jonson (1572–1637) and the architect Inigo Jones (1573–1652) collaborated to produce some splendidly extravagant masques, but the two best-known literary examples are Shakespeare's masque in *The Tempest* featuring the Roman goddesses Ceres and Juno, and John Milton's *Comus* (1634).

In 1642 when the Puritans closed the theatres in England, masques were banned and so the genre never developed. But it had a considerable influence on later drama, particularly on staging techniques. For example, Inigo Jones had introduced the proscenium stage and this was widely adopted for the production of plays when the theatres reopened at the Restoration.

mass noun = UNCOUNTABLE NOUN.

masterpiece

an outstanding piece of work by a writer or artist. *Don Quixote* (1605 and 1615) is Cervantes' masterpiece.

material

the information, traditional tale, legend etc that is the basis for a literary work.

maxim

a brief statement of a general truth; it is based on experience of life and includes or suggests advice, e.g. *The higher you climb, the further you fall*. See APOPHTHEGM.

maximizer

an adverb or adverbial phrase (an *intensifier*) that affects the meaning of a sentence by increasing the force of part of it as much as possible, e.g. *entirely, altogether, most willingly*, or *in every way*, as in *I agree entirely* or *I like it in every way*. Maximizers are the strongest form of amplifier. See MINIMIZER.

means, adverb of

an adverb or adverbial phrase that describes the method or means used to do something, as in *We can't cure it medically, Let's go by car* and *I signed it with his pen*. See MANNER.

measure = METRE.

medieval drama

drama created and performed during the Middle Ages (1000–1500 AD) in Europe, especially religious drama.

From the 10th century, words were added to the chants sung in churches as verbal elaborations and these developed into short plays performed by the clergy. These plays were first performed in Latin but gradually the people's own language was introduced, for example Middle English in England. Performances had earlier taken place inside the churches but they gradually passed out of the hands of the clergy and were taken into open public places, such as market squares, by ordinary people. Local trade guilds became the controllers of these productions. See MYSTERY PLAY.

Apart from religious drama, on festival days a large amount of folk drama and dance was also performed and included dramatizations of traditional tales, such as those about Robin Hood, and the early forms of masques (see MUMMERY). See MIRACLE and MORALITY PLAY.

medieval romance

stories of the adventures of chivalrous and gallant knights and heroes
that first appeared in France in the 12th century but quickly spread
across Europe. By the 13th century, romances in Middle English were
becoming popular in England. Many of them were based on French
originals, especially on the 'chansons de geste'. There were three
topics: *England*, using traditional tales of folk heroes, *antiquity*, using
stories such as the legends from ancient Greece, Rome and Troy
including Chaucer's *Troylus and Cryseyde* (c. 1385), and *Britain*, using
Arthurian legends including *Sir Gawain and the Green Knight* (14th
century) and Sir Thomas Malory's *Le Morte Darthur* (1469–1470). See
COURTLY LOVE.

meiosis = LITOTES   /mie-**oh**-sis/

melodrama

a play, film or story with exaggerated emotions and sensationalism,
and often with exaggerated action. **melodramatic** adjective.

Melodrama in classical Greek theatre was a romantic and sensational
drama with music and song (*melodrama* in Greek means 'song
drama'). Music remained an essential element up to the 19th century.
Modern melodrama developed in Italy towards the end of the 16th
century at about the same time as classical opera; the music composer
Handel referred to his compositions as opera or melodrama. French
playwrights two hundred years later established a separate genre by
excluding music while elaborating the dialogue and including the exaggerated or sentimental elements. Characters have extreme personalities, good or evil, there is always a great deal of emotion and action,
and the plays and stories usually have happy endings. From the 19th
century melodramas have been very popular and many established
plays are still performed, including *Sweeney Todd, the Demon Barber
of Fleet Street* (1847).

Today, melodrama is used mainly in film or on television but some
excellent 20th century examples can still be seen on stage including
Edgar Wallace's *The Case of the Frightened Lady* (1931), Jean Paul
Sartre's *Crime Passionel* (1948) and Joe Orton's *Loot* (1965).

Melodrama can also refer to exaggerated and insincere emotional
behaviour.

memoirs

an account of thoughts, experiences and events during a period or
lifetime written from the personal viewpoint of the writer. Memoirs
are similar to an autobiography, but the emphasis is less on the self and
more on the people one has met and the events one has lived through.

Most memoirs are produced from a diary or journal that has been dutifully maintained to provide the intimate detail and anecdotal references that make good memoirs interesting. Almost any person who becomes well known in public life now publishes her or his memoirs.

Mermaid, the

a tavern (a kind of pub) that once stood in central London on the north side of the river Thames at Blackfriars. It was the meeting-place of many writers during Shakespeare's time, including Shakespeare himself, Donne, Marlowe, Jonson, Beaumont and Fletcher. It had become one of the first literary 'clubs', having been established by Sir Walter Raleigh in about 1603. Leading poets and playwrights would gather here every first Friday of the month.

It is praised in a famous quote from Beaumont in a poem to Ben Jonson: 'What things have we seen done at the Mermaid!' and John Keats also wrote his poem *Lines on the Mermaid Tavern* (1818).

meta language

a set of terms or symbols used to describe and discuss a language, especially a foreign language. Meta language is often used in textbooks on linguistics or in teachers' guides to language learning courses.

metaphor

a figure of speech in which a person or thing is described by comparison with someone or something else – by implication and not by using *like ...* or *as ...* , e.g. *You're a feather in my arms.* (*You're as light as a feather* is a simile). See SIMILE. **metaphorical** adjective.

A metaphor has been called a **compressed simile** and there is much truth in this because whereas a simile makes a comparison between two people, objects or ideas that do not seem to have anything in common (*A woman is like a feather*), a metaphor goes one stage further and unites the comparison in a single idea (*The woman is a feather*). See DIMINISHING METAPHOR.

The following is a good example of a metaphor from Shakespeare's *Henry IV Part I*:

> To put down Richard, that sweet lovely rose,
> And plant this thorn, this canker Bolingbroke.

Metaphors are very common in everyday conversation, and many are so common, e.g. *to take the bull by the horns*, that they have lost any strength or quality and are sometimes referred to as **dead metaphors**. Writers use metaphors a great deal but good writers search for fresh, original comparisons or creative adaptations of well-known metaphors. If these new metaphors are too farfetched, they may not succeed but if they are clever, apt and easily understood they add richness to the writing, as in this one (referring to the sky as a blanket) from T E Hulme's *The Embankment* (1912):

> O, God, make small
> The old star-eaten blanket of the sky,
> That I may fold it round me and in comfort lie.

A **mixed metaphor** is a mixture of two unrelated figures of speech in one statement, e.g. *A cat may be as poor as a church mouse but it may look at a king.* Most are considered unsatisfactory in the imagery they try to present but others show great creative and literary skill, as in Hamlet's *to take arms against a sea of troubles.*

metaphysical

describes verse that is philosophical and concerns thoughts and feelings about the nature of existence or the origin and structure of the universe.

The term refers particularly to the 17th century English poets Herbert, Crashaw, Vaughan, Maxwell, Cowley and the greatest of them all, John Donne. The verse is intellectual, analytical and passionate, the imagery is elaborate, the expression is extravagant and the themes include the physical world, love, death and religious devotion.

This opening stanza of Donne's *The Sunne Rising* (1633) is typical:

> Busie old foole, unruly Sunne,
> Why dost thou thus,
> Through windowes, and through curtaines call on us?
> Must to thy motions lovers seasons run?
> Sawcy pedantique wretch, goe chide
> Late school boyes and sowre prentices,
> Goe tell court-huntsmen that the King will ride,
> Call countrey ants to harvest offices;
> Love, all alike, no season knowes, nor clyme,
> Nor houres, dayes, moneths, which are rags of time.

metonymy   /mi-**ton**-i-mee/

a figure of speech in which the name of something is used to represent a more general but closely-related thing, e.g. *the stage* used to represent the whole field of dramatic performances, or *the crown* to represent a monarch or royal power.

metre

the organization of rhythm in verse into various regular patterns or units. In English verse, these units are based on stress, and it is the combination of stressed and unstressed syllables into the various patterns or units that gives each poem its rhythm or metre. **metrical** adjective.

Each unit is called a **foot** or **metrical foot** and this is the basic unit of rhythm in English poetry.

Many combinations of syllables or feet are possible but the most common is the *iamb* or *iambic foot*, which is a 2-syllable foot, an unstressed syllable followed by a stressed syllable as (˘ ‾) as in this well-known line from Aphra Behn's *The Moor's Revenge* (1677):

Ĭ ōwe | ă dūt|ў, whēre | Ĭ cān|nŏt lōve. |

Other popular forms are:

a the *anapaest* or *anapaestic foot*, which is a 3-syllable foot, two unstressed syllables followed by a stressed syllable as (˘ ˘ ‾), as in these lines from Byron's *The Destruction of Sennacherib* (1815):

Thĕ Āssȳr|ĭăn cāme dōwn | lĭke ă wōlf | ŏn thĕ fōld, |
Ănd hĭs cō|hŏrts wĕre glēam|ĭng ĭn pūrp|lĕ ănd gōld. |

b the *dactyl* or *dactylic foot*, which is a 3-syllable foot, a stressed syllable followed by two unstressed syllables as (‾ ˘ ˘), as in this extract from Lord Tennyson's *Charge of the Light Brigade* (1854):

Fōrwărd, thĕ | Līght Brĭgăde, |
Chārge fŏr thĕ | gūns, hĕ săid. |

c the *spondee* or *spondaic foot*, which is a 2-syllable foot with both syllables stressed (‾ ‾), as in this line from John Milton's *Paradise Lost* (1667):

Rōcks, cāves, | lākes, fēns, | bōgs, dēns | ănd shādes | ŏf dēath

d the *trochee* or *trochaic foot*, which is a 2-syllable foot, a stressed syllable followed by an unstressed syllable as (‾ ˘), as in these lines from Milton's *L'Allegro* (1632):

Cōme ănd | trīp ĭt | ās yĕ | gō |
Ōn thĕ | līght făn|tāstĭc | tōe |

This process of analysing metrical patterns is called *scansion*.

Metrical feet are often used in combination with each other rather than forming a complete poem on their own. As well as variety in types of feet, there can be variety in the number of feet in a line of verse:

a *monometer*	one foot
a *dimeter*	two feet
a *trimeter*	three feet
a *tetrameter*	four feet

a *pentameter*	five feet
a *hexameter*	six feet
a *heptameter*	seven feet
an *octometer*	eight feet

Modern poetry is much less likely to use metrical forms as rigidly as earlier poetry. Modern poets often experiment freely with metrical forms. See FREE VERSE.

microfiche   /mie-kroh-feesh/

a piece of film on which text is reproduced in very small letters that can be read only when the film is enlarged onto a screen. It is ideal for storing information, for example the contents of a catalogue that needs to be referred to regularly.

mid-Atlantic

the form of English produced as a mixture of British and American English including vocabulary, pronunciation and syntax.

middlebrow

describes a person with an average or general intellectual, literary or artistic taste, or literature, music, painting etc produced to appeal to such a person. See HIGHBROW, LOWBROW.

Middle English

the kind of English used between about 1100 and 1500; it gradually developed into Modern English.

The Middle English period can be divided into two parts. The *Anglo-French period* dates from the successful Norman invasion of England in 1066 to about 1350. During this period, a French dialect introduced by the Norman settlers predominated. This influence was particularly evident in the Norman monasteries that were established across England and became centres of intellectual life. This period was followed by the *Anglo-Saxon period* between about 1350 and 1500 when the native Anglo-Saxon or Old English predominated again. This second period is very important in the history of English literature. There is almost no record left of literature written in English during the first period.

The earliest poems in English are influenced very strongly by French themes and verse forms. The late literature from the Anglo-Saxon period includes folk ballads, mystery plays, morality plays, and various forms of medieval religious drama and the masques. This is not only the age of Chaucer's *The Canterbury Tales* (c. 1387) and *Troylus and Cryseyde* (1385), but also Langland's poem *Piers Plowman* (?1360–1399). In Scotland, William Dunbar and Robert Henryson, known as the Scottish Chaucerians, were writing. At the end of the period, Sir Thomas Malory produced his fine prose piece *Le Morte Darthur* (1469–1470).

middle rhyme = INTERNAL RHYME.

mid position

the position of a word or phrase, e.g. of an adverb, between the subject and the main verb in a sentence, as in *They **totally** disapprove of your plan*. See END and INITIAL POSITION.

millboard   See BOARDS.

Miltonic sonnet   See SONNET.

mime

drama in which actors use movement and gestures, not words. Mime can also refer to an actor who is skilled at mime. Mime originated in Greece about 500 BC and developed as a comic portrayal of everyday life. However, it later became bawdy and sensual and so was driven into obscurity by the Catholic church.

Mime continued to be performed by wandering players throughout Europe in medieval times and it influenced masques, mystery plays and much traditional folk drama of that period, especially mumming plays (see MUMMERY). In Shakespeare's *Hamlet*, the travelling players mime the action before their intended performance. At about this time, mime was enjoying a revival in Italy in the 16th century where it formed an important part of commedia dell'arte.

Today, it continues to form part of traditional pantomime and has influenced comic methods such as slapstick, although it is also popular as a genre in its own right. Mime is particularly popular in France where it is highly regarded as a dramatic form with Marcel Marceau (b. 1923) established as the greatest mime in the world.

mimesis   /mi-**mee**-sis/

the use of imitation in literature to represent human behaviour or the natural world.

Mimesis is used most often in literary criticism with reference to the ancient Greek philosopher Aristotle's *Poetics* (4th century BC) in which he refers to assessment of dramatic construction and content as an imitation of reality. **mimetic** adjective.

minimizer

an adverb or adverbial phrase (an *intensifier*) that affects the meaning of a sentence by reducing the force of part of it as much as possible, e.g.

scarcely, in the slightest as in *I **scarcely** knew him* or *She didn't care in the slightest*. Minimizers are the strongest form of downtoner. See MAXIMIZER.

minstrel

a travelling musician and poet who was very popular in Europe in the 13th and 14th centuries. He was an entertainer who travelled from one market town to another carrying news and gossip as well as entertaining people with his songs, stories and poems while he played a small drum (called a tabor) or a small harp. See TROUBADOUR.

Many minstrels travelled between large cities carrying news and spreading popular ballads and stories throughout Europe. The invention of printing at the end of the 15th century caused the gradual demise of the minstrel.

minuscule

a small cursive letter or style of writing that developed from majuscules between the 7th and 9th centuries AD, used in medieval manuscripts. See MAJUSCULE, UNCIAL.

miracle play

a kind of non-scriptural drama from the late Middle Ages in Europe that developed out of the mystery plays. The plots were based on the life of a saint, the story of a miracle or a particular miraculous act by the Virgin Mary (called a *virgin play*).

Although they were very popular, very few examples survive. The best known is a collection of forty-two miracle plays from the late 14th century in France, *Miracles de Notre Dame*. Miracle play is often used interchangeably with mystery play. See MORALITY PLAY.

miscellanea

a collection of a variety of examples, especially different kinds of literary works.

mise en scène   /meez aan **sen**/

the arrangement of scenery and properties on the stage for a play, or the set for a film.

misnomer

a wrong or inappropriate term or name given to a person or thing.

misprint

a mistake in the printed text of a book, journal etc. **misprint** verb.

misquote

to quote an author, text or speech incorrectly. **misquotation** noun.

missal

a book with all the prayers, church services etc for masses during the whole year.

mixed metaphor   See METAPHOR.

mnemonic   /ni-**mon**-ik/

any device used to help a person to remember something, e.g. the statement *Every Good Boy Deserves Fun* used to remember the notes on the lines in written music (EGBDF).

mock-epic or mock-heroic

describes a kind of satirical poem that uses the structure and pompous style of classical epic verse but has a trivial theme.

The most famous example is probably Alexander Pope's *The Rape of the Lock* (1712 and 1714). Shorter poems of a similar satirical style are also described as mock-epic. Lewis Carroll's nonsense poem *The Hunting of the Snark* (1876) is mock-epic.

modal auxiliary verb, modal auxiliary or modal verb

an auxiliary verb that has its own meaning but also modifies the meaning of a main verb in a sentence; *can, could, may, might, must, need, ought, shall, should, will* and *would* are modal auxiliaries, and *dare* and *used to* are also sometimes referred to as modal auxiliaries.

All modal auxiliaries (except *dare* and *used to*) have a meaning related to possibility, probability or certainty, as in *I might come, You could be wrong* and *You must be her sister*. Each verb also has its own meaning or usage; many are related to permission or obligation, as in *May I come in?, You must pay to enter, You'll need a passport*, or to ability, as in *Can you cook?, You ought to be able to do it*, or to willingness, as in *I would if I could*.

modern classic

a literary work, especially a novel, by a modern writer that is considered to have excellent qualities that will make it a classic work in the future.

Modern English

the kind of English used since 1500 that has developed from Middle English. Of course, the English language continues to adapt, change and develop but this is generally more to do with the expansion of vocabulary and usages rather than significant changes in grammatical structure.

Modern English can also refer to the period since the First World War (1914–1918), a time that is characterized by experimentation and innovation in literature. There can be no precise definition of this use of modern; there are no unifying features because it continues to be so varied.

modernism

the movements and tendencies in literature and art during the 20th century, especially the rejection of rigidly traditional or conventional styles and a deliberate emphasis on experimentation and free expression.

modifier

a word or phrase that describes, limits or changes the meaning of another word. Adjectives are modifiers of nouns. Adverbs can modify an adjective, as in *a very bad headache*, another adverb, as in *He came too late*, a verb, as in *Suddenly we saw it* or a clause, as in *It's late; nevertheless I'll phone him.* **modification** noun. **modify** verb.

monody

a song that mourns a person's death and expresses feelings of grief and loss. It dates back to classical Greek tragedy where the monody was sung by one person. See DIRGE, ELEGY, LAMENT, THRENODY. There have also been attempts at lighthearted monody; one of S T Coleridge's early poems is called *Monody on a Tea Kettle* (1790).

monograph

an essay on a single topic or theme.

monologue

a long speech made by one person; it can be part of a drama or a complete poem, play etc. *A Light Woman* (1855) by Robert Browning is a monologue. Tom Stoppard's short play *New-Found-Land* (1976) consists almost entirely of monologue. See DRAMATIC MONOLOGUE.

monometer

a line of verse with one metrical foot as in the first six lines of Ogden Nash's *The Guppy* (1949):

> Whales have calves, |
> Cats have kittens, |
> Bears have cubs, |
> Bats have bittens. |

Swans have cygnets, |
Seals have puppies, |
But guppies just have little guppies.

monostich   /mon-*a*-stik/

1 a line of verse.
2 a poem that consists of one line.

monosyllable

a word with one syllable, e.g. *cup*. **monosyllabic** adjective.

montage   /mon-taaz*h*/

a process used in art to create a scene or atmosphere; a set of pictures
are grouped together or superimposed on each other. It is also a
technique used in filming by using a series of short pictures that
quickly follow each other.

Montage is sometimes used to refer to similar devices used by an
author when writing a descriptive scene.

mood

1 the general atmosphere created in a literary work that often
produces a particular feeling in the reader or audience, e.g. fearful,
gloomy, lighthearted.
2 categories of verb forms used to show command or request (the
imperative mood), to state a fact (the *indicative mood*) or to show
conditions, doubt etc (the *subjunctive mood*), e.g. **Come** *here!*, **Don't**
be late!, *Man is mortal* and *I'd apologize if I* **were** *you.*

morality play

a kind of drama that dates from the late Middle Ages in Europe, about
1400 to 1500; it developed from the mystery plays and the miracle
plays.

The plays were allegories in which virtues and vices such as Patience,
Mercy, Greed or Lust are the main characters, usually with good and
evil forces caught up in a spiritual struggle. Although the earlier plays
were typically naive, they were popular because of their familiar characterization and vigorous action, and because they dealt with the single
issue that dominated Christian spiritual concern at the time, the
struggle between God, man and the devil. The best-known example
from this early period is *Everyman* (15th century).

Morality plays from the 16th century had become much more
sophisticated and increasingly included political or social issues rather
than religious ones; Sir David Lindsay's *Ane Pleasant Satyre of the
Thrie Estaitis* (c. 1540) is a typical example. But they continued to

examine or portray different kinds of human nature and this dramatization of real contemporary life was the foundation of English
comedy.

From the middle of the 16th century, morality plays lost their popularity, especially in Elizabethan times. However, their influence is
obvious in many plays of this period, including Marlowe's *Dr Faustus*
(c. 1601).

morpheme

a speech element that has meaning or a grammatical function and
which cannot be separated into smaller parts, e.g. *book* has one morpheme; *books* has two morphemes: book-s; *bookings* has three morphemes: book-ing-s. See LEXEME, LEXICON (3), PHONEME.

morphology

the study of the ways in which words are formed in a language and the
classification of patterns of inflections, how parts combine etc. See
SYNTAX (2).

mother tongue

the language that a person learns as a child and uses while growing up
at home. It is also called a *first language*.

motif   /moh-**teef**/

a recurring theme or idea in a literary work or one that links several
literary works. Motifs can be identified as a part of the plot, a type of
character or situation, or even the type of imagery or phrasing. See
LEITMOTIF.

mot juste   /moh **zh**oost/

a French phrase meaning 'the appropriate word or phrase', used to
refer to particularly apt vocabulary in a description etc.

mot propre   /moh **prop**-*ra*/

a French phrase meaning 'the correct word or phrase', used to refer to
vocabulary that is particularly suitable and therefore essential to
choose.

movement

1 the action in the plot of a literary work, especially when it is strong
and obvious. A play that lacks movement is often criticized as being
slow and boring.
2 a recognizable new development or trend during a period of literary
activity, as in the *free verse movement* in contemporary poetry. Some
movements have been set up deliberately to influence change, a well-

known example being the *Oxford movement* (1833–c. 1845) which was committed to the reform of the Church of England and produced ninety learned essays. See SCHOOL.

A group of British poets in the 1950s is sometimes referred to as **the Movement** because of their distinctive qualities of traditional structure and interest in human experiences in the natural world rather than spiritual or mental concerns. Poets such as Philip Larkin (1922–1985), John Wain (b. 1925) and Kingsley Amis (b. 1922) have produced poetry that is typical of this group.

MS, MSS, ms, mss   See MANUSCRIPT.

muckrake

to find out and publicize the faults and wrongdoings of a well-known person or organization, especially one with power or influence. **muckraking** noun.

mudsling

to accuse an opponent, especially a political opponent, of doing wrong or bad things.

multi-word verb

any verb that contains several words, e.g. *go away*, *get down to it* or *run out on her*. See PHRASAL, PREPOSITIONAL and PREPOSITIONAL PHRASAL VERB.

mumbo-jumbo

meaningless language, especially because it is too complicated or technical, in other words it uses obscure and difficult vocabulary.

mummery or mumming play

a kind of early and simple folk drama that was usually performed by masked or disguised players (called *mummers*) who entered buildings, gave a performance, collected money and then moved on. See MASQUE.

Either all or most of the play was performed as a mime with stock characters such as a fool, a doctor and a knight called St George (he is killed in the play and then revived by the doctor). The play was performed on festival days, especially in spring and after funerals; the play's theme of struggle, death and resurrection is clearly appropriate.

There is much evidence that mummeries were performed regularly up to about a hundred years ago and there is a description of a typical performance in Thomas Hardy's *Return of the Native* (1878).

muse

1 the goddess who inspires an individual writer or artist but especially a poet.

2 one of Zeus' nine daughters in ancient Greek mythology; each was responsible for a particular art or science but traditionally they are considered to have inspired and protected poets and so poets have traditionally asked for help from the muses when writing. The usual names for the nine muses are: *Calliope* (epic verse), *Clio* (history), *Erato* (love lyrics), *Euterpe* (music), *Melpomene* (tragedy), *Polyhymnia* (religious verse), *Terpsichore* (choral dance), *Thalia* (comedy) and *Urania* (astronomy).

musical or musical comedy

a modern form of light entertainment that developed in the United States of America from light opera, burlesque and vaudeville. It had become a recognizable dramatic form by the beginning of the 20th century.

Musicals include a spoken dialogue with songs from individual characters or the whole cast, and orchestral music and dance. The earlier ones placed separated songs and dances between episodes in the spoken dialogue. *Showboat* (1927) changed the style of future musicals by integrating the songs with the dialogue. The staging and costumes in musicals are elaborate in order to make a great visual spectacle. The storylines are usually romantic and light and usually have a happy ending.

Musicals became the most popular form of theatrical entertainment in the past sixty years attracting huge audiences most of whom have had no other experience of the theatre. Many musicals have been made into successful films that have brought them worldwide popularity and established the songs and music as classic standards. Television has also been responsible for their enormous popularity. There are many examples including *South Pacific, Carousel* and *Hello, Dolly!* Some highly successful musicals are adaptations of classic drama, including *Kiss Me Kate* (1948) based on Shakespeare's *The Taming of the Shrew*, *West Side Story* (1957) using the story themes from Shakespeare's *Romeo and Juliet*, and *My Fair Lady* (1956) adapted from G B Shaw's *Pygmalion* (1912). See SONG.

The audience expectations of large casts and extravagant sets have made musicals extremely expensive to produce and, although there are occasional revivals of old favourites, new ones are now seldom written. However, there has been success in Europe with an adaptation of the American model which uses less glitter but more serious plots or themes and more sophisticated choreography, especially those concerning historical episodes or characters that make pertinent comments about society today. *Les Misérables*, based on Victor Hugo's novel of 1862, is a typical example.

music drama

an opera in which the plot and characters have the same importance as the music and singing. Wagner coined the term as a fitting description of his later operas.

mystery fiction

novels, stories or plays in which the plot involves the solving of a mystery, usually a crime. Like detective fiction, which is the main form of mystery fiction, there is a reversal of the usual plot sequence and the catastrophe occurs at the beginning. See DETECTIVE and SPY FICTION.

mystery play

a kind of religious drama developed in Europe in the Middle Ages (1000–1500) that became the most important dramatic form of the period.

Plays that had developed inside churches as part of religious services were increasingly performed outdoors in open squares by ordinary people. Local craft and trade guilds took over responsibility for them and organized performances into annual events. *Mystery* at that time could also mean 'guild'.

By the 14th century, there were large numbers of these plays covering all aspects of the Bible from the Creation through the story of Christ's Life to the Last Judgement. Each guild took responsibility for one play or episode and the complete cycle of plays or episodes was performed at the feast of Corpus Christi, sixty days after Easter.

These mystery plays were performed on a wheeled stage (a wagon) and when the performance was over it moved on to another spot in the town where the performance began again. In this way, over a period of one or two days, the complete cycle could be seen by everyone. The wagon had a curtained scaffold for the stage while the lower part was used as a dressing-room. Performances became increasingly elaborate with attention paid to costumes, scenery, and even stage machinery and lighting effects. Comic scenes were added which did not always meet with the approval of Church officials.

The guilds took their responsibilities very seriously and large numbers of people were involved in performances; for the audience it was a chance for entertainment and spectacle that had become the highlight of each year. The plays were written in rhyming verse, unpolished but strong. There are several complete cycles in existence today, all of which originated in a particular town. *The York cycle*, the largest, contains forty-eight episodes.

Mystery plays were a central part of medieval life for more than four hundred years; the Reformation in the 16th century put an end to the function and purpose of the mystery plays. And by then morality plays had become more popular. See MORALITY PLAY.

myth

an anonymous tale about a superhuman being that is used to explain natural phenomena and social customs. They have their origins in preliterate society and primitive belief. Myths try to explain or describe the creation of the world, and the purpose of existence and death. Many give an account of the lives of heroes and heroines in which personalities and feelings are described and explored. See LEGEND.

Myths are not concerned with actual history or with morality. They are the product of whole communities or regions rather than individuals and every country or group has its mythology.

Writers often use myths, especially the rich store in ancient Greek and Roman mythologies, as themes or episodes. Some writers, William Blake (1757–1827) in particular, have adapted and combined old myths to create a personal mythology. W B Yeats (1865–1939) also used ancient Celtic myths and folktales in his *A Vision* (1925).

N

narrative

the part of a literary work that gives an account of events or tells the story. The term is also used to mean a story.

Narrative verse is any poem that tells a story; it has a long history and has been extremely popular throughout many cultures. Today, it has been largely superseded by the novel. Epics and ballads are well-known types of narrative verse, although many poems do not fit easily into either category. The ancient Greek poet Homer's *Iliad* and *Odyssey* are early examples. Chaucer's *The Canterbury Tales* (c. 1387) and Milton's *Paradise Lost* (1667) are also narrative verse, together with S T Coleridge's *The Rime of the Ancient Mariner* (1798) and Tennyson's *The Idylls of the King* (1842–1885). There are many other examples, including from contemporary poets Robert Frost's *A Hundred Collars* (1914) and W H Auden's *Letter to Lord Byron* (1937).

narrator

1 a person who recites a story.

2 the character in a literary work who tells the story, either as an observer or as one of the characters involved in the action.

naturalism

a kind of fiction that describes life and the natural world in an objective and scientific way rather than involving the spiritual or supernatural. See REALISM. Writers of naturalist works pay great attention to social environment and to the critical assessment of human weaknesses. **naturalist** adjective and noun.

Émile Zola is acknowledged as giving the greatest expression to naturalism in novels like *Thérèse Raquin* (1867) and *Nana* (1880). Zola had a profound influence on later European writers, especially in Germany where a naturalist movement flourished in Berlin and Munich. Sherwood Anderson (1876–1941) was a prominent American naturalistic writer. Naturalism is obvious in the works of many novelists and dramatists including Tolstoy and Ibsen, Strindberg and Chekhov.

near rhyme = HALF-RHYME.

negative

describes a verb form in a sentence with *not, neither* etc to show denial, refusal etc, e.g. *I do not like it, She won't tell, will she?* See AFFIRMATIVE.

negritude

an awareness of Black, especially African, culture and heritage in a literary work. The term was coined by the French poet Cesaire and the Senegalese poet Senghor in the 1930s. Negritude has always been more closely associated with French-speaking than with English-speaking African writers.

neoclassicism or Neoclassicism

the style in literature and the arts, especially architecture, during the period from the Restoration (1660) to about 1750. **neoclassical** adjective. **neoclassicist** noun.

The principal writers of this period were great admirers of classical Greek and Roman literary works and so they modelled themselves on these writers. They believed that literature is an art form that must be studied, that it has rules to be learned and followed. They believed strongly in reason and logical order (the 18th century is also known as the *Age of Reason*) and their favourite subject was mankind, not so much a person as an individual but as a member of an ordered society, with responsibilities towards that society. They recognized a person's place in the Great Chain of Being, above animals but below the angels, and while acknowledging and celebrating mankind's achievements felt it important for us to realize our limitations and not overreach ourselves. Neoclassicists scorned those who lived by excess or attempted to destroy the harmony and discipline of society. Satire was a weapon frequently and very skilfully used to express this scorn.

The neoclassicists' belief in reason and order is evident in the style of their writing as well as its subject-matter; it is polished, balanced and socially correct. They favoured respect for the three dramatic unities of action, time and space (see UNITIES) as principles set down by the ancient Greek philosopher Aristotle. Their choice of the highly-principled but potentially limiting metrical form, the heroic couplet, is also significant. However, at its best neoclassical writing is far from limited; it is witty, original and highly imaginative.

Some of the major writers of the period were the poet, dramatist and essayist Oliver Goldsmith (c. 1730–1774), the poet and critic Samuel Johnson (1709–1784), the essayists Joseph Addison (1672–1719) and Sir Richard Steele (1672–1729), the poet and dramatist John Dryden (1631–1700), and the poets Alexander Pope (1688–1744) and Jonathan Swift (1667–1745) who dominated the later period, often referred to as the Augustan Age of neoclassicism.

neologism   /ni-**ol**-*a*-dgizm/

a newly-coined word or phrase; it can be a new word or an old one given a new meaning. *Negritude* is a neologism. Current advances in technology have forced the rapid introduction of a range of neologisms for the computing industry.

new comedy

comedy produced in ancient Greece between the 3rd and 4th centuries BC after the decline in Greek power. Gone was Aristophanes' political satire and lyric beauty; in its place were complicated plots and intrigues, usually romantic tales with happy endings and at least one marriage. Stock characters included cunning servants and boastful soldiers; the humour was often farcical. Menander (342–291 BC) was a popular writer of new comedy although very few complete plays of his survive; *The Curmudgeon* is one. See OLD COMEDY.

New comedy influenced several Roman playwrights, including Plautus and Terence, who in turn influenced Tudor and Elizabethan drama. Shakespeare's *The Comedy of Errors* is based on a play by Plautus. New comedy also influenced the later comedies of manners.

new criticism, the

the approach to literary criticism developed principally in the United States of America from the 1920s that considers any literary work as an object to be studied in its own right, with great attention to a detailed examination of the text and a disregard for the personality of the author. New criticism has no fixed system but is more a set of approaches used to uncover the essential merits of literature. This approach to literary criticism is popular today.

newsletter

a printed leaflet or pamphlet that is circulated to members of a group.

Historically, newsletters were handwritten circulars giving news of proceedings in Parliament and the High Court that were sent out to subscribers twice a week. They were produced by Henry Muddiman in the late 17th century, the journalist who was also responsible for the *Oxford Gazette*. See GAZETTE.

newspeak

insincere statements used by politicians and bureaucrats that is deliberately ambiguous or evasive. The term was coined by George Orwell in his novel *Nineteen Eighty Four* (1949).

nocturne

a lyric poem about night or dreaminess that contains speech sounds that express nocturnal qualities. Nocturne usually refers to a piece of piano music with dreamy qualities.

Nō drama or Noh drama

the formal and classical Japanese drama developed in the 14th century for the nobility. It involves music, chanting and stylized dancing with only male actors, including those playing the parts of women. In any production there are never more than six actors who are nearly always masked. Scenery is very limited but the traditional costumes are extremely elaborate. A Nō performance usually lasts about seven hours with several comic interludes that sometimes mock the Nō drama itself.

These dramas, usually with religious or ethical themes, are credited to the work of a writer called Kwanami and his son Seami, and there are thought to be about three hundred examples. The content and staging of them was established by the early 17th century and has not changed since then; they are therefore described as a fossilized dramatic form. Nō drama continues to attract large numbers in Japan. See KABUKI.

Western playwrights have shown interest in Nō drama and some have been influenced by it. Ezra Pound adapted some of the plays, and writers such as Bertolt Brecht and W B Yeats used Nō techniques. The American playwright Thornton Wilder's *Our Town* (1938) contains obvious Nō influences. Recent visits to Europe of Nō productions met with critical acclaim.

nom de plume = PEN-NAME.

nominative = SUBJECTIVE.

nonassertive   See ASSERTIVE.

nonce word
>a word deliberately invented for a particular occasion or purpose. *Newspeak* is a nonce word invented by George Orwell in his *Nineteen Eighty Four* (1949) to describe lack of sincerity and evasion in political speech.

nondefining relative clause = NONRESTRICTIVE RELATIVE CLAUSE.

nonfiction
>any writing or publication about facts, not novels, stories, drama or poetry. Nonfiction includes biographies, reference books, textbooks, guidebooks, coffee-table books etc.

nonfinite
>describes a form of a verb or verb phrase that is not finite, e.g. *to laugh*, *laughing*. It cannot be used with a subject to form a sentence or clause. See FINITE, PARTICIPLE.
>
>A **nonfinite clause** contains a nonfinite form of a verb, as in ***Listening to her lecture*** *made me want to read the book myself*. See FINITE CLAUSE.

nonidentifying relative clause = NONRESTRICTIVE RELATIVE CLAUSE.

nonrestrictive
>describes any part of a sentence that is not grammatically essential to its meaning, as in *That book,* ***with its bright green cover,*** *is a prize I won many years ago* or ***Of course,*** *I insisted on an apology*. See RESTRICTIVE.

nonrestrictive relative clause
>a relative clause that does not identify the person or thing being referred to (but does add information) and can be omitted leaving the rest of the sentence complete and with its meaning. Commas are generally used, as in *My neighbour,* ***who is a splendid cook,*** *is giving a party on Saturday*. See RESTRICTIVE RELATIVE CLAUSE.

nonsense verse

a kind of light verse in which the meaning or storyline is absurd or illogical. Most nonsense verse is characterized by a strong rhythm and often contains tongue twisters, a mixture of languages, malapropisms or nonce words.

These verses are typically English although German writers have tried them. Limericks are a particular form of nonsense verse. Edward Lear wrote the best-known collection of limericks but also composed many nonsense poems or songs including *The Dong with the Luminous Nose* (1877) and *The Owl and the Pussy-cat* (1871). Lewis Carroll also produced several outstanding nonsense poems including *The Hunting of the Snark* (1876). See JABBERWOCKY. Here is a typical nonsense verse illustrating the extraordinary imagination of Mervyn Peake (1911–1968), *Little Spider*:

> Little spider
> spiding sadly
> in the webly
> light of leaves!
> Why deride a
> spide's mentadly
> when its hebly
> full of grieves?
> Little spider
> legged and lonely
> in the bony
> way of thieves
> Where's the fly-da
> on the phonebly?

non sequitur   /non **sek**-wi-ter/

a sentence that has no connection in meaning, logic or relevance to the sentence in front of it.

nonstandard

describes an idiom, word, spelling etc that is not considered as correct or acceptable by educated users of a language. *I **ain't** got any* and *William, Ben and **me*** contain nonstandard usages. See STANDARD.

notebook

a small book used to record information, ideas etc.

noun

a word used to name or refer to a person, thing, idea etc, e.g. *woman, garden, beauty, greatness*.

Some nouns have a plural form, e.g. *women*, others are uncountable and cannot be used in the plural, e.g. *greatness*.

Some plural nouns are used with a singular verb, e.g. *athletics, politics*, and others can be used with a singular or plural verb according to meaning, e.g. *My family lives in London* (singular, referring to all the members as a group) and *My family are football addicts* (plural, referring to each member within the group). See ABSTRACT, COLLECTIVE, COMMON, CONCRETE, COUNT, DEFINITE, DEFINITE PLURAL, EPICENE, PROPER and UNCOUNTABLE NOUN; DEVERBAL, GENITIVE, GERUND and VERBAL.

A **noun clause** is a clause which functions as a noun, as in *He asked me what I'd like to do next*. A **noun phrase** is a phrase which functions as a noun, as in ***The tall man standing in the queue** turned round and walked away*.

novel

a long literary work of fiction in prose that is published as a book. The novel is a relatively new literary genre in the history of literature and yet it is enormously popular, probably the most popular literary form today. There is so much variety and scope for the novel that it is only possible to deal with it briefly here. This enormous variety also makes it very difficult to describe precisely what a novel is. It can be described as 'an extended narrative' written in prose with a plot or plots, characters and settings. The possibilities of creating different plots, characters or settings are limitless.

Although narrative has existed for a very long time, earlier ones tended to be written in verse form, e.g. Chaucer's *The Canterbury Tales* (c. 1387). An early prose narrative by Sir Philip Sidney, a pastoral romance called *Arcadia* (1590) does not really qualify as a forerunner of the novel. In England, we must consider John Bunyan's *The Pilgrim's Progress* (1678) and Daniel Defoe's *Robinson Crusoe* (1719) and *Moll Flanders* (1722) as early novels. Other well-known examples are Samuel Richardson's *Pamela* (1740 and 1741) and *Clarissa Harlowe* (1747 and 1748). From that time the novel flourished.

An interesting aspect of the growth and development of the novel is that it has been international; every continent has produced major novelists. It is impossible to review every country and so we must confine ourselves to Britain.

Two acclaimed novelists of the middle 18th century are Henry Fielding (1707–1754) and the Irish writer Laurence Sterne (1713–1768). Jane Austen (1775–1817) and the Scottish author Sir Walter Scott (1771–1832) dominate the early 19th century but the mid to late

19th century sees a dramatic growth in the novel; George Eliot (1819–1880) and Charles Dickens (1812–1870) are the two giants of the period. At that time, novelists tended to write very long novels published in serial form. These met with huge popular success. Thomas Hardy (1840–1928) was a very popular late 19th century author who published his great novels in this way. Joseph Conrad also published his *Lord Jim* (1900) in serial form. It is notable that the novel has established women as writers far more than any other literary form.

In the 20th century, novelists began to try out new techniques and perhaps this is best demonstrated by the works of the Irish author James Joyce (1882–1941) and Virginia Woolf (1882–1941) experimenting with streams of consciousness. Today, the novel is still very popular especially following the advent of paperback publishing that has brought books to a much wider audience. Some people think that television is destroying the market for novels; others consider that television serials or dramatizations greatly increase the demand for particular novels and their authors. See ANTINOVEL, EPIC and GOTHIC.

novelette

a short novel or extended story written in prose. It contains more characters and a more complicated plot than the short story but it is not as long or complex as a full-length novel. Ernest Hemingway's *The Old Man and the Sea* (1952) is a fine example.

novella

a narrative tale. The novella is particularly associated with popular tales that link moral or satirical comments, as in the works of the Italian writer Boccaccio and his *The Decameron* (1349–1351). As late as the early 19th century, the novella became a recognized genre, especially in Germany where it continues to be popular. The accepted characteristics of the German novella are that each one is concerned with a single event or situation and that it has a surprising consequence or finale.

Novella is now often used interchangeably with novelette.

number

1 the grammatical forms of a noun, pronoun, verb etc used to show how many people, things or ideas are being referred to. This includes singular and plural forms of nouns and pronouns. For most verbs in English number changes only in the present tense third person singular, e.g. *He laughs.*

One important consideration about style is to avoid a change in number when constructing a sentence. *One works in order to live, in fact we must* is not balanced and *We work in order to live, in fact we must* is much better.

nursery rhyme

a short traditional poem or song for young children. The origins of these rhymes are unclear but over eight hundred are thought to exist in English alone. Many were first part of old oral tradition, others are satirical comments on a social condition or political event of the period, others are counting or spelling rhymes and jingles, skipping rhymes, tongue-twisters or verbal games.

The earliest collections of English nursery rhymes are *Tommy Thumb's Pretty Song Book* (1744) and *Mother Goose's Melody* (1781). New rhymes continue to be composed and some achieve lasting popularity; A A Milne's *When We Were Very Young* (1924) and *Now We Are Six* (1927) contain several rhymes that have become established favourites.

object

a noun, pronoun or noun phrase used to complete the meaning of a transitive verb, as in *I saw **him** in the distance*. See CLAUSAL, DIRECT and INDIRECT OBJECT.

object complement

a noun or noun phrase that identifies or completes the sense of an object by describing or explaining it, as in *I consider her book **a masterpiece***. See SUBJECT COMPLEMENT.

objective

the form of a noun or (more often) a pronoun when it is the object in a sentence, as in Look at ***her***, *Give **them** a wink* and *To **whom** are you referring?* See SUBJECTIVE.

objectivity

the qualities in a literary work that indicate the writer has deliberately removed her or his personal thoughts, feelings and attitudes.

It is often very important for the writer to be objective in order to have the freedom to develop characters or describe situations that would otherwise be avoided or seem artificial or forced. In other literary works, the impact of the writer's personality and opinions can make an important contribution to its merits. See SUBJECTIVITY.

obloquy   /ob-la-kwee/

a defamatory or abusive statement made against an individual.

occasional verse

verse composed to commemorate an occasion such as an important
historical event; it can be serious or light. The poet laureate is committed to writing verse for official occasions such as royal weddings,
births, coronations and jubilees.

Gerard Manley Hopkins' *The Wreck of the Deutschland* (1875)
was written in memory of five Franciscan nuns who drowned on
7 December 1875. A modern example of occasional verse is W H
Auden's *In Memory of W B Yeats* (1939).

octave or octet

a set of eight lines of verse that can be either a complete stanza or the
first eight lines of a sonnet. See OTTAVA RIMA, SONNET.

octometer

a line of verse with eight metrical feet. See METRE.

octosyllabic

describes a line of verse with eight syllables. The octosyllabic couplet
was popular in medieval verse. It is evident in Chaucer's works and
was also used by John Milton, Ben Jonson, William Wordsworth,
Lord Byron and many other English poets. Here is an example from
Andrew Marvell's *The Garden* (c. 1651):

> How vainly men themselves amaze
> To win the Palm, the Oke, or Bayes;
> And their uncessant Labours see
> Crown'd from some single Herb or Tree.

ode

a kind of lyric poem that expresses strong emotion and usually
addresses a particular subject.

Odes have a long history originating in the **Pindaric odes** of the
ancient Greek poet Pindar (c. 522–442 BC) written to celebrate public
occasions such as victories at the Olympic Games. The seriousness of
the subject-matter often demands a more majestic style than a simple
lyric and a sustained treatment of the subject; this means that an ode
can be lengthy with an intricate arrangement of verse patterns. Pindar's
odes were based on the movement and songs of the Chorus in classical
Greek tragedy: each ode was divided into three sections which corres-
ponded to the movements of the Chorus as they chanted (see ANTIS-
TROPHE, EPODE, STROPHE). English Pindaric odes modelled on this

formal pattern are Thomas Gray's *The Progress of Poesy* (1754) and *The Bard* (1757).

In the 1650s, Abraham Cowley, experimenting with the ode form, produced odes which, although Pindaric in subject and tone, had irregular verse patterns. This flexibility proved influential; an excellent example is Wordsworth's ode *Intimations of Immortality from Recollections of Early Childhood* (1807) in which no two verses are exactly the same in structure. This type of ode is referred to as an **irregular ode**.

The other classic influence in the writing of odes was the ancient Roman poet Horace (65–8 BC) who admired Pindar's odes but chose more personal and reflective subject-matter, and used a uniform pattern in each verse. The Italian scholar Carducci (1835–1907) composed many odes inspired by Horace. John Keats' ode *To a Nightingale* (1819) is a fine example in English.

Oedipus theme   /ee-di-p*as*/

In ancient Greek mythology, one of the most powerful stories is that of Oedipus who unknowingly murders his father and marries his mother. The story is well known to us through the ancient Greek playwright Sophocles (c. 496–406 BC) and his play *Oedipus the King*. *Oedipus complex* is a term used in modern psychology to describe a child's emotional attachment to a parent of the opposite sex and rejection of the other parent. **Oedipal** adjective.

We can see the reworking of the Oedipus theme in modern literature where a man has an excessively close relationship with his mother while feeling hostility towards his father. D H Lawrence's *Sons and Lovers* (1913) is an obvious example.

oeuvre   /er-vr*a*/

1 a particular literary work or work of art.
2 all the works produced by a writer, painter, composer etc.

off-Broadway

describes staged productions in New York City in theatres that are outside the Broadway district. These are associated with low-cost, experimental productions in small buildings. See BROADWAY.

off-the-cuff

describes a casual statement made without thinking, planning or examining facts. It usually refers to a remark expressing an opinion, a guess at a likely result, a suggestion etc.

off-the-record

describes a statement or answer given unofficially or informally and not meant to be published or recorded.

of-genitive   See GENITIVE.

old comedy

comedy produced in Greece in the 5th century BC. It had its origins in the fertility festivals in honour of Dionysus, the Greek god of vegetation who was also considered to give rewards of pleasure (wine and luscious fruits were an important part of Greek vegetation) and even to be a god of drama.

Such comedies were characterized by often savage personal and political satire and lyric beauty with a Chorus who played an important part in the action. Only plays by Aristophanes (c. 448–c. 380 BC) are left to us from this period. See NEW COMEDY.

Old English

The earliest period of the English language from about 450 AD (when England was invaded by Germanic tribes, the Angles and the Saxons – for this reason it is also referred to as *Anglo-Saxon*) to 1066 (the successful Norman French invasion of England).

Literature remained an oral tradition until the establishment of Christianity in about the 7th century when monasteries developed into centres of learning and monks began to copy and write manuscripts. Bede, the 8th century monk, wrote his *Ecclesiastical History of the English People* (c. 731) in Latin. However, some Anglo-Saxon literature was also written down; the late 10th century epic *Beowulf* is the best-known example, but there were also the laments of *The Wanderer* and *The Seafarer*. Old English literature also included biblical and religious narratives.

Central England was the first centre for English literature but the famous King Alfred the Great (c. 849–901) was himself a writer and supported literature in his kingdom of Wessex in southwest England. Here many Latin texts were translated into Old English and *The Anglo-Saxon Chronicle* was revised. Because of this, the dialect used in this area became the chief influence on the development of the English language.

After the Norman conquest in 1066, the influence of Norman French eclipsed Old English for over a century. See MIDDLE ENGLISH.

omnibus

describes a single volume that contains all the literary works of a particular author, or works that relate to a particular theme, e.g. *an omnibus edition* of Shakespeare's plays or of modern detective stories.

one-act play

a drama that has one act only. It has grown in popularity since the late 19th century although the short dramas that were performed after longer plays in the 18th century may also be considered as one-act plays.

Experimental theatre in the early 20th century gave the genre further encouragement and many modern dramatists have used it including Strindberg, W B Yeats, Samuel Beckett and Harold Pinter. Beckett's *End Game* (1958) is an excellent example.

The one-act play is the dramatic equivalent of the short story in that it often limits the plot to a single incident and involves only a few characters.

one-liner

a witty comment or joke that is brief and apt, usually an immediate reply. The writer and film director Woody Allen has produced many brilliant examples, such as his remark when being driven with his girlfriend in a taxi in New York: *You're so beautiful I can hardly keep my eyes on the meter.*

onomastic   /on-*a*-**mas**-tik/

of or referring to proper names.

onomatopoeia   /on-*a*-mat-*a*-**pee**-*a*/

the formation of a word with a sound that imitates the action or noise, e.g. *buzz, plop, hiss.* It is used as a kind of figure of speech in which the choice of words conveys a particular meaning or atmosphere, for example using long sounds such as -*z*-, -*th*- and -*m*- to convey lazy or dreamy qualities, or short ones such as -*t*-, -*p*- and -*k*- to convey a sharp or hurried quality.

Onomatopoeia can work in individual words, as in this excerpt from Vernon Scannell's *A Case of Murder* (1965):

> The cat, half through, was cracked like a nut
> And the soft black thud was dumped on the floor

or more subtly as in the following line from Tennyson's *The Gardener's Daughter* (1842) where the repetition of -*m*- suggests the sound of humming insects:

> The lime a summer home of murmurous wings

op. cit.

an abbreviation of the Latin *opere citato* meaning 'in the book, article, journal etc that has already been referred to', used in books when giving the reference to the source of a quotation etc. See IBID., ID.

open couplet

a couplet in which the meaning is not complete in the first two lines but depends on a third or fourth line. Here is an example from John Milton's *L'Allegro* (1632):

> Oft listening how the hounds and horn
> Cheerly rouse the slumbering morn
> From the side of some hoar hill.

opera

1 a musical drama in which the words are sung, with an orchestra playing the music.

Opera was developed from chanted tragedy, especially in the form of classical Greek tragedy. Modern opera began in Italy in 1600 and spread to England within the following hundred years; it was strongly influenced by the masques of the period. In the mid 17th century, there were notable operatic adaptations of Shakespeare's tragedies although the dialogue was spoken. The opera's rise in popularity coincided with a decline in ordinary drama.

In more recent times there have been interesting collaborations between playwrights and composers, the works of Bertolt Brecht and Kurt Weill being well-known examples including *The Threepenny Opera* (1928). There have also been adaptations of novels and stories by operatic composers such as Benjamin Britten's operatic adaptation in 1954 of Henry James' ghost story *The Turn of the Screw* (1898). However, there are very few examples of playwrights or poets who have written operas. See COMIC and GRAND OPERA; OPERA BOUFFE, OPERETTA.

2 the plural form of *opus*.

opera bouffe   /op-*a*-r*a* boof/

a kind of light opera that was popular in France in the 18th century. It is considered to have influenced the development of the comic operas of the late 19th century in England written and composed by Gilbert and Sullivan.

operetta or light opera

a kind of lighthearted opera with a spoken dialogue. See COMIC OPERA.

opus

(two *opuses* or *opera*)
a literary work or musical composition.

oral tradition

literature that is spoken and not written down. It developed before literacy and was being passed from one community to another by travelling pedlars, singers and reciters, or passed down from one generation to the next.

Obviously, each story, poem or song went through many changes since there was no fixed form and the imagination and skill of the actor or singer had an enormous influence on the script. The ancient Greek poet Homer's epics belong to oral tradition.

In England and Scotland, ballads are a significant part of oral tradition because they were popular when only a tiny fraction of the population could read or write. In any society where there is not universal literacy there is a strong oral tradition.

oration

a formal speech meant to encourage listeners to believe or do something. Oration in drama can express powerful emotive appeal and it is therefore very popular with audiences. Shakespeare's magnificent example in his *Julius Caesar* is Mark Antony's oration to the people of Rome over the body of the murdered Julius Caesar.

oratory

the style of speech used in orations.

originality

the quality in a literary work produced by the writer being creative, innovative and experimental. Originality can refer to subject-matter, style or structure.

orthography

1 a form of spelling considered to be correct.
2 the principles used in a particular system of spelling.
orthographic adjective.

otiose   /oh-**ti**-ohs/

describes a verbose style of speaking or writing that seems to have no practical purpose or point.

ottava rima   /oh-**taa**-va **ree**-ma/

a kind of Italian verse form with eight lines and an *a b a b a b c c* rhyme scheme. It was first used in England by Thomas Wyatt (?1503–1542) and was later used by Byron as the verse form for his epic satire *Don Juan* (1819–1824). Here is one stanza:

> I would not imitate the petty thought
>   Nor coin my self-love to so base a vice,
> For all the glory your conversion brought,
>   Since gold alone should not have been its price.

> You have your salary; was't for that you wrought?
>   And Wordsworth has his place in the Excise.
> You're shabby fellows – true – but poets still
>   And duly seated on the immortal hill.

outline

a brief account of the main features of a plan, plot, scheme etc; it can be produced as a series of notes rather than as a set of complete sentences. See SYNOPSIS.

oversimplify

to attempt to describe, state or analyse something in simple language but to such an extent that the result is an incorrect or distorted version of the original. **oversimplification** noun.

overstate

to exaggerate when making a statement, or use too much emphasis or vocabulary that makes it too important. **overstatement** noun.

overwrite

to use too many elaborate or sophisticated words when shorter sentences and simple vocabulary will do.

oxymoron   /ok-si-**maw**-ron/

a figure of speech in which a phrase combines two contradictory words to create a special meaning or idea, e.g. *a wise fool* or *a living death*.

P

padding

redundant material in a speech or piece of writing used to make it longer, appear more detailed or seem more authoritative.

Padding usually contains vague terms and unnecessary vocabulary. See BOMBAST, OTIOSE, WAFFLE, WORDY.

paean   /**pee**-yan/

a song of joy or praise. In ancient Greece, a paean referred to an ode sung by a Chorus in praise of Apollo but it was later used of other gods and often used before or during a military attack or after a victory.

Today, paean can refer to any song or hymn of praise.

paeon   /pee-yan/

a metrical foot in classical verse with one stressed syllable and three unstressed syllables in various combinations (called the *first, second, third* and *fourth paeon*). Gerard Manley Hopkins (1844–1889) often experimented with it, as in *The Windhover* (1877):

> My heart in hiding
> Stirred for a bird, – the achieve of, the mastery of the thing.

pageant

1 an elaborate spectacle or procession that commemorates an event, with historical costumes, dancing and singing, and often a set of dramatic scenes performed as a pantomime on a series of floats.
2 a wheeled stage (like a wagon) used to perform mystery plays in medieval Europe. It had two 'floors', the upper used as the stage and the lower as a dressing-room.
3 a dramatic performance that took place on a pageant (2).

palimpsest

a piece of papyrus, vellum etc used more than once to produce a manuscript, the previous text being erased by washing, rubbing or scratching. This was a common practice because materials were scarce and expensive before paper was invented. Fortunately, the earlier text was often not erased completely so that some have survived beneath later manuscripts.

palindrome

a word, phrase or sentence that reads the same both ways, e.g. *level* or *Madam, I'm Adam*.

palinode

a piece of writing, especially a poem, in which the writer takes back an opinion, belief etc mentioned in an earlier piece of writing.

pamphlet

a small book without a cover or with paper covers. The term first referred to an essay or treatise on a contemporary topic supporting a particular point of view. One of the earliest writers of political pamphlets was George Savile (1633–1695).

Many established authors wrote pamphlets, especially in the 18th and 19th centuries about controversial political issues. Jonathan Swift wrote several pamphlets with the intention of drawing attention to the sufferings of the Irish people: *The Drapier's Letters* (1724), the *Short*

View of the State of Ireland (1728) and *A Modest Proposal* (1729). Today, a pamphlet can be any informational booklet.

pamphleteer

a person who writes or produces pamphlets.

panegyric   /pan-i-**dgi**-rik/

a formal speech or piece of writing, usually a poem, that contains extravagant praise of a person or organization.

pantomime

a kind of drama for children with farce, stock characters, colourful costumes and topical humour. It is particularly popular around Christmas time. In ancient Rome, pantomime referred to an actor in mime and until recently the term was interchangeable with mime.

In modern pantomime, the main boy character is played by a girl in boy's costume. The stock character of the 'Dame', a silly older woman, is always played by a man, usually a well-known comedian. Traditional or fairy tales provide the favourite storylines, e.g. *Cinderella*, *Sleeping Beauty* or *Hansel and Gretel*.

paperback

a book published in a thin cardboard cover. It is produced cheaply by using less expensive paper to give it a cheap price for mass sales. The vast majority of novels are now sold in paperback editions, and school textbooks have created another enormous market for paperback publishers. See HARDBACK.

papyrus   /pa-**pie**-ras/

a kind of paper made from the inside stem of a reed plant grown in southern Europe and North Africa. It has now been replaced by paper made from wood pulp or synthetic materials. However, there are many ancient documents in archives that were produced on papyrus. See PALIMPSEST.

parable

a short narrative used to illustrate a moral or religious situation. Unlike a fable, the characters are people. The best known are those attributed to Jesus Christ in the New Testament. See FABLE (1).

paradigm   /**pa**-ra-diem/

1 a particular pattern, model or example in a literary work.
2 a systematic arrangement of all the inflected forms of a verb.

paradox

a statement that seems contradictory but is also true, e.g. *I always tell lies*. It has often been used in literature from ancient Greece to modern times, as in Shakespeare's *Julius Caesar* when Brutus calls out to the dead Caesar, *O Caesar thou art mighty yet!* Paradox is very common in metaphysical poetry, such as in John Donne's *The Canonization* (1633) or Andrew Marvell's *A Dialogue between the Soul and the Body* (c. 1650).

A paradox may sometimes appear in a single phrase, as in *magnanimous despair* from Marvell's *The Definition of Love* (c. 1651) or *And having nothing, yet hath all* from Sir Henry Wotton's *The Happy Life* (1651).

In science fiction there is the common paradox of time travel, for example a person who travels into the past and kills his mother or father while they are still children cannot possibly have existed to travel from the future to the past.

paragram

a kind of pun obtained by changing a letter or letters, as in Shakespeare's *Julius Caesar* when Cassius says

> Now it is <u>Rome</u> indeed, and <u>room</u> enough
> When there is in it but one man only.

Paragrams are often used in children's jokes. See CONUNDRUM.

paragraph

a subsection in a piece of prose that contains several sentences and usually deals with one idea or piece of information.

Paragraphs are marked by beginning each one on a new line, and often with the first word of the new line set in from the lefthand side or with extra space between the previous line and the new line.

paragraphia

the habit of writing a different word or letter from the one intended. It can be caused by a mental disorder or brain injury, but is also the result of having to use the word often in hurried writing so that the error becomes a habitual one.

paralinguistics

the study of nonverbal speech elements such as intonation, gesture or facial expressions.

paralipsis   /pa-ra-**lip**-sis/

(two *paralipses*)
a kind of rhetorical device in which an idea is emphasized by presenting it as too obvious to be stated or discussed, as in the use of . . . *not to
mention . . .* .

parallelism or parallel structure

the balanced arrangement of phrases or sentences so that they have
similar constructions and are of equal importance. The intention is to
present ideas in a coordinated way in order to reflect that they have
equal status.
   Parallelism is found in early English verse, e.g. *Beowulf* (late 10th
century) and has been used by several writers throughout the history
of literature. The American poet Walt Whitman (1819–1892) often
used this technique in his works.

paraphrase

a statement of the meaning of a piece of writing using different vocabulary and sentence structure from the original. This often involves
expanding the original text in order to make the sense clear. For
example, a passage that uses advanced and technical vocabulary may be
paraphrased for the general reader, or a poem may be paraphrased in
prose. **paraphrase** verb.

parataxis   /pa-ra-**tak**-sis/

the positioning of main clauses together to form a sentence without
using a conjunction, as in *I didn't phone – it was easier to write a letter*
or *Don't pay for it yet; wait until you get the bill.*

parchment

1 the skin from animals, especially sheep and goats, that has been
treated for binding books, or in earlier times for making manuscripts.
2 a kind of thick, pale yellow paper used as writing paper, for official
documents etc.

pardoner

a person in medieval times who was licensed to sell Roman Catholic
indulgences. The payment freed the purchaser from certain religious
obligations. These indulgences were sold up to the Reformation when
the establishment of Protestant churches made them unnecessary.
   In Chaucer's poem, *The General Prologue to the Canterbury Tales*
(c. 1387), one of the pilgrims is a pardoner. Far from being a respect-
able church official, he shows how the position was open to abuse; he
is an unscrupulous man who prospers because of people's ignorance
and makes money selling false indulgences.

parenthesis

(two *parentheses*)
the punctuation marks (and) used to separate a phrase, word or
sentence in a piece of writing. The text in parentheses can contain an
example, date, explanation, additional information, suggestions for
further research, a cross-reference etc, as in ... *the use of oxymoron
(e.g. 'the sound of silence') in his songs* ..., ... *by William Shakespeare
(1564–1616)* ... and ... *in Wordsworth's poetry (see 'The Prelude')* ....
    In some cases, as in the first example above, parentheses can be
replaced by commas.

parenthetical element

the part of a statement that is enclosed in parentheses, or in commas or
dashes used like parentheses.

Parnassian School

the poetic movement in France in the later 19th century that emphasized conventional structure and restricted emotional expression.
    Members of this school, such as Théophile Gautier (1811–1872),
Henri Leconte de Lisle (1818–1894), Paul Verlaine (1844–1896) and
Stéphane Mallarmé (1842–1898), were committed to objective
approaches that removed the writer's personal feelings and concentrated on careful craftsmanship. Their verse was a reaction to the
Romantic poetry of Alphonse de Lamartine (1790–1869), Victor Hugo
(1802–1885) and others.

parody

a piece of writing that imitates or mocks the style, structure, thoughts,
tone etc of another writer or literary or artistic movement. The intention is to criticize by exaggerating certain features. It is often described
as the literary equivalent to the cartoon in art.
    Fielding's novel *Shamela* (1741) is a parody of Richardson's *Pamela*
(1740 and 1741). Stella Gibbons' *Cold Comfort Farm* (1932) is a parody of Mary Webb's novels.

paronym   /pa-ra-nim/

a word with the same root as another, e.g. *deity* and *deify* from Latin
deus (God). **paronymous** adjective.

parrot-fashion

without any attempt to understand, analyse or concern oneself with
whether one agrees. It is used when a person repeats what another
person has said or written.

participle

a nonfinite verb form used to form certain compound tenses, e.g. *selling* or *sold* as in *am **selling*** and *was **sold***. A participle can also be used as an adjective, as in *I saw the **broken** window* or ***Running** water is safer to drink*. See PAST and PRESENT PARTICIPLE. **participial** adjective.

A **participial clause** contains a participle instead of a finite verb form, as in ***Seeing her all alone**, I decided to ask her to dance with me* and *I left the room, **shocked by her rudeness**.*

particle

any word, usually a short one, that is not a verb, subject or object but is essential to the meaning of a sentence or has an essential grammatical function, e.g. as part of a multi-word verb, as in *make **up** a story*. See ADVERBIAL and INFINITIVE PARTICLE.

particularizer

an adverb or adverbial phrase (an *adjunct*) used to show that what is being stated affects a particular example or group but not exclusively, e.g. *especially* or *mainly*, as in *The literature courses are **especially** relevant to foreign students* or *I'm **mainly** interested in novels set in West Africa*. See EXCLUSIVE.

partitive

describes a word or phrase used to restrict a statement to only a part of what is being referred to, as in *I'd like **a piece of** cake*, *That's **an interesting item of** news*, *I'd like **a glass of** milk*, *Don't plant it in **clay** soil* and *I prefer **French** cooking*.

part of speech

a category of words that share the same grammatical function. The main parts of speech in English are *noun, pronoun, verb, adjective, adverb, preposition* and *conjunction*.

part work

a literary work produced or published in separate sections, usually a large reference work produced and sold as a series of magazines that can be collected and fastened together as a single volume inside a cover.

passage

a section, especially a fairly short one, taken from a longer speech or piece of writing.

passim

a Latin word used in footnotes to indicate that the example or point referred to occurs in several pláces in the book or article mentioned. See SIC PASSIM.

passion play

a religious drama about the Crucifixion of Jesus Christ. It was first performed in Siena, Italy in the 13th century.

Later in many European cities it formed part of the Corpus Christi cycle of mystery plays. (Corpus Christi is a Christian festival dating from 1264 observed on the first Thursday after Whitsun; religious drama was often included in the celebrations.)

The passion play has remained popular in southern Germany, Austria and Switzerland. The best-known production is that given once every ten years in Oberammergau, Bavaria; in 1633 the local villagers vowed to perform the passion play regularly in order to avoid the plague, a disease that was killing enormous numbers of people in Europe at that time.

passive

a form of a verb in which the grammatical subject is the person or thing affected by the verb. Some of the passive forms of the verb *break* are *is broken, was broken, was being broken, has been broken, will be broken* and *will have been broken*.

Passive forms are made by using forms of *be* with a past participle:

present	present form of *be* + a past participle, as in *It is cooked.*
present continuous	present form of *be* + *being* + a past participle, as in *It is being cooked.*
present perfect	*has/have been* + a past participle, as in *It has been cooked.*
past	*was/were* + a past participle, as in *It was cooked.*
past continuous	*was/were* + *being* + a past participle, as in *It was being cooked.*
past perfect	*had been* + a past participle, as in *It had been cooked.*
future	*will be* + a past participle, as in *It will be cooked.*
future continuous	*will be* + *being* + a past participle, as in *It will be being cooked.*
future perfect	*will have been* + a past participle, as in *It will have been cooked.*

Passive forms of the perfect continuous tenses are rare; they are formed by adding *being* to the perfect passive forms, as *It has been being cooked, It had been being cooked, It will have been being cooked.*

Passive *-ing*-forms are often used, as in *Having been broken, the stick was useless.*

Passives often use *by* ... as in *It was written by Shakespeare* (see AGENT) but there are several other forms, e.g. *Shakespeare will be studied in detail next year, I was given another month to pay, It will be noted that some examples are less obvious* and *You're advised to apply as soon as possible.* See ACTIVE.

The passive is particularly effective when the writer or speaker wishes to focus on the object of the sentence rather than the person or thing responsible for the action of the verb, e.g. *The poem was written when Keats was only twenty-three, The goal was scored in the last minute of the game* or *She was born in 1882.* Often the person or thing responsible for the action is irrelevant and not mentioned at all as in the last two examples (who scored the goal or who the mother was is not the point of interest).

Intransitive verbs cannot be used in the passive (without an object there is nothing to use as the subject in a passive construction) and many verbs that refer to conditions or states rather than action have no passive forms: *I had a wash, That dress suits you* and *We've missed the start of the film* cannot be used in the passive.

passive vocabulary

the words, expressions etc that a person understands but does not use. See ACTIVE VOCABULARY, IDIOLECT.

past conditional tense = PERFECT CONDITIONAL TENSE.

past continuous tense

the verb form used to talk about an action or situation that continued during a period in the past. It is formed by using *was* or *were* and a present participle (...*ing*), as in *I was lying in bed when the phone rang* or *What were they discussing last night?*

pasteboard   See BOARDS.

pastiche   /pa-**steesh**/

a literary work that is a mixture of styles, especially one that is a parody of another writer or group of writers.

pastoral   /**paa**-sta-ral/

describes a piece of writing, usually a poem, concerned with the life of a shepherd and the simple joys of living in the countryside. It depicts rural life in an idealistic way without the rush, corruption or material competitiveness typical of urban living. It shows a harmony with the natural world and a desire to return to a state of simple pleasures and peace. See BUCOLIC, SYLVAN.

Pastoral writing is evident in earliest literary culture including ancient Greece and Rome. In Europe in the Middle Ages (1000–1500), pastoral themes were very common, no doubt encouraged by religious interest and the portrayal of Jesus Christ as the good shepherd to his flock, the people.

At the time of the classical revival, between the mid 16th and mid 18th centuries, many pastoral poems, plays and novels were written including Edmund Spenser's *The Shepheard's Calendar* (1579), Sir Philip Sidney's *Arcadia* (1590) and Ben Jonson's unfinished play *The Sad Shepherd* (1640). In many instances, the writing is artificial with shepherds using the language of educated speakers and dressed in formal urban clothes.

Because pastoral refers to content rather than structure, it is used of a very wide range of writing, even to pastoral elements within a literary work, such as in John Milton's *L'Allegro* (1632). Shakespeare's *As You Like It* is sometimes called a *pastoral romance* and Milton's *Lycidas* (1637) is a classic *pastoral elegy*.

pastorale   /pa-stα-**raal**/

a musical play with a pastoral theme that was very popular in the 16th century.

pastourelle   /pa-stα-**rel**/

a medieval narrative poem in which a knight or poet courts a young shepherdess; the outcome is usually unsuccessful and the arrival of the shepherdess's father or brother ends the dialogue. Pastourelles were an obvious influence on pastoral elements in Elizabethan drama.

past participle

the form of a verb used to form the perfect tenses, as in *They have just left*, *We had **arrived** early* and *You'll have **finished** by tomorrow*. It is used to form the passive, as in *The play was **written** by Oscar Wilde* and can also be an adjective, as in *a **hurried** speech*. See PRESENT PARTICIPLE.

past perfect continuous tense

the verb form used to talk about an action or situation that continued until a particular time in the past. It is formed by using *had been* and a present participle (*…ing*), as in *She **had been** studying all night and was fast asleep at her desk*.

past perfect simple tense = PAST PERFECT TENSE.

past perfect tense
the verb form used to talk about an action or situation that had already happened when mentioning a time in the past. It is formed by using *had* and a past participle, as in *When we arrived, the meeting **had** already finished*.

past progressive tense = PAST CONTINUOUS TENSE.

past simple tense = PAST TENSE.

past tense
the verb form used to talk about an action or situation completed in the past. It is formed by using the past form of the verb without any form of *be* or *have*, as in *He **jumped** over the wall, I **slept** well* and *We often **wrote** to each other*.
The past tense can also have meanings related to the present or future, as in *It's time you **decided** what to do* or *If I **had** the money, I would visit India*. See HYPOTHETICAL PAST TENSE.

pathetic fallacy
the tendency of a writer to give inanimate objects human emotions. The term was first used by John Ruskin in 1856 as a derogative but it is now used simply as a descriptive label.
Pathetic fallacy has been used widely in literature from the earliest times. Here is a familiar example from a speech by Romeo in Shakespeare's *Romeo and Juliet*:

> Arise, fair sun, and kill the envious moon
> Who is already sick and pale with grief,
> That thou her maid art far more fair than she.

pathos
the feelings of pity, tenderness or sympathy which an author, by using skilful description, arouses in the reader or audience.
Charles Dickens' novels contain many scenes of pathos; the death of Little Nell in his *The Old Curiosity Shop* (1840–1841) is usually mentioned as being too sentimental for modern taste. Shakespeare achieves pathos more subtly, as when King Lear holds his dead daughter Cordelia in his arms at the end of *King Lear*.

patois /pat-waa/
a local spoken dialect, especially one used by uneducated people and considered to include substandard grammar. Patois refers particularly

to such dialects in the French language but is now often used to describe the form of any language used by a group such as a profession.

patron or patroness (female)

a wealthy person of high social rank (and therefore influential in public life) who gives money to a writer or artist and encourages her or his success.

Many political leaders and members of royal families have been patrons of the arts from ancient civilizations down to the present day. It was a familiar feature of medieval Europe and without patrons in Elizabethan times it is doubtful whether drama would have flourished. Lord Southampton was Shakespeare's principal patron; the Countess of Bedford was John Donne's patroness.

In return for a patron's support, writers and artists often dedicated their works to the patron. As a system, it has its advantages and disadvantages: for many writers and artists the only way to earn a living was with the support of a patron, but the patron was able to impose her or his own taste.

The growth of the publishing industry led to a decline in patronage for writers but in modern times large businesses are being encouraged to act as patrons for individual theatres, productions, exhibitions etc. **patronage** noun.

pause

a point in a plot that provides a 'rest' from the action so that the reader or audience can reflect on the plot in preparation for the climax. Often, a pause will contain a review or an explanation of events. In drama, a pause is usually a period of silence. See PREGNANT PAUSE, TABLEAU.

A pause in the middle of a line of verse is called a *caesura*.

pedant

a pedantic person.

pedantic

describes speech, writing or a person with an exaggerated concern for academic learning shown by the use of far too much, often irrelevant, detail, long and difficult vocabulary and unnecessary classical references. Persistent attention and analysis is needed to uncover the meaning or purpose of the speech or text; the writer or speaker is more determined to show off her or his academic knowledge than to make an interesting point.

pejoration

a change in the meaning or use of a word so that it takes on a pejorative sense. For example, 'melodrama' can be used either in its historical descriptive meaning or in its modern pejorative sense.

pejorative

describes a word or phrase that has an unpleasant or derogatory meaning or usage. In *a hard mother*, 'hard' is pejorative.

Pejorative prefixes, e.g. *mal-* or *mis-*, are common in English.

PEN

the International Association of Poets, Playwrights, Editors, Essayists and Novelists.

pen-name

a pseudonym used by an author.

penny dreadful

a cheap published novel or story that was very popular in the 19th century in Britain; each plot involved mystery, adventure or violent action and was written in a sensational emotive style.

There was never any idea that these novels were serious literature. In North America, such fiction was called *dime novels*. See BLUE BOOK (1).

pentameter

a line of verse with five metrical feet. See IAMBIC PENTAMETER, METRE. Here is an example from Dylan Thomas' *After the Funeral (In Memory of Ann Jones)* (1938):

> After | the fu|neral | , mule prai|ses, brays, |
> Windshake | of sail | shaped ears, | muffle-|toed tap |

perfect conditional tense

the verb form used in some conditional sentences. It is formed by using *should have* or *would have* and a past participle. See THIRD CONDITIONAL.

perfect infinitive

1 the verb form used to refer to a time earlier than that of the main verb. It is formed by *have* and a past participle, as in *You ought **to have warned** us, We were **to have begun** last week* or *I could **have killed** her*.
2 the infinitive *to have* and a past participle, e.g. **to have written** or **to have been warmed**.

perfect rhyme

a rhyme that has an exact repetition of the vowel sounds and final consonant, e.g. *cat/mat, ceiling/feeling, relation/elation.*

perfect tense = PRESENT PERFECT TENSE. See FUTURE, PAST and PRESENT PERFECT TENSE.

period

a number of years considered as a group when describing or classifying special features associated with that time, e.g. *the Renaissance period.*

periodical

a publication, especially a journal, that is published each month, quarter etc. The content is much more serious than a magazine and is usually concerned with literary, political or social issues. See JOURNAL (2).

Periodicals first appeared in the 17th century and literary periodicals became popular a hundred years later, especially with the *Monthly Review* (1749–1845) and the quarterly *Edinburgh Review* (1802–1929).

Today, periodicals are less popular because of literary coverage by television and the review sections of serious newspapers, and also because they are expensive to produce. However, the *Times Literary Supplement, New Statesman, Encounter* and others continue to be popular.

period piece

a piece of writing in the style of a particular period such as the Victorian period.

periphrasis   /pa-**rif**-ra-sis/

an indirect or roundabout way of saying or writing something. It is a device often used by authors to add humour or to gain an emotive response, as in the use of *old Ocean, hoary sire* for 'the sea'. See CIRCUMLOCUTION.

peroration

the conclusion to a speech or piece of writing in which the main points are summarized and emphasized in order to make an emotional appeal to the audience.

per pro   See PP (2).

person

the way a verb or personal pronoun is changed in form according to whether the subject is the person speaking (see FIRST PERSON), the person spoken to (see SECOND PERSON) or the person spoken about (see THIRD PERSON).

persona

(two *personae*)
1 a character in a drama, novel etc, as in *dramatis personae*.
2 in literary criticism, persona is used to refer to the narrator or speaker in a poem, novel or story.

personal pronoun

a pronoun that changes its form according to whether it is the subject or object of a sentence. Each personal pronoun in English has two forms, *subjective* as in *I, he, she, we, they* and *objective* as in *me, him, her, us, them. You* and *it* have no change in form.

personification

a figure of speech in which inanimate or abstract things are given qualities or attributes of a living being. It is very common in both verse and prose. Here is a fine example from T S Eliot's *The Love Song of J Alfred Prufrock* (1917):

> The yellow fog that rubs its back upon the window-panes,
> The yellow smoke that rubs its muzzle on the window-panes,
> Licked its tongue into the corners of the evening,
> Lingered upon the pools that stand in drains
> Let fall upon its back the soot that falls from chimneys,
> Slipped by the terrace, made a sudden leap,
> And seeing that it was a soft October night,
> Curled once about the house, and fell asleep.

persuasion

the devices used in a literary work to encourage the reader or audience to do something; the most powerful examples combine an effective intellectual argument with emotional appeal. Shakespeare's finest example of persuasion is Mark Antony's speech to the citizens of Rome after Julius Caesar's murder in his play *Julius Caesar*. In his *Henry V*, Henry V's speech to his army to fight the battle at Agincourt contains very strong persuasive emotional appeal.

Petrarchan conceit   See CONCEIT.

Petrarchan sonnet   See SONNET.

philology

an old-fashioned word meaning the study of historical and comparative linguistics. **philological** adjective. **philologist** noun.

phone

a single speech sound; it is either a consonant or a vowel.

phoneme

one of the speech sounds in a language that distinguishes one word from another, e.g. *g* in *give* is a different phoneme from *g* in *gene*. See ALLOPHONE, MORPHEME, POLYPHONE. **phonemic** adjective.

Phonemic phonetic alphabets use one letter or symbol for each phoneme, e.g. *g* can be written in phonetics as /g/ as in *give* or /dʒ/ as in *gene*.

phonetics

1 the study of speech production.
2 the method of writing down a language using symbols to represent each speech sound.

A phonetic spelling is a way of writing a language so that the spelling corresponds consistently to a sound when it is spoken. Spanish uses phonetic spelling, English does not.

phonology

1 the study of speech sounds in a language.
2 a system of speech sounds.
phonological adjective.

phrasal verb

a multi-word verb that contains an adverbial particle; its meaning is different from the meanings of the words used to form it. A phrasal verb can consist of either an intransitive verb and an adverbial particle, e.g. *go off* and *run out*, or a transitive verb and an adverbial particle where the object can be placed either after the verb, as in *write the message down* or after the particle, as in *write down the message*. See PREPOSITIONAL VERB.

Phrasal verb is often used interchangeably with multi-word verb.

phrase

any group of words that has a particular meaning or function in a sentence but does not contain a finite verb, e.g. *in order to, the evening before last, to put it another way, realizing her sorrow* and *angered by his refusal*. See CLAUSE.

phrase book

a book that lists frequently used sentences and their equivalents in another language. They are usually produced for tourists.

picaresque novel   /pi-k*a*-**resk**/

a novel in which a rogue of low social rank experiences many adventures during which he satirizes the higher social classes.

The genre seems to have its origins in Spain in the 16th century (the Spanish for 'rogue' is *picaro*). Cervantes' *Don Quixote* (1605 and 1615) is a classic example and was soon translated from Spanish into English. It influenced writers elsewhere in Europe including the French writer Alain-René LeSage and his *Gil Blas* (1715), the English writer Daniel Defoe and his *Moll Flanders* (1722) and the German writer Thomas Mann and his *Confessions of Felix Krull* (1954).

pictograph

a picture, or a symbol based on a picture, used to represent a word or phrase, as used in Chinese or Japanese writing.

pidgin English

a dialect of English used in parts of Papua New Guinea, Australasia, West Africa and the Caribbean in which there are obvious elements of other languages. The mixture is of adapted English vocabulary with the simplified grammar of the mother tongue. It was used originally for trading purposes. Pidgin is an oral dialect; where it has become the main language, for example in the Caribbean, it is Creole.

Here is an example of pidgin English from Australasia of the opening lines of the Lord's Prayer:

> Fader bilong mifelo – yu stop long heven – Ol i santuim nem bilong yu – Kingdom bilong yu i kam – Ol i hirim tok bilong yu long graund olsem long heven . . .

Pindaric ode   See ODE.

pirate

1 a person who uses or produces another person's literary work without permission or any legal right to do so.
2 to publish a literary work without the legal right to do so.

pl.

an abbreviation of *plural* or *plate*.

plagiarism

/**play**-dgi-*a*-rizm/

the act of stealing and using the ideas, style, plot, phrasing etc from another literary work and pretending it is your own. See IMITATION.

Plagiarism is often not intentional and can be unconscious imitation or reproduction. Many literary works are based on earlier ones. Using earlier literary works as a source material is not criticized as plagiarism since the new piece of writing is clearly an undisguised attempt to reproduce the story or idea in an original way. For example, Shakespeare used Arthur Brooke's *Tragicall Historye of Romeus and Juliet* (1562) which in turn had used a story that had appeared in Italy in various forms a hundred years earlier.

Throughout history there have been writers who stole material from others and reproduced it as their own. This is very different from using earlier material as a source for one's own work. **plagiarize** verb.

plain English

simple, straightforward and usual vocabulary and syntax, not jargon or technical language or complex formal phrasing.

plaint

a poem that is a lament, e.g. Milton's *On the Death of a Fair Infant Dying of a Cough* (1628).

plate

a print taken from a photograph, woodcut e.g. used as an illustration in a book. See BOOKPLATE.

platitude

an ordinary and dull remark or statement, especially one produced by a writer as if it is interesting. Many idiomatic expressions have become platitudes, e.g. *It never rains but it pours.* Some famous writers are guilty of platitude. **platitudinous** adjective.

play

a dramatic work written to be performed by actors and actresses. See DRAMA.

playbill

a poster that advertises the production of a play.

playhouse

a theatre.

playlet

a short play.

playwright

a person who writes a play.

Until the 16th century, authorship of plays was unimportant. Performances were of traditional or standard plots with constant creative interpretations and adaptations by the actors. At that time plays written to be performed were not considered as literary as books written to be read. It was at about the time of Shakespeare that playwrights were becoming respected and acclaimed. It is evidence of Shakespeare's enormous popularity while he was alive that his plays were published under his own name.

Since the 17th century, playwrights have held their place in literary history although there is a trend today to consider the theatrical director, rather than the playwright, as the key person in a successful production.

plot

the series of incidents and episodes that form the storyline of a literary work. The arrangement is designed to achieve the greatest interest before the climax and denouement. The portrayal of characters and the creation of a particular atmosphere are essential ingredients of a plot. See SUBPLOT.

The plots of earlier works were easier to place in categories such as tragedy and comedy; modern literature is much more flexible and a rigid definition of a plot as a definite storyline in a particular time sequence cannot be used of novels such as James Joyce's *Ulysses* (1922) or Virginia Woolf's *The Waves* (1931).

pluperfect = PAST PERFECT TENSE.

plural

the form of a word used to refer to more than one, e.g. *those, several, personae, billets doux.* See DEFINITE and ZERO PLURAL, SINGULAR.

poem

a literary composition in verse form. **poetic** adjective.

poet

a writer of poems.

poetaster   /poh-i-tas-ta/

a writer of inferior poems. Ben Jonson's comedy *The Poetaster* (1601) satirizes conflicts between poets (himself and his contemporaries, but disguised in the play as classical Roman poets Horace, Virgil and others). Sections of the play are deliberately written in ridiculous verse.

poethon
/**poh**-*a*-thon/

a new term for a poetry recital that lasts for many hours, usually twenty-four. It has become a popular event at festivals where both new and established poets can read their works.

poetic diction

the language selected to suit different kinds of verse, e.g. the use of classical references, or the use of romantic imagery in pastoral poetry. It is judged according to its suitability and effectiveness.

During earlier periods, for example in the 18th century in England, established principles for good poetic diction provided very restricted options for selection and order based on narrow expectations of culture and elegance. This led to the use of archaic and Latin words and elaborate wording to convey simple things, e.g. *bleating kind* for 'sheep' or *cleave with pliant arm thy glassy wave* from Gray's *Ode on a Distant Prospect of Eton College* (1742) for 'swimming in a river'.

Wordsworth rebelled against this artificial language and said in his preface to the second edition of his *Lyrical Ballads* (1800) that poets should use everyday language. However, poetry of the 19th century still contained much pedantic, artificial and archaic phrasing.

Modern poets write with much greater freedom, but even today there are those who attempt to establish an ideal poetic diction that sets down rules for problems such as the use of jargon, regional and international variants and obscure technical terms.

Here are two examples that show how much diction is a conscious choice on the poet's part and how important it is to get the diction right. The first example is from the opening of Gerard Manley Hopkins' *That Nature is a Heraclitean Fire and of the Comfort of the Resurrection* (1888):

> Cloud-puffball, torn tufts, tossed pillows flaunt forth, then chevy on an air –
> built thorough fare: heaven-roysterers, in gay-gangs they throng; they glitter in marches.
> Down roughcast, down dazzling whitewash, wherever an elm arches,
> Shivelights and shadowtackle in long lashes lace, lance, and pair.

This diction is highly appropriate to the subject of the poem; Heraclitus (c. 535–475 BC) taught that everything is in a state of flux, and here

Hopkins catches the sense of permanent movement. It is, however, extraordinary diction, even containing made-up words (e.g. the compound *shivelights* made up of 'shive' and 'lights'). It is very powerful and absolutely original.

The second example is a complete contrast. It is the opening of the modern poet Michael Rosen's lighthearted poem *Go-kart* written for children in which the poetic diction has been chosen to represent the everyday speech of a young child:

> Me and my mate Harrybo
> we once made a go-kart,
> Everyone was making go-karts
> So we had to make one.
> Big Tony's was terrific,
> Big Tony was terrific
> because Big Tony told us he was.
> What he said was,
> 'I am TERRIFIC'
> and because Big Tony was VERY big
> no one said,
> 'Big Tony
> You are NOT terrific'.
> So,
> Big Tony was terrific
> and Big Tony's go-kart was terrific.
> And that was that.

poetic drama

drama written in verse with poetic qualities such as rhythm, alliteration and strong imagery. It is often blank verse, as in Shakespeare's plays, but poetic drama of the Restoration was written in heroic couplets. T S Eliot's *Murder in the Cathedral* (1935) and *The Family Reunion* (1939) are two fine modern examples. Poetic drama is written to be performed on stage. See CLOSET DRAMA.

poetic licence

the practice of abandoning usual or conventional rules about grammar, meaning, pronunciation etc; it is a common feature of poetry.

poetic prose   See PROSE.

poetics

the study of the principles and rules of poetry. The ancient Greek philosopher Aristotle's *Poetics* (4th century BC) is the classic model.

poet laureate   /poh-it law-ri-at/

the poet in Britain who is given the official responsibility to write poems on special occasions such as coronations, royal weddings and births, jubilees etc. The first poet to be given the post was Ben Jonson in 1616. Each poet has the position for his own lifetime; no woman has yet been appointed poet laureate.

poetry

a literary composition that uses metrical form and communicates strong emotions in an imaginative way, often with the arrangement of vocabulary in lines with special patterns. Most poetry is filled with imagery and a range of figures of speech, with vocabulary selected for rhythm and connotation. The purpose is to affect the reader's imagination with sincere personal expression; some poems are written to entertain and are humorous or lighthearted.

Poetry can be divided into basic types of pattern, e.g. epic, lyric, ode or sonnet, and also into various moods, e.g. pastoral, elegiac or satirical.

polemic

a controversy or argument that concerns politics or religion. A well-known example is John Milton's pamphlet on censorship *Areopagitica* (1644).

polyglot

1 a person who can speak and write several languages.
2 describes text written in several languages.

polyphone

a letter that has more than one speech sound, e.g. 'g' as in *good* or *giraffe*. See PHONEME. **polyphonic** adjective.

Polyphonic prose is prose that includes basic poetic elements such as alliteration and a rhythmical pattern. Amy Lowell's *Can Grande's Castle* (1918) is a notable example.

pornography

a piece of writing (or a painting, film etc) created to encourage interest and excitement in sexual activities. It is a matter of personal taste combined with the general moral code of each period that determines whether pornography is obscene, vulgar, immodest or improper. **pornographic** adjective.

The Italian writer Boccaccio's *The Decameron* (1349–1351) is acknowledged as a classic literary work but it is also considered by many to be pornographic. Cleland's *Fanny Hill* (1748–1749) was banned as pornographic in 1749 and an unabridged version published in 1963 was seized by the police.

portmanteau word

a word created by joining the beginning of one word to the end of another, e.g. *heliport* from 'helicopter' and 'airport'. Many writers create words in this way, particularly James Joyce in his *Finnegans Wake* (1939) and Lewis Carroll in his *Through the Looking Glass* (1872).

positive degree or positive form

the form of an adjective or adverb that is not the comparative or superlative, e.g. **good** (positive) (*better* is the comparative and *best* is the superlative) or **bad** (positive) (*worse* is the comparative and *worst* is the superlative).

possessive

the form of a word used to show possession. **Possessive adjectives** are *my*, *your*, *his*, *her*, *its*, *our*, *their*. **Possessive pronouns** are *mine*, *yours*, *his*, *hers*, *its*, *ours*, *theirs*. A noun used with -'s shows possession, as in *that **boy**'s nose*. See GENITIVE.

posthumous

describes a literary work that is published after the death of the author.

postmodifier

a word or phrase placed after the noun it modifies, as in *The results **expected** didn't happen after all*, *A friend **of yours** phoned you earlier* and *A writer **like that** should be honoured*. See PREMODIFIER. **postmodification** noun.

postscript

a comment or note added at the end of a letter, essay or document. The abbreviation of *postscript* is **PS**.

poststructuralism   See DECONSTRUCTION.

potboiler

a literary work produced quickly in order to make money; it usually has little literary merit.

PP

1 an abbreviation meaning 'pages'.
2 an abbreviation of the Latin phrase *per pro* meaning 'by proxy', used when signing a letter etc on behalf of the person who is sending it.

PPS

an abbreviation of *post postscript*, used to label a comment added after a postscript. See PS.

practical criticism   See APPRECIATION, FOUR MEANINGS.

pragmatics

the study of elements in a language that cannot be separated from its use or those who use it.

preamble

an introductory part to an official document such as a legal contract. It contains essential background information so that the decisions, opinion etc can be understood.

precept = MAXIM.

precis or précis

a short summary that includes the main points or details given in the longer version, often in a more logical order.

predeterminer

a determiner used in front of another determiner, as in ***all** the people* or ***half** an hour*.

predicate

everything in a sentence that says something about the subject including the verb, object etc. In other words, it is one of the two divisions of a sentence (the other being the subject), as in *The boy **stood on the burning deck**.*

predicative

describes an adjective placed after the verb in a sentence. In *She's **beautiful**,* the adjective *beautiful* is in the predicative position. Many adjectives, e.g. *asleep* or *awake*, can only be used in this position. See ATTRIBUTIVE.

predicator

the part of a clause or sentence that contains the verbal element, as in *During the past year the young woman, in an effort to earn money, **had been writing** articles for her local newspaper.*

preface

a statement by the author at the beginning of a book; it explains its purpose, acknowledges any help, provides personal information, describes reasons for any limitations etc. G B Shaw's prefaces to some of his plays are essays rather than prefaces. See FOREWORD.

prefix

a group of letters (an *affix*) put at the beginning of a word to make a new word with a different meaning, as in *pre-Raphaelite*, *uncountable*, *subplot*, *coordinating*. See SUFFIX.

pregnant pause

a point in the action of a drama where there is a deliberate period of silence and no action; it is full of meaning. It can be a time when the audience is able to read a character's mind, or reflect with the character on a statement or a piece of action, or realize the inevitability of a forthcoming action and become anxious. Modern playwrights, Harold Pinter and Samuel Beckett in particular, have made extensive use of pregnant pauses. See SUBTEXT.

prelude

a short poem that acts as an introduction to a longer piece.

premodifier

a word or phrase placed before the noun it modifies, as in *a different subject*, *a rather peculiar style*, *That's absolute rubbish* and *It's a newly-discovered cure*. See POSTMODIFIER. **premodification** noun.

preparatory object

the pronoun *it* used when the object of a sentence is an infinitive or a *that*-clause, as in *I can't do it* and *We made it clear that lateness is unacceptable*.

preparatory subject

the pronoun *it* used in the initial position when the subject of a sentence is an infinitive or a *that*-clause, as in *It's easy to understand why you don't like her novel* and *It's obvious that you don't like me*.

preposition

a word or phrase used to show the relationship between a noun or pronoun and another word in a sentence, e.g. *in*, *at*, *for*; it is usually placed before the noun or pronoun, as in *lived in Rome*, *write to her* and *fall off the wall*. **prepositional** adjective.

A **prepositional phrase** is a preposition together with the noun or pronoun it is related to and any modifiers, e.g. *at an important meeting*. Prepositional phrases can be used as an adjective or adverb and also as a noun. In the example *Can you help me **with this essay?***, the prepositional phrase is adverbial (explaining in what way you can help). A prepositional phrase can also refer to a preposition that is formed as a group of words, e.g. *in front of*.

prepositional phrasal verb

a multi-word verb that contains an adverbial particle together with a preposition, as in *You'll never **get away with** it* or *They **came out against** violence*.

prepositional verb

a multi-word verb that contains a preposition; its meaning is different from the meanings of the words it contains. A prepositional verb must consist of a transitive verb and a preposition; the preposition always comes before the object, e.g. **go on** *the stage* or **run through** *your speech*. See PHRASAL VERB.

prepositive

describes the position in front of another word, as used by prefixes and premodifiers.

pre-Raphaelites, the

a group of artists (who included Dante Gabriel Rossetti, John Millais and Holman Hunt) who wanted to return to the simplicity of Italian painting as it was before the time of Raphael (1483–1520) and the Renaissance.

This association influenced poets such as Christina Rossetti (1830–1894), William Morris (1834–1896) and Dante Gabriel Rossetti himself (1828–1882) who was a poet as well as a painter.

These poets had great respect and love for beauty but they had failed to find it in their own industrial society; instead they looked back to medieval times, and their work is characterized by medieval features such as archaic words and archaic poetic forms; their poems are often melancholic. Religious language is often used, yet there is also a richness and sensuousness in the themes and the styles which caused them to be criticized as the *fleshly school of poetry*.

presage   /pre-sidg/

a warning or indication of something, usually evil or bad, that is about to happen.

prescriptive grammar

a system of grammar with fixed rules; it rejects structures that, although used, break these rules. The widely used *I'd hoped to have finished by then* is wrong according to prescriptive grammar because the rule states that the perfect infinitive *to have finished* cannot be used after a perfect tense (*had hoped*); the infinitive *to finish* is considered correct, as in *I'd hoped to finish by then*.

present conditional tense

a verb form used in some conditional sentences. It is formed by using *would* or *should* with a bare infinitive (the verb without *to*). See SECOND CONDITIONAL.

present continuous tense

the verb form used to talk about an action or situation that is happening now. It is formed by using the present tense of *be* and a present participle (...*ing*), as in *I am enjoying her book*.

The present continuous tense can also be used to talk about a future action that has been planned or arranged, as in *They're leaving tomorrow*. You can also use *going to* and a verb (*They're going to leave tomorrow*). See FUTURE TENSE.

Some verbs, e.g. *want, love, agree*, cannot be used in the present continuous tense; use the present tense, e.g. *I love most of his poetry*.

present infinitive = INFINITIVE.   See PERFECT INFINITIVE.

present participle

the form of a verb ending in -*ing* used to form the continuous tenses, as in *She is writing, She was writing, She has/had been writing, She will be writing, She will have been writing* etc.

The present participle can be used as an adjective, as in *a singing policeman* or in adjectival or adverbial phrases, as in *Holding the door open with his foot, he picked up the letter*. See -ING-FORM, PAST PARTICIPLE.

present perfect continuous tense

the verb form used to talk about an action or situation that started in the past and is continuing now or is still relevant (it may have stopped or not stopped). It is formed by using *has been* or *have been* and a present participle (...*ing*), as in *I've been reading all evening* and *It's been raining*.

present perfect simple tense = PRESENT PERFECT TENSE.

present perfect tense

the verb form used to talk about an action or situation that was started in the past but continues or is relevant now. It is formed by using *has* or *have* and a past participle, e.g. *I **haven't read** her latest novel, She **has hurt** her leg and can't play* or *We **have tried** many times.*

present progressive tense = PRESENT CONTINUOUS TENSE.

present simple tense = PRESENT TENSE.

present tense

the verb form used to talk about an action or situation that happens all the time or is repeated regularly, and to give advice or instructions. It is formed by using the present tense forms without any form of *be*, as in *He **writes** well, We usually **eat** dinner at 8 o'clock* or ***Sign** your name here.*

The present tense can be used to talk about a future arrangement or plan that cannot be changed, as in *The film **starts** at 8 o'clock.* It is also used for some verbs, e.g. *want, like, agree,* that cannot be used in the present continuous tense, as in *I don't **agree** that he writes well* or *They **want** to use the library.*

press release

a prepared statement or announcement circulated to the media, e.g. a publicity announcement about a forthcoming event.

preterite = PAST TENSE.

primary auxiliary

any of the auxiliary verbs used to form tenses, the negative or questions, i.e. *be, do* and *have.* See MODAL AUXILIARY.

primary source

a direct and firsthand source of information such as written records, a conversation with the writer, a taped speech or a diary. See SECONDARY SOURCE.

primary stress

the strongest emphasis given to a syllable in a spoken word, e.g. *pamphlet*/**pam**-flit/, *pastiche* /pa-**steesh**/. See SECONDARY STRESS.

primer

a school textbook that explains and practises the basic elements of a course of study. The term was first used to refer to the prayer book used before the Reformation and later for any book that contained daily prayers.

Such books were often used to teach children how to read and gradually the meaning altered from its religious connotations to its educational one. See HORNBOOK.

print run = RUN.

problem play

1 a drama in which moral problems related to life are examined, e.g. Shakespeare's *King Lear*.

2 a drama in which moral, social or political problems are examined together with possible choices of solutions. See PROPAGANDA NOVEL. Writers such as the Norwegian dramatist Henrik Ibsen (1828–1906) and G B Shaw (1856–1950) wrote excellent examples of the problem play.

Similarly, the **problem novel** deals with political or religious problems with the purpose of criticizing social morality. Samuel Butler (1835–1902), Charles Dickens (1812–1870) and the American novelist John Steinbeck (1902–1968) are notable authors.

proem   /**proh**-em/

a preface or introduction to a literary work.

profanity

a piece of obscene, irreverent or abusive vocabulary. **profane** adjective.

profile

a short but careful biographical sketch of an individual, or a brief description of a place, organization etc. **profile** verb.

pro-form

a word used as a substitute for another word or phrase, as in '*Can I borrow your bike?*' '*I haven't got one.*' See SUBSTITUTION.

progressive tenses = CONTINUOUS TENSE. See FUTURE, PAST, PRESENT and FUTURE PERFECT CONTINUOUS TENSE.

prolegomenon   /proh-la-**gom**-i-nan/

(two *prolegomena*)
a foreword or introduction to a literary work or to a section of it, especially a long critical treatise on its subject-matter.

prolepsis   /proh-**lep**-sis/

(two *prolepses*)
1 a literary device in which objections or criticisms are anticipated and answered before an opponent can put them forward.

2 a literary device in which a future event is introduced as if it has already happened, as in Keats' reference to *a murder'd man* in his poem *Isabella* (1820).

prolixity

a style of writing that is too long and wordy so that it is boring and difficult to understand.

prologue

the beginning of a literary work that acts as an introduction, especially to a play.

Prologues were popular during the 17th and 18th centuries but a well-known earlier example is Chaucer's Prologue to his *The Canterbury Tales* (c. 1387). Shakespeare's *Hamlet* also includes a prologue. See EPILOGUE.

pronominal adjective

a possessive pronoun that modifies a noun, as in *They arrived **this** morning* or *That's **my** book.*

pronoun

a word used instead of a noun or noun phrase, e.g. *he, she, it, they, them, theirs, yours.* In English, pronouns have three forms (called *cases*):

subjective (used to refer to the subject);
objective (used to refer to the object);
possessive (used to show possession), e.g. *him, his.*

See DEMONSTRATIVE, EMPHATIC, INDEFINITE, INTERROGATIVE, PERSONAL, POSSESSIVE, RECIPROCAL, REFLEXIVE and RELATIVE PRONOUN.

pronouncement

a formal or official announcement of a decision or judgement.

proof

a copy of the text of a piece of writing after it has been set by a printer or keyed into a computer.

proofread

to read proofs and insert corrections and amendments. **proofreader** noun.

propaganda

information that is carefully written, organized and distributed in order to help or damage a political policy, group, government etc.

A **propaganda novel** examines moral, social or political ideas in a critical way (like a problem novel) but also firmly chooses one preferred system and attempts to convince the reader either using direct argument or, more usually, by subtle persuasion, e.g. Harriet Beecher Stowe's *Uncle Tom's Cabin* (1852) about black slaves in America.

proper noun or proper name

a noun that is the name of a person, place or thing, e.g. *Shakespeare, Rome, Earth*. See ONOMASTIC.

proscenium

the part of a stage between the opening or curtain and the front edge. It can also refer to the opening itself. See MASQUE.

prose

a literary composition that is not poetry and usually presents ordinary or conventional grammatical structure. It is written in sentences that follow each other in blocks of text, although there are special features of arrangement such as paragraphs or dialogue. Essays, stories and novels are written in prose. Earlier drama was highly influenced by poetry but modern plays are usually written in prose.

Poetic prose describes prose that has clear evidence of poetic influences such as assonance, alliteration, imagery and rhythm; it is often found as a section of a long work which is included in order to obtain a particular emotive effect.

prose poem

a piece of writing produced as prose but which contains very significant poetic characteristics, especially metrical form, figures of speech, internal rhyme and strong imagery.

prosody

the study of the theory and features of verse, especially metrical form, rhyme and stress. **prosodic** adjective.

prosopopoeia = PERSONIFICATION   /pros-*a*-p*a*-**pee**-*a*/

protagonist

the main character in a play, novel etc or in a major episode. If the plot concerns conflict, the main character who opposes the protagonist is called the antagonist. If the protagonist is a hero or heroine, the villain is the antagonist. In some literary works, the protagonist can be an antihero. See ANTAGONIST.

proverb

a short saying that expresses concisely a general truth or observation about life; it cannot usually be attributed to a particular author having been passed down into the language from oral tradition.

Proverbs usually give advice, hope or a warning, e.g. *A stitch in time saves nine* or *Every cloud has a silver lining*, and are often characterized by alliteration or internal rhymes. See APHORISM, EPIGRAM. **proverbial** adjective.

PS = POSTSCRIPT.   See PPS.

psalm   /saam/

a religious song of praise, especially one of the lyrical compositions in the *Book of Psalms* of the Old Testament. **psalmic** adjective.

psalter   /sawl-ta/

1 a book of psalms, especially those from the Old Testament.
2 a book with psalms set to music.

pseudonym

a fictitious name used instead of a person's real name. When used by an author, a pseudonym is also called a *pen-name* or *nom de plume*. See ALLONYM.

There are numerous examples of authors who have used pseudonyms including Molière (Jean Baptiste Poquelin), George Eliot (Mary Ann Evans) and Mark Twain (Samuel Clemens). **pseudonymous** adjective.

psycholinguistics

the study of the psychology of language including the mental processes of acquiring language and producing speech.

psychological novel

a novel that is more concerned with the emotions and thoughts of the characters than the action; therefore, characterization is considered much more important than the plot.

Writers since the mid 19th century have produced psychological novels, including George Eliot, and novelists such as Charles Dickens and Joseph Conrad have included strong elements of this genre. Virginia Woolf's *To the Lighthouse* (1927) is a more recent and fine example of a psychological novel.

Puck

a mischievous spirit. He was well-known in traditional folklore but is now best-known as a character in Shakespeare's *A Midsummer Night's*

Dream. Puck, acting on Oberon's orders, plays an active and crucial part in the plot. He has various magical powers, such as the ability to assume various disguises:

> Sometime a horse I'll be, sometime a hound,
>   A hog, a headless bear, sometime a fire,
> And neigh, and bark, and grunt and roar and burn
> Like horse, hound, hog, bear, fire at every turn.

He is essentially a good spirit, but his love of mischief is shown in these lines:

> And sometimes lurk I in a gossip's bowl
> In very likeness of a roasted crab;
> And when she drinks, against her lips I bob,
> And on her withered dewlap pour the ale.

puff
a piece of writing that praises a person, book, product etc.

pulp
describes any literary work, but especially a novel, that has few literary qualities and is published as light reading material. It is usually produced as a cheap paperback.

pun
a figure of speech that is a play on the dual or multiple meanings of a word or the similarity of sound between different words. A well-known literary example is from Shakespeare's *Romeo and Juliet* in one of Mercutio's speeches after he has been stabbed:

> Ask for me tomorrow and you shall find me a <u>grave</u> man.

Hilaire Belloc has left us with a witty pun among his *Epigrams* (1923) in his *On his Book*:

> When I am dead, I hope it may be said
> 'His sins were scarlet, but his books were <u>read</u>'.

See CONUNDRUM, PARAGRAM.

punctuation
the use of symbols in a written language that are not letters and are not spoken but are necessary to provide pauses, intonation and meaning. The common punctuation marks in English are the *full stop, question mark, exclamation mark, comma, semicolon, colon* and *inverted commas*.

purist

a writer or academic who emphasizes the correct use of grammar, spelling, vocabulary, pronunciation and style. Because purists often insist on formal or traditional usage that can be inappropriate and because they are often so rigid, the term is frequently used derogatorily.

Today, there is far greater emphasis on flexibility and experimentation.

Puritanism

the religious and political movement that originated in England in the 16th century and later spread to North America. Puritans supported strict Christian moral and spiritual principles, and campaigned against what they judged to be permissive. They were able to take over the government of England in 1649 after the civil war but had already banned public performances and closed all the theatres; the theatres remained closed until 1660 when the Puritans were defeated and King Charles II was restored to the throne. See COMMONWEALTH.

Puritans admired and supported the poetry that reflected their own beliefs; they considered Shakespeare and his fellow writers as decadent and praised the work of writers such as Henry Vaughan, Andrew Marvell and Jeremy Taylor.

purple passage, purple prose or purple patch

a passage in a literary work that is filled with elaborate phrasing and metaphor and is intended to produce a strong emotive response. Because these passages are usually overwritten and artificial, the term is now always derogatory.

putative author

the person who claims, or is claimed, to have written a literary work that has been written by another person.

pyrrhic   /pi-rik/

a metrical foot with two unstressed syllables ($\smile$ $\smile$). It is rare in English verse unless it is combined with other kinds of metrical feet. See SPONDEE.

QED

an abbreviation of the Latin phrase *quod erat demonstrandum* meaning 'which was to be proved or demonstrated', used to indicate that a statement has just been shown to be true.

qq.v.   See Q.V.

qualifier = MODIFIER.

qualitative

describes the particular characteristic of a speech sound that distinguishes it from any other. There is a qualitative difference between the sound *e* in *ten* and the sound *e* in *tea*. See QUANTITATIVE.

quantifier

a word or phrase that shows number or amount, e.g. *some, many* and *a lot of*. Some quantifiers modify plural nouns, e.g. *a few oranges, several rooms*; others modify uncountable nouns, e.g. *a little sugar, a lot of milk*; and others can be used with plural or uncountable nouns, e.g. *some oranges* and *some butter* or *plenty of carrots* and *plenty of food*.

quantitative

describes the difference in length between one vowel sound and another, or the same vowel sound followed by a different consonant. There is a quantitative difference between *oo* in *food* (long) and *oo* in *boot* (short). See QUALITATIVE.

quartet

1 four lines of verse produced as a stanza or a definite section of a poem. Shakespearian sonnets contain three quartets followed by a rhymed couplet. See QUATRAIN.
2 four novels written as a set with a shared theme, setting etc. Lawrence Durrell's *The Alexandria Quartet* (1957–1960) is well known and Paul Scott's *Raj Quartet* that includes *The Jewel in the Crown* (1966), *The Day of the Scorpion* (1968), *The Towers of Silence* (1971) and *A Division of the Spoils* (1975) is a hugely successful portrait of the last period of British rule in India.

quarto

1 a book produced by using sheets of paper that have been folded twice to produce four leaves or eight pages.

2 the form, using paper folded twice, in which the early editions of Shakespeare's plays were printed separately. During his lifetime, *Good Quartos* (reliable texts) of 14 plays were produced and *Bad Quartos* (corrupt and unreliable texts) of the others were produced later. The *First Folio* (1623) contained all the plays printed as separate quartos. See FOLIO (2).

quatrain

a stanza with four lines; it can have any rhyme scheme or it can be unrhymed; it is the most common form of stanza in English verse.

Here is an example from Adrienne Rich's *Aunt Jennifer's Tigers* (1951):

> Aunt Jennifer's fingers fluttering through her wool
> Find even the ivory needle hard to pull.
> The massive weight of Uncle's wedding band
> Sits heavily upon Aunt Jennifer's hand.

Queen's English, the = KING'S ENGLISH.

question

a sentence used to obtain information or some kind of similar response. Questions are usually asked to find out who? what? when? where? why? how? can? will? which? or do? See RHETORICAL QUESTION, STATEMENT.

question mark

the punctuation mark **?** used at the end of a question in English, e.g. *What would you like?* It can also be used at the end of a statement in order to show that it is meant as a question (called a *declarative question*) and so is spoken like a question, e.g. *So he told you he wasn't coming?*

question tag

an expression such as *won't she?*, *have they?*, *didn't he?*, *can it?* used at the end of a statement in order to change it into a question, as in *He did do it, didn't he?* or *You haven't sold it, have you?* A question tag is formed by using an auxiliary verb (*can*, *do*, *have* etc) and a pronoun.

Note that the auxiliary verb used in the first part is the same verb used in the question tag. Also, if the verb in the first part is positive, the verb in the question tag is negative and if the verb in the first part is negative, the verb in the question tag is positive. See SHORT ANSWER.

quintet or quintain

a stanza that contains five lines; it can have any rhyme scheme or it can be unrhymed. A common example is any limerick. Here is an example of a quintet from John Masefield's *Cargoes* (1902):

> Quinquereme of Nineveh from distant Ophir
> Rowing home to haven in sunny Palestine,
> With a cargo of ivory,
> And apes and peacocks,
> Sandalwood, cedarwood, and sweet white wine.

quip

a clever or witty reply, especially a sarcastic comment. See BON MOT.

quotation

1 a word, phrase, passage, stanza etc reproduced from another literary work or speech, especially as an example of a literary or grammatical feature, or used to explain or support a point of view or idea. Many quotations from poetry or drama are learned and remembered because they are excellent examples of the author's skill or style.

It is important that a quotation in an essay is both relevant and appropriate, and the best ones are short and memorable, e.g. *Nothing great was ever achieved without enthusiasm*, from R W Emerson (1803–1882), the American philosopher and poet.

2 a speech made by a character in a story or novel; it is printed with quotation marks.

quotation marks or inverted commas

the punctuation marks " and " (*double*) or ' and ' (*single*) used at the beginning and end of a written quotation. They are also called **speech marks** when they enclose written speech, as in '*Come as soon as you can,*' *she said.*

Single quotation marks are the most usual style in British English, but double quotation marks are used if there is a quotation inside another one, as in '*I've already explained that, she shouted "There he is!" and the man ran into the crowded market,*' *she said.* Double quotation marks are the most usual style in American English.

quotation title

a title of a literary work that is a quotation from another one, e.g. Ernest Hemingway's *For Whom the Bell Tolls* (1940) uses a phrase from Donne's *Devotions* (1624):

> And therefore never send to know for whom the bell tolls;
> it tolls for thee.

Quotation titles have become extremely popular in the 20th century.

q.v.

an abbreviation of the Latin phrase *quod vide* meaning 'which see', used with a cross-reference. The plural form is **qq.v.**

R

Rabelaisian   /rab-*a*-**lay**-zi-*an*/

describes writing that contains coarse humour, especially using witty satire with extravagant words and structures. The term is after François Rabelais (?1494–1553) the French satirist and physician whose best-known works *Gargantua* (1532) and *Pantagruel* (1534) were written in this style.

rap

a monologue in verse form with a recurring energetic rhythm and, usually, simple patterns of end rhyme. It originated in the Caribbean and is most popular as a narrative recited against a background of pre-recorded soul music. **rap** verb **rapper** noun.

Rap has obvious roots in oral tradition, chants, speech, calypso, reggae and soul. Explicit vocabulary, humour and wit as well as anger and references to social oppression and racism are typical. Rappers frequently employ Afro-Caribbean dialect for its rich sounds and in-tonations that can be repeated and remoulded in endlessly creative ways.

Benjamin Zephaniah (b. 1958) is probably the most respected rap poet; first recognized in the early 1980s as a performer he produced his first book *Pen and Rhythm* (1982) and successful records including *Big Boys Don't Make Girls Cry*.

Many rappers are renowned for their ability to ad-lib at public performances, either to soul music or unaccompanied. And many poems written by contemporary black poets can be recited as raps. Linton Kwesi Johnson (b. 1952) is not always regarded as primarily a rap poet but some of his works demand to be read aloud in a bold rap style and have been recorded. This short excerpt from his *Di Great Insoreckshan* (1983) is typical and is also an example of the effective use of Afro-Caribbean dialect:

> it woz April nineteen eighty-wan
> doun inna di ghetto of Brixton
> dat di babylan dem cause such a frickshan
> an it bring about a great insoreckshan
> an it spread all ovah di naeshan
> it woz a truly histarical okayjan

rationalism

any way of thinking that depends on independent reasoning and logic to justify opinions and beliefs, not personal feelings, traditional or conventional influences or intuition. Such rational thought was particularly popular in England in the 18th century. See ENLIGHTENMENT, NEOCLASSICISM.

realism

the way of presenting life and the natural world as they are and without idealistic or romantic colouring. See NATURALISM. Realism insists on objective, accurate and detailed description with an emphasis on ordinary familiar events rather than the strange or heroic.

Arnold Bennett's *Clayhanger* series of novels (1910–1916) is a portrait of life in the sordid environment of industrial urban centres in central England; these novels include intimate description but very little critical commentary.

Received Pronunciation

the way of speaking English used by educated speakers from the southeast of England. This pronunciation was used as a model for phonetic presentation of spoken English but there is now greater flexibility concerning correct speech. See KING'S ENGLISH.

The abbreviation for Received Pronunciation is **RP**.

reciprocal pronoun

a pronoun used to show that the action is given and received by each member of a plural subject, e.g. *each other* and *one another* as in *We argued with **each other*** and *They ignored **one another***.

recto

a righthand page in a book; it always has an odd number printed on it. See VERSO.

red herring

something, e.g. irrelevant information or a deliberate diversion, used to mislead the reader or listener, or take away attention from the correct line of enquiry.

reductio ad absurdum   /ri-**duk**-ti-oh ad ab-**ser**-dʌm/

a method used to prove that a logical proposition is wrong by showing that when taken to its extreme the inevitable results are absurd. For example, you would agree that rest is good for you but if you remain without exercise or movement for too long, you will become very ill.

redundant

describes text, especially vocabulary or information, that is not necessary because it repeats other text without adding anything new or significant. This often refers to the multiple use of synonyms in a passage. See TAUTOLOGY.

reflex

a word, or part of a word, that is derived from a related form at an earlier stage in the development of a language, e.g. *think* is a reflex of Old English *thencan*.

reflexive

the verb form used to refer back to the subject of a sentence or clause. It is formed by using a transitive verb and a reflexive pronoun, e.g. *She washed herself quickly*.

reflexive pronoun

a pronoun used as the direct object to form the reflexive, e.g. *myself, itself, themselves, ourselves*, as in *I hurt* **myself** and *We enjoyed* **ourselves** *so much*. See EMPHATIC PRONOUN.

Reformation, the

the religious and political movement that began in the 16th century in Europe in order to challenge the power and control of the Roman Catholic Church. The movement was led by Martin Luther (1483–1546), the German theologian, who was dissatisfied with many aspects of the Catholic Church. His break with Rome led to the establishment of Protestantism which was considered by its supporters as a reformed religion – hence the name Reformation. The Reformation was the religious expression of the effects of the Renaissance in Europe. See RENAISSANCE.

King Henry VIII (1491–1547), father of Elizabeth I, brought the Reformation to England when he broke with the Catholic Church for political reasons. From that time, Protestantism became the country's religion with the monarch as the head of the Church, not the Pope.

The inevitable effects on life at that time are reflected in a great deal of the literature of the period, including the work of poets such as Edmund Spenser (?1552–1599). During this period, the Bible was translated from Latin into English and many sermons were also produced in English. The Reformation was popular in England at the time; it encouraged a growth in nationalism, and less strict religious and moral controls made a favourable setting for the rewards of the Renaissance and the birth of Elizabethan drama. See ELIZABETHAN.

refrain

a phrase or sentence that is repeated regularly in a poem, usually at the end of each stanza.

Refrains were used by the earliest poets, probably because of the early traditional device in which a poem was recited with the audience or Chorus repeating the refrain as a group. See CHORUS. Refrains are most common in ballads. Some are exact repetitions of a fixed phrase or line of verse while others include small but significant changes. In the following traditional ballad, *The Twa Sisters o' Binnorie*, the refrain is the 2nd and 4th line and is repeated in all twenty-eight verses:

> There were twa sisters sat in a bower,
>> Binnorie, O Binnorie,
> A knight cam' there, a noble wooer
>> By the bonnie mill-dams o' Binnorie.

register

the form of a language used by a social group or in a particular social setting, e.g. *informal*, *formal*, *slang*. Register can also include language used by a profession or for a particular subject-matter, e.g. *journalese*.

regular

describes a noun or verb with forms that follow the usual pattern or rules.

The regular plural of a noun is formed by adding *-s* or *-es*. Most verbs are regular; for example, they form the past tenses by adding *-d* or *-ed*. See IRREGULAR.

reinforcement tag

a word or phrase used to emphasize or identify the subject, as in *They're all the same, **those people**, It's a pleasant city, **is Budapest**, It was a silly joke, **that one** and You've a good chance of winning, **you have**, if you try*.

relative clause

a subordinate clause introduced by a relative pronoun (*who*, *that*, *which* etc), as in *The person **who wrote it** is already famous, The copy **that I remember** had a green cover* or *It's the only pot **which wasn't sold***. See NONRESTRICTIVE and RESTRICTIVE RELATIVE CLAUSE.

relative pronoun

a pronoun used like a conjunction to introduce a relative clause, e.g. *who*, *that*, *which*, as in *She's the person **who lent me this book***. See RELATIVE CLAUSE.

relief

emotional relaxation during a play that is a deliberate part of the play and is achieved by including an episode, scene or speech that provides a rest from the main action. See COMIC RELIEF.

Renaissance, the

the rebirth (or renaissance) of artistic, literary and academic interest and creativity that marks the transition from Medieval Europe to the modern world. It began in Italy in the 14th century and swept across Europe, reaching England by the 16th century. This was a period when there were many travellers all over Europe as well as great navigators who sailed the world discovering new continents and returned with stories of unimagined beauty and opportunity.

The introduction of printing in Europe at this time led to the written word becoming available to an ever-increasing number of literate and inquisitive people. Science made huge leaps forward producing the works of great scientists such as Copernicus and Galileo. At the same time, religious thinkers were demanding reforms from a Roman Catholic Church which held on firmly to its traditional strict morality and power; from these demands came the Reformation.

The Renaissance was characterized by a renewal of interest in ancient Greek and Roman culture, and scholars translated and studied the classics. It was also a period of liberal thinking and new standards were reached in scholarship, art, poetry, drama and literary criticism. An extraordinary swell of creative activity, combined with a remarkable number of talented artists and writers, has left its legacy in great art and literature; Leonardo da Vinci, Michelangelo and Raphael were painters of the Renaissance, Dante and Petrarch were writing in Italy followed by Erasmus in the Netherlands and later Shakespeare in England.

rendition

a performance or interpretation of a dramatic role, musical composition, style of writing etc.

repertoire

all the dramatic roles, plays, songs, poetry etc that an individual or group has practised and can perform.

repertory company

a theatrical company that gives performances of several different plays during a particular period rather than repeated performances of one play. Each actor in the company has the opportunity to play a variety of major and minor roles, and there may be several producers and directors.

repetition

the use of the same word, phrase, speech sound etc in a poem, speech etc. Repetition is an essential ingredient of features such as rhyme, alliteration and onomatopoeia; it is often crucial for rhythmic patterns, can help unify structure and can be used for effective emphasis or to clarify the meaning or purpose of a piece of writing. See the first example given at CAESURA.

reported speech = INDIRECT SPEECH.

requiem
a mass for the dead, especially one set to music. Benjamin Britten's *War Requiem* (1961), composed to mark the consecration of the new Coventry Cathedral (1962), combines the liturgy with settings of poems by Wilfred Owen (1893–1918).

resolution = FALLING ACTION.

Restoration, the
the period in English history that begins when King Charles II was restored to the throne (1660) and when Puritanism was defeated. It is considered to have lasted until the end of the 17th century before the beginning of the Georgian period.

Theatres, closed by the Puritans in 1642, were reopened and drama flourished. The notable writers of this period are John Dryden (1631–1700), Samuel Pepys (1633–1703) and later William Congreve (1670–1729), but Dryden is acknowledged as the outstanding poet of the Restoration. See GEORGIAN.

Restoration comedy (the comedies of manners written during this time) characterizes this period; witty and stylish comedies about marital infidelity in upper-class society. Congreve's *Love for Love* (1695) and Wycherley's *The Country Wife* (1675) are well-known examples. See SENTIMENTAL COMEDY.

restrictive
describes any part of a sentence that is grammatically essential to its meaning. See NONRESTRICTIVE.

restrictive relative clause
a relative clause that identifies the person or thing being referred to and cannot be omitted without making the rest of the sentence incomplete or changing its meaning, as in *He's the person **who gave her flowers*** or *Here's the dog **that bit the postman***. Unlike a nonrestrictive relative clause, commas are not used. See NONRESTRICTIVE RELATIVE CLAUSE.

retort
an immediate and witty reply, especially to an accusation or during an argument.

retraction

a formal statement that an earlier accusation, statement of fact etc is not true. **retract** verb.

revenge tragedy

a form of Elizabethan drama established by Thomas Kyd's *Spanish Tragedy* (?1594). The dominant theme is the revenge of a father for his son, or a son for his father, with the need to act honourably in the inevitable conflict between duty and love.

Earlier revenge tragedies were dramatic and violent; although audiences loved them, serious critics were much less enthusiastic. Shakespeare's first attempt, *Titus Andronicus* (?1594), was strongly influenced by Kyd's play but he was later to write the greatest revenge tragedy of all, *Hamlet* (?1603).

Other notable tragedies with revenge as a central theme are Marlowe's *The Jew of Malta* (?1592) and later Webster's *The Duchess of Malfi* (?1614). A modern example is the American playwright Arthur Miller's *A View from the Bridge* (1955).

review

a critical assessment of the merits and faults of a literary work or a dramatic production or performance.

There have been many periodicals produced or noted for literary reviews; the *Edinburgh Review*, a quarterly periodical produced between 1802 and 1929, is a well-known example. Today, reviews in newspapers reach a much wider readership.

review copy

a free copy of a book sent by the publisher to a person who will write a critical review for a newspaper or periodical, or for television or the radio.

revue

a form of light entertainment that contains songs, dances and comic sketches based on contemporary events and public figures. There is no link between the various elements that make up a revue.

rhapsodist

a professional person in ancient Greece who recited poetry, especially epics written by Homer.

rhapsody

1 an emotional expression in writing or speech of great enthusiasm for a person or thing, e.g. T S Eliot's *Rhapsody on a Windy Night* (1917).

2 an epic poem, or part of one, that was recited by a rhapsodist in ancient Greece.
rhapsodic adjective.

rhetoric

the study of the principles and theory concerning the use of language to present facts and ideas logically and convincingly, especially in order to persuade the reader or audience. Chaucer uses rhetoric in his *Nun's Priest's Tale* (c. 1387).

In ancient Greece and Rome, philosophers, writers and orators set down specific rules for acceptable rhetoric. Works by the ancient Greek philosopher Aristotle, e.g. *Rhetoric* (4th century BC), and later the ancient Roman Cicero, e.g. *De Oratore* (1st century BC) and others influenced rhetoric until as late as the 19th century.

Five fundamental features were considered essential; relevant facts, logical and appropriate arrangement, a relevant style, an efficient system for memorizing the text and a good technique for delivering a speech.

rhetorical device

the use of well-chosen vocabulary in a deliberate arrangement in order to gain a particular effect. This may include repetition or rhetorical questions. Rhetorical devices are used to affect the way in which the text of an argument is presented but are not meant to change the meaning of the text.

Sixty-four rhetorical devices are described in the *Rhetorica ad Herennium* (1st century BC) and were adopted later in medieval books on rhetoric. Chaucer makes free use of them in his *The Franklin's Tale* (c. 1387). When the Franklin introduces himself and says

> But, sires, bycause I am a burel man
> At my bigynnyng first I yow beseche,
> Have me excused of my rude speche.

> (burel = homely)

he is in fact using the rhetorical device 'diminutio' (a confession of modesty and inadequacies) which is suggested as a way of gaining the audience's sympathy at the start. A modern equivalent of 'diminutio' might be *Unaccustomed as I am to public speaking . . . .*

rhetorical question

the kind of question made without expecting or needing an answer because it is self-evident, e.g. *Are we expected to accept mass persecution rather than struggle for democracy?* It is a common device in public speeches because it can make a stronger impression on the audience than a direct statement.

rhyme

the repetition of identical or similar speech sounds, especially in poetry. Not all poetry contains rhyme (blank verse and free verse do not) but it has always been popular; Chaucer wrote in rhyme in the 14th century. At its best, rhyme adds to our enjoyment of poetry by unifying the poem and by repeating harmonious sounds that become a central part of the rhythm; at its worst, it can become monotonous.

Of the various kinds of rhyme in English poetry, the most common is *end rhyme* (rhyme which occurs at the end of a line). Here is an example from James Kirkup's *Thunder and Lightning* (1959):

> Blood punches through every vein
> As lightning strips the windowpane.
> Under its flashing whip, a white
> Village leaps to light.

Rhymes which are one syllable with a strong stress, like those above, are called *masculine rhymes*. They are also *true rhymes* because the final consonants are also identical. See EYE, FEMININE, HALF and INTERNAL RHYME. See also ASSONANCE.

rhyme royal or rhyme-royal

a stanza with seven lines in iambic pentameters and the rhyme scheme *a b a b b c c.*

It is probably named after King James I of Scotland who used it in his *Kingis Quair* (1423–1424) (see CHAUCERIAN), but it had been used much earlier by Chaucer in his *Troylus and Cryseyde* (c. 1385) and several of his *Canterbury Tales* (c. 1387). Thomas Wyatt and Edmund Spenser tried rhyme royal and Shakespeare used it in his poem *The Rape of Lucrece* (1594). It has also been tried by modern poets including William Morris and John Masefield.

rhyme scheme

a convenient way to show the pattern of rhyme in verse. Each rhyme sound is given a letter, the first being '*a*', the second '*b*' and so on. So, in the example from Kirkup's poem above (see RHYME), the rhyme scheme is *a a b b.*

This is a useful shorthand when describing the structure of verse that rhymes.

rhyming slang = COCKNEY RHYME.

rhythm

the pattern of movement in a piece of writing created by stressed and unstressed syllables, by different vowel lengths, by intonation and by repetition.

Rhythm is like the beat in music or the blood pulse in our bodies. In most poetry, especially in the kinds that are not free verse, there is a fixed or regular pattern that can be described as particular types and combinations (see METRE). Rhythm, although it may be irregular, is also important to free verse because it gives it unity. Our appreciation of rhythm is more instinctive than conscious but successful rhythm is crucial to our enjoyment of poetry.

Rhythm and meaning often go hand in hand. Tennyson's *The Charge of the Light Brigade* (1854), written in memory of the men who died in the military charge against the Russian army at Balaclava in the Crimean War, successfully captures the rhythm of marching:

> 'Forward, the Light Brigade!
> Charge for the guns!' he said:
> Into the valley of Death
>   Rode the six hundred.

A completely different rhythm, regular and light, is used by Spike Milligan for his entertaining poem *Silly Old Baboon* (1968):

> There was a Baboon
> Who, one afternoon,
> Said, 'I think I will fly to the sun.'
> So, with two great palms
> Strapped to his arms,
> He started his take-off run.

The heat and the slow, deliberate movement of a snake are successfully evoked by the rhythm in D H Lawrence's poem *Snake* (1923):

> He lifted his head from his drinking, as cattle do,
> And looked at me vaguely, as drinking cattle do,
> And flickered his two-forked tongue from his lips, and mused
>   a moment,
> And stopped and drank a little more,
> Being earth-brown, earth-golden from the burning bowels of
>   the earth
> On the day of Sicilian July, with Etna smoking.

Finally, another complete contrast. The following poem has a jaunty, punchy rhythm and cries out to be read aloud. See RAP. It is Benjamin Zephaniah's *I love me mudder* (1987):

I love me mudder and me mudder love me
we come so far from over de sea,
we heard dat de streets were paved with gold
sometime it hot sometime it cold
I love me mudder and me mudder love me
we try fe live in harmony
you might know her as Valerie
but to me she is my mummy.

ribaldry

language that contains indecent, crude or obscene humour or mockery.
ribald adjective.

rigmarole

confused, pointless and often lengthy language.

rime riche /reem **reesh**/

(two *rimes riches*)
a rhyme in which words or syllables have identical sounds, e.g.
deceive/receive, or *bear/bare*.

ringbinder See BINDER (2).

rising action

the events in the plot of a literary work, especially a drama, that come
immediately before the climax. It includes events that increase excitement and lead to complications or conflict and finally to the turning-
point of the action. See FREYTAG'S PYRAMID.

roman

describes the style of type generally used in books. See ITALIC.

roman à clef = KEY NOVEL. /roh-**maan** aa **kle**/

(two *romans à clef*)

romance

a medieval narrative in prose or verse that deals with exciting and
chivalric adventures by heroes. Romances were written in vernacular
languages, not Latin. They began in France in the 12th century but
quickly spread across Europe and became extremely popular. The
earliest known *verse romance* in English is *King Horn* (late 13th century). Material for the plots was mostly traditional myths and legends;
in England, the adventures of King Arthur and the Knights of the
Round Table were the most popular subject-matter. The conventions

of courtly love and the poetry of the troubadours were also conventional ingredients. See COURTLY LOVE. *Sir Gawain and the Green Knight* (14th century) is a well-known verse romance and at the end of the 14th century Thomas Malory's masterpiece *Morte Darthur* was produced.

The romance was influential in Renaissance literature; notable examples are Edmund Spenser's poem *The Faerie Queene* (1589–1596) and Sir Philip Sidney's *Arcadia* (1590) in prose.

There was a revival of interest in the romance during the Romantic period at the turn of the 19th century. Keats' *The Eve of St Agnes* (1820) has many romantic echoes. Later, Tennyson used the Arthurian legend for his poem *Idylls of the King* (1842–1885). See ROMANTIC PERIOD.

In modern times, a romance is usually a love story, especially a sentimental one, but it can also be any adventure that includes a love theme.

romance language

a modern language derived from Latin including *Italian*, *French*, *Spanish*, *Portuguese* and *Romanian*.

roman-fleuve   /roh-maan **flerv**/

(two *romans-fleuves*)
a series of novels, or one long novel, that deals with characters who are members of a particular family or social group; the plot covers many years or several generations.

These novels were very popular during the 19th century with Trollope's *Barchester* series (1855–1867) a typical example. In the 20th century, notable works are John Galsworthy's *The Forsyte Saga* (1922), Antony Powell's *A Dance to the Music of Time* (1951–1975) and Paul Scott's *Raj Quartet* (1966–1974). See SAGA (2).

Romans-fleuves are currently extremely popular and several have been adapted as television serials, including Barbara Taylor Bradford's series *A Woman of Substance* (1979) and *Hold The Dream* (1985) and Shirley Conran's long novel *Lace* (1982).

romantic comedy

a comedy that uses love as the main theme; in former times it often involved a heroine dressed as a man and love between the main characters is made difficult by mistaken identity and misunderstandings. There is a reconciliation and a happy ending.

Romantic comedy was a favourite with Elizabethan audiences and Shakespeare wrote several, including *As You Like It* and *A Midsummer Night's Dream*.

Romantic period

the period from about 1789 (the French Revolution) to about 1830 during which writers and artists concentrated on feelings and interests rather than structure and order. It was to some extent a reaction against the neoclassical period that preceded it. The principal Romantic poets were Wordsworth, Blake, Coleridge, Byron, Shelley and Keats. The main novelists were Sir Walter Scott and Jane Austen. Lamb, Hazlitt and de Quincey were important essayists. In his preface to the second edition of *Lyrical Ballads* (1800) Wordsworth stated several of his beliefs about writing poetry and these are considered to be a statement of the Romantic movement.

Whereas neoclassicists chose people in their social setting with responsibilities towards society as a major theme, the Romantics were interested in each person as an individual, often in isolation from society. Wordsworth's decision in his *The Prelude* (1805) to write about himself rather than other people was revolutionary, as was his interest in childhood experiences. Whereas the neoclassicists believed it necessary for a person to recognize personal limitations, the Romantics felt that people have infinite capabilities and must never cease striving and aspiring for whatever they want. This was partly an effect of the French Revolution whose motto of freedom for the individual was an inspiration.

Nature, too, was a source of inspiration for the Romantics but not just as an end in itself; they felt an empathy with nature and used it as a projection for examining their own inner state. Romantics often looked back to earlier times; mythology, medievalism and the supernatural were of particular interest and they sometimes reworked traditional tales and folk ballads.

The neoclassicists had believed that literature was an art to be studied with rules to be learned. The Romantics rejected this and placed greater emphasis on imagination which for them was an active force, creating strong and fresh poetic ideas and images out of what they saw and heard. Neoclassicists had relied on a poetic vocabulary that was elevated above ordinary discourse but the Romantics preferred ordinary language as more compatible with their interest in ordinary men and women. The conventional ode and heroic couplet were replaced by the sonnet, blank verse, Spenserian stanza and numerous experimental forms.

rondeau

(two *rondeaux*)

a French poem made up of usually fifteen lines (but sometimes thirteen) divided into three stanzas with a short refrain at the end of the second and third stanzas (i.e. lines nine and fifteen of the full-length rondeau). The rhyme scheme is *a a b b a a a b C a a b b a C* (*C* is the opening words of the first line used as the refrain).

The rondeau was popular in France in the 16th century but did not receive any special attention in England until the 19th century. Here is an example by Austin Dobson from that period:

> "You bid me try, Blue-Eyes, to write
> A Rondeau. What! – forthwith? – to-night?
>   Reflect. Some skill I have, 'tis true: –
>   But thirteen lines! – and rhymed on two!
> "Refrain", as well. Ah hapless plight!
>
> Still there are five lines, – ranged aright.
> These Gallic bonds, I feared, would fright
>   My easy Muse. They did, till you –
>   You bid me try!
>
> That makes them eight. The port's in sight: –
> 'Tis all because your eyes are bright!
>   Now just a pair to end in 'oo' –
>   When maids command, what can't we do.
> Behold! – the RONDEAU, tasteful, light,
>   You bid me try!

rondel

a variation of the rondeau made up of thirteen lines divided into three stanzas with a rhyme scheme *A B b a a b A B a b b a A* (*A* is the opening line of the poem used as the refrain). Sometimes only the final line of the refrain (*B*, not *A*) was repeated at the end to produce a poem of thirteen lines.

Rose, the

the theatre opened in 1592 on the south bank of the River Thames near London Bridge. This area of London was familiar as a centre for public entertainment with its bear garden, amusement parks, taverns and theatres. The Rose was managed by Philip Henslowe until 1603. Shakespeare is known to have acted there although he had much closer links with the Globe theatre, assembled in the same area in 1599. See HOPE.

Although the site of the Rose has been efficiently recorded, the surviving foundations and some structures were not discovered until very recently when excavations for building an office-block revealed them.

rounded

1 describes a character in a literary work who is portrayed in such a way that it is as complex and interesting as necessary, in other words the portrait is 'complete'. See CHARACTER SKETCH.

2 describes any speech sound produced by the lips shaped like an O, e.g. *oo* as in *boot* and *oh* as in *boat.*

roundel

a variation of the rondeau made up of eleven lines divided into three stanzas with the rhyme scheme *a b a C   b a b   a b a C* (C is the first words of the opening line used as the refrain). A C Swinburne (1837–1909) who wrote *A Century of Roundels* (1883) was responsible for popularizing roundels.

roundelay

a simple medieval song with a refrain to which people used to dance. It is similar to the rondel in verse structure although the refrain is sometimes shorter.

Roundelay is also used interchangeably with rondeau or roundel.

RP = received pronunciation.

rubric

1 an initial letter or title in a book or manuscript, especially one produced using red ink.
2 a heading in a book or manuscript that is a set of instructions or rules.

run or print run

the number of copies of any publication, e.g. a book, magazine or leaflet, produced in one impression.

rune

1 a character or symbol from an ancient Germanic alphabet that was itself based on ancient Greek and Roman alphabets. These runes were suitable for carving on stone or wood and several were considered to have magical powers.

Runes were used in Scandinavia from about the 3rd century AD and in England during Anglo-Saxon times (from about the 5th century) but were replaced by the Roman alphabet.
2 a kind of ancient Finnish poem that includes curious or magical symbols.

running head

a heading at the top of each page in a book. It can be the title of a chapter or section, the first and last words on the page of a dictionary etc.

run-on

text printed as sentences that follow each other without any breaks to start a new line or paragraph.

run-on line

a line of verse without a grammatical stop at the end. See ENJAMBEMENT.

S

saga

1 a medieval story written in Iceland about the adventures of a hero, especially a hero who belongs to an influential family. They were first written down in the 12th century but belonged to oral tradition for a long time before then.

Many similar historical narratives from oral tradition also became known as sagas, particularly tales of actual historical figures such as royalty and warrior leaders.

2 (also **saga novel**) a long story or series of books that are about the lives of members of the same family, often covering several generations. There are many modern examples including John Galsworthy's *The Forsyte Saga* (1922), the Canadian novelist Mazo de la Roche's *Jalna* series of 16 novels (1927 onwards), and Barbara Taylor Bradford's *A Woman of Substance* (1979). See ROMAN-FLEUVE.

3 a long account about events that occurred over a long period of time.

salon

a formal social gathering (or the private house where it is held) for major writers, artists and thinkers.

Salons were very popular in France until the Revolution (1789) but in England the tavern, coffee-house or club has been preferred. However, in the mid 18th century gatherings at the homes of Mrs Elizabeth Vesey and Mrs Elizabeth Montagu can be described as salons. See BLUESTOCKING.

sapphic   /sa-fik/

a quatrain named after the ancient Greek poetess Sappho (late 7th century BC). It consisted of three lines of eleven syllables with the metrical pattern ⎺ ˘ | ⎺ ⎺ | ⎺ ˘ ˘ | ⎺ ˘ | ⎺ ˘ followed by a final line of five syllables with the metrical pattern ⁻ ˘ ˘ | ⁻ ˘. Although it is a difficult form, many English and American poets have tried it including Sir Philip Sidney, Tennyson, Swinburne and the modern American poet Ezra Pound.

Here is an example from Sappho's *The Moon* in which the translator T F Higham has been faithful to the metrical pattern of the original:

> Bright stars, around the fair Selene peering,
> No more their beauty to the night discover
> When she, at full, her silver light ensphering,
> Floods the world over.

sarcasm

a mocking, spiteful or ironic way of writing or speaking in order to be insulting or critical. See IRONY.

satire

a piece of writing, or a speech, in which public personalities, current affairs, human weaknesses, stereotypical heroes etc are mocked using sarcasm and irony. The term is also used to label the sarcastic and ironic style used. See LAMPOON. **satirize** verb.

satirical comedy

a play which exposes and mocks stupidities and bad behaviour in society, often by concentrating on particular individuals.

The ancient Greek playwright Aristophanes (c. 450–380 BC) is the earliest-known writer of satirical comedy; his *The Wasps* and *The Birds* are two examples. In England, Ben Jonson's *Volpone* (1606) and *The Alchemist* (1610) are well-known satirical comedies, but the truly great writer in this field was the French dramatist Molière who wrote *Le Bourgeois gentilhomme* (1670) and *Le Malade imaginaire* (1673).

satirist

a person who uses satire in her or his work.

Saxon See ANGLO-SAXON.

scansion

the analysis of the metrical pattern of a poem so that the types and number of metrical feet in each line are identified. These are often given technical names, such as *iambic pentameter* or *dactylic hexameter*. Stressed syllables are marked by ⁻ and unstressed syllables by

˘, as in a scansion of these lines from Keats' sonnet *O Solitude* (1816):

Ŏ Sŏl|ĭtū͞de! | If͞ I͞ | mŭst wi͞th | the͞e dwe͞ll, |
Lĕt i͞t | nŏt be͞ | amo͞ng | the͞ jumb|lĕd he͞ap. |

See FOOT, METRE, STRESS.

scenario

an outline or summary of the plot of a play, story, film etc, especially one that includes details of the order and types of scenes, information about the characters etc. A scenario is particularly useful to a producer who is organizing a production for theatre, film, television or radio.

scene

1 a division of an act of a play, e.g. Shakespeare's *Romeo and Juliet* is divided into five acts and Act 1 is divided into five scenes. These subdivisions occur when the scenery changes to show that the events happen in a different place, or when the scenery is the same but the characters change and there is a development in the plot. See ACT (1).
2 a particular event in a play, such as the *balcony scene* in Shakespeare's *Romeo and Juliet*.
3 the setting for the plot of a play; in *Romeo and Juliet* the scene is set in Verona, northern Italy.

scholasticism

the system of philosophical and religious teaching in western Europe during the Middle Ages (1000–1500) which lost its popularity because of the Renaissance. It used the ancient Greek philosopher Aristotle's methods of accurate formal reasoning to explain and debate Christianity.

The earlier period of scholasticism was dominated by academics such as Pierre Abélard (1079–1142) in France (who is considered to be responsible for scholasticism), the Italian Peter Lombard (c. 1100–1160) who worked in Paris and later by the Italian philosopher Thomas Aquinas (c. 1225–1274) whose writings continue to influence Roman Catholic theologians.

Towards the 14th century, scholastic debate became preoccupied with trivial matters and was giving place to the new scientific reasoning of the Renaissance. Whereas scholastics attempted to use logical argument to justify and prove facts, the new thinkers such as Sir Francis Bacon (1561–1626) favoured philosophical proof by drawing a conclusion from a set of premises that are based on experience and scientific experiment.

school

a group of influential writers, artists etc who share the same style, objectives or principles, e.g. the pre-Raphaelites. Since a school depends on the energy and interest of active members, it often lasts only a short time; however, its influence can last much longer and this can produce a movement. See MOVEMENT (2).

science fiction

a story or novel in which modern science and technology make a major contribution to the plot; the setting is usually in the future and the storyline is usually an adventure with imaginative guesses about technical and scientific developments.

Science fiction is very popular in Britain and North America but it is not a recent genre. Although the American writer Edgar Allan Poe (1809–1849) is often described as the first science fiction writer, the French novelist Jules Verne's *Voyage au centre de la Terre* (1864) and the English author H G Wells' novel *The War of the Worlds* (1898) are the early science fiction classics. See FANTASY.

The abbreviation for science fiction is **SF**.

Scottish Chaucerians   See CHAUCERIAN.

screed

a lengthy piece of writing or speech, especially one considered to be too long.

screenplay

the script of a film or television drama; it includes directions for camera work and the props in the same way as a play includes stage directions.

sea shanty = SHANTY.

secondary source

an indirect source of information such as the research undertaken by another person, a published reference, comment from other writers etc. See PRIMARY SOURCE.

secondary stress

the weaker emphasis given to a syllable in a long word that has a strong stress on another syllable when it is spoken. In *terminology*, there is secondary stress on 'term' and primary stress on 'nol' (the other syllables are unstressed). See PRIMARY STRESS.

second conditional

the structure of a conditional sentence used to talk about a hypothetical or unlikely situation and the likely result.

if-clause PAST TENSE	main clause *would* + infinitive without *to*.
If I was rich,	*I would buy a sports car.*
If he loved her,	*he would marry her.*

The second conditional is also used to give advice, as in *If you practised more, you would win* or *If I were you, I would apologize.* See SUBJUNCTIVE.

In some cases *unless* can replace *if* but the structure changes, as in *He wouldn't marry her unless he loved her.*
See FIRST, THIRD and ZERO CONDITIONAL.

second language

a language that is not a mother tongue (a *first language*) but is widely used by people in a community for commerce, education etc, especially in a place where there are several mother tongues. English is a common second language in many countries.

second person

a form of a pronoun or verb used to refer to the person or thing, or people or things, being spoken to, as in *You are wrong.* See FIRST and THIRD PERSON.

section

a set of pages in a book that have been produced by folding and trimming a sheet of paper. See SIGNATURE.

section mark

the mark § put in printed text to mark a section or to indicate a footnote.

semantics

1 the study of the meanings of words and also changes in meanings, or the connections between sentence structure and meanings.
2 the study of signs and symbols and what they stand for.

semicolon

the punctuation mark ; used
a to separate main clauses in a sentence that has no coordinating conjunction, as in *Go by bus; it's the easiest way to get there.*
b to separate main clauses joined by *however, nevertheless, therefore* etc, as in *He didn't write the letter; however he did phone her.*

c to separate sections of a list or series, as in *We need ten shirts, all large; four pairs of socks, red and white if possible; eight pairs of shorts, five large, three medium; one referee's whistle.*

d to separate parts of a sentence that already uses commas, as in *We are willing to accept your fee, whether it's bigger than our budget or not; you have the skills, we need them.*

A semicolon can replace a colon in many structures and a dash can often replace a semicolon. See COLON, DASH.

semiliterate

1 describes a person who has poor reading and writing skills, or who can read but not write.

2 describes a person who has not read many books and is poorly educated.

sentence

a group of words that contains a subject and a finite verb; it can be a statement, question, command or exclamation. Written sentences always begin with a capital letter and end with a full stop, question mark, exclamation mark or quotation mark.

Every sentence can be divided into two parts, subject and predicate. See CLEFT, COMPOUND and SIMPLE SENTENCE.

sentence connector

a word or phrase used to introduce a sentence in order to show a link between it and the previous one, as in *We didn't get the tickets we'd hoped to get.* **On the other hand**, *we did see the performance.*

sentiment

an expression of deep feeling such as pity, sadness or love as a response to a piece of writing, a painting etc or as described by the writer or artist.

sentimental comedy

a kind of comedy that developed in England in the 18th century as a reaction to Restoration comedy. It rejected a focus on vices and coarse humour and preferred to stress virtue and suffering.

In sentimental comedy, the plots were simple and the characters were uncomplicated caricatures of honourable heroes or villains. Virtue was always victorious. Sir Richard Steele's *The Conscious Lovers* (1722) is a typical example. These plays had ceased to be written by the end of the 18th century and are rarely performed nowadays. See SENTIMENTAL NOVEL.

sentimentalism

exaggerated sentiment, especially when this is deliberately encouraged by a writer or expressed in a piece of writing. Sentimentalism is common in modern melodrama.

sentimental novel

a kind of novel produced in England in the 18th century as the equivalent of sentimental comedy on the stage. Samuel Richardson's *Pamela* (1740 and 1741) is considered to have begun the genre which includes novels such as Oliver Goldsmith's *The Vicar of Wakefield* (1766).

Like the comedies, these novels attempt to show that honour and virtue are justly victorious over unkind personal attack. Many later novels contain sentimental episodes, e.g. Little Nell's death in Charles Dickens' *The Old Curiosity Shop* (1840–1841).

serenade

a romantic song to be sung at night under a woman's window.

serious theatre

productions of plays, including both tragedy and comedy, considered to be of literary merit. See LIGHT ENTERTAINMENT.

sermon

a formal speech or essay about moral behaviour or religion, especially one based on a passage from the Bible.

Sermons were the main means of moral education in Europe up to the 18th century, the period when the Church controlled public life; preachers enjoyed great influence and many writers were preachers by profession, including John Donne (1572–1631) and John Bunyan (1628–1688). Other preachers have achieved lasting fame because of their sermons or their influence on the Christian church, John Wesley (1703–1791) in particular.

serpentine verse

a line of verse or a stanza that begins and ends with the same word.

sestet

a stanza, or section of a poem (e.g. the last section of a Pindaric ode) with six lines. See SONNET.

set piece

1 a piece of writing, often in a conventional and formal style, on a particular theme and often intended to impress the reader.

2 a piece of scenery on stage that is independent of the rest of the set.

setting

1 the surroundings for the action of a play or story. This can include the geographical and physical details, the historical period, the status or professions of the main characters or the social or political environment.

2 in dramatic productions, setting is used to refer to the stage scenery and furnishings.

SF = SCIENCE FICTION.

shaggy dog story

a kind of joke that is a long story with a boring and weak ending – a deliberate anticlimax. The sequence of events is always unlikely and various episodes have little or no connection with the actual story.

Shakespearian sonnet   See SONNET.

shanty or sea shanty

a song sung by sailors while working on board sailing ships.

Many are traditional songs passed down from earliest times, e.g. *Blow the Man Down*. The purpose was to coordinate the movements of a team of sailors in the same way as Black workers in the United States of America sang together in the cotton fields or while building the railways.

Shavian

of or like the literary works of the Irish writer G B Shaw (1856–1950), especially his ideas, humour and satire.

short answer

a short reply made up of a noun or pronoun and an auxiliary verb, as in *'Who would like another cake?' 'I would.'* or *'Can I leave early?' 'No, you can't.'* See QUESTION TAG.

short measure

a stanza with four lines and the rhyme scheme *a b c b*. It is often used for hymns, as in this example written by Percy Dearmer:

> O Holy Spirit, God
> All loveliness is thine;

Great things and small are both in
Thee
The star-world is thy shrine.

short novel = NOVELLA.

short story

a narrative in prose that is shorter than a novel. It is a difficult genre to
define precisely – exactly how short is short? – but Edgar Allan Poe
(1809–1849), who is often described as the originator of the modern
short story, gave a useful definition saying that the short story is a
prose narrative, often concentrating on a 'certain unique or single
effect' which could be read at one sitting of half an hour to two hours.

The genre is highly flexible. It shares many of the characteristics of
the novel although it has fewer characters and incidents, perhaps only
one or two characters or one incident. There is often an interesting and
surprising ending to the story.

The short story is extremely popular and there are many skilled
writers worldwide. Influential short story writers include the Russian
Anton Chekhov (1860–1904), the Frenchman Guy de Maupassant
(1850–1893), the American O Henry (1862–1910), Katherine Mans-
field (1888–1923) and the Irish writer Liam O'Flaherty (1897–1984).

Many modern novelists have also written excellent short stories;
D H Lawrence (1885–1930), Aldous Huxley (1894–1963) and Doris
Lessing (b. 1919) are just three examples.

short syllable

a syllable in classical verse that is short in duration. It is marked by the
symbol ˘. See IONIC, LONG SYLLABLE.

sic

a Latin word meaning 'thus' or 'so', used in brackets, often square
brackets, in a piece of writing to indicate that the text may be mis-
spelled or odd but is an accurate presentation of the original. See SIC
PASSIM.

sick verse

verse that is cynical, unkind or macabre and is poetry's equivalent of
drama's black comedy.

It became fashionable in the 15th century when Europe suffered
many wars and plagues; the French writer François Villon (1431–?) is
the best-known writer of that period. Sick verse was also popular in
the 19th century and is included in the work of poets such as Robert
Browning, Robert Graves and John Betjeman.

sic passim

a Latin phrase meaning 'thus everywhere or throughout', used to indicate that the spelling or odd vocabulary occurs in this form throughout the text. See SIC.

signature

one sheet of paper that is folded after printing to make a set of pages. See SECTION.

simile   /**sim**-i-lee/

a figure of speech in which a person or thing is described by comparison with another using *like* ... or *as* ... ; the comparison is usually between things that do not seem to have much in common, e.g. *He's as timid as a mouse.* See EPIC SIMILE, METAPHOR.

In our attempt to describe another person, idea, experience etc we often make comparisons with something else and similes form a constant part of our everyday speech. Many similes are so common that they have become clichés, e.g. *as old as the hills.*

Writers are interested in creating new similes as a way of making description more vivid and of adding richness and interest to their work. Sometimes similes can be so farfetched that they are not very successful, but when they are well chosen they add so much to our enjoyment of literature. Here is a very early simile from Chaucer's *The Canterbury Tales* (c. 1387) in which he is describing the Pardoner:

> The Pardoner hadde heer as yelow as wax,
> But smothe it hang as dooth a strike of flax.

Sylvia Plath's (1932–1963) poetry is full of vivid and unusual similes. Here is just one, taken from *Tulips* (published 1965):

> They have propped my head between the pillow and the sheet-cuff
> Like an eye between two white lids that will not shut.

And D H Lawrence's satirical poem *How Beastly the Bourgeois is* (1929) is filled with similes. Here is a short excerpt:

> Nicely groomed like a mushroom
> standing there so sleek and erect and eyeable –
> and like fungus, living on the remains of bygone life.

Here is Hotspur in Shakespeare's *Henry IV Part I* speaking of a lord who visited him at the scene of the battle:

> Came there a certain lord, neat and trimly dress'd,
> Fresh as a bridegroom, and his chin new-reap'd
> Show'd like a stubble-land at harvest-time.

Prose is equally rich in similes. Here is an example from Gerald Durrell's *My Family and Other Animals* (1956) in which he is describing the arrival in his house of huge numbers of mantises (a kind of winged tropical insect with a long body and a raised head with bulging eyes):

> At night they would converge on the house, whirring into the lamplight with their green wings churning like the wheels of ancient paddle-steamers.

simple sentence

a sentence with one clause, e.g. *He read the book.* See COMPOUND SENTENCE.

simple tense   See FUTURE, PAST and PRESENT SIMPLE TENSE.

Singspiel   /**zing**-shpeel/
a kind of German comic opera that was popular around the end of the 18th century.

singular

the form of a word used to refer to one person, thing or idea, e.g. *this, child, persona, billet doux.* See PLURAL.

sitcom = SITUATION COMEDY.

situation

1 the general circumstances or conditions that are the background to a story or drama as it begins.
2 the circumstances in which a particular incident or event happens during the story or drama.

situation, comedy of

a kind of comedy that relies on ridiculous or unlikely situations, coincidence, mistaken identity etc. There is often no strong interest in the characters but a great deal of interest in the complexities of the plot. Sheridan's *School for Scandal* (1777) is an excellent example. Shakespeare's *Comedy of Errors* is also a comedy of situation.

situation comedy

a television or radio series that is a light comedy about the everyday lives of a set of characters in a neighbourhood or family. Each episode of the series is a separate story. It is often abbreviated to **sitcom**. See SOAP.

sketch

1 a brief description or outline, e.g. of a character or plot; it includes the main facts.

2 a short comic act as part of a revue.

skit

a short satirical sketch, especially one that is part of a revue or a written one produced as a satirical description of a person or group.

slander

a spoken statement about a person that is defamatory and untrue. See LIBEL.

slang

vocabulary that is not used in formal, educated, serious or even general conversation or writing, e.g. *the fuzz* (the police), *bread* (money). Slang is used in very informal situations or in casual light conversation, especially by young people.

A notable characteristic is that slang words and phrases are fashionable for a short time only and therefore are often inappropriate in literary works. However, slang can be important for convincing dialogue.

slant = SOLIDUS.

slapstick

a kind of comic act using clumsy actions, practical jokes and rough behaviour. Typical actions are falling or slipping, being hit by a falling object, throwing water or bumping against a closed door.

It is a common and popular feature of farce and pantomime, and has been responsible for the success of many silent films and the comedians who acted in them.

soap or soap opera

a television or radio series that is a continuous story about the lives of a set of characters in a neighbourhood or family. See SITUATION COMEDY.

sob fiction

fiction that includes exaggerated sadness or suffering to arouse pity or sympathy.

sobriquet or soubriquet   /soh-bri-kay/

a well-known nickname for a person or place, such as *the Bard* for Shakespeare or *the Big Apple* for New York City. Sobriquets are often amusing or witty.

sociolinguistics

the study of language in its social context, for example the influence of social factors such as class, rural or urban settings, age etc.

sociological novel

a novel that uses broad social conditions as a main interest or theme, for example many novels by Charles Dickens, John Steinbeck's *Grapes of Wrath* (1940) or Alan Paton's *Cry the Beloved Country* (1948). See PROBLEM NOVEL.

soft

describes *c* or *g* pronounced from the front of the mouth as *s* as in *centre*, *ch* as in *change*, *sh* as in *champagne* or *dg* as in *generous*. See HARD.

solecism   /sol-i-sizm/

a nonstandard or unconventional grammatical usage, especially one that is often used, such as *She don't like them oranges* (instead of *She doesn't like those oranges*).

solidus

(two *solidi*)
the short slanted stroke / used in printing
a to separate alternatives, e.g. *and/or*
b to separate sections of a group, e.g. *13/2/92*
c at the beginning and end of a separate section, e.g. *bathos* pronounced /**bay**-thos/
d to separate metrical feet, as in the opening lines of *Night Thoughts* (1962) by Stevie Smith:

> There were thoughts / that came / to Phil /
> And Oh / they made / him feel / quite ill. /

e to print fractions, especially one using large numbers, e.g. *179/360*.
f to mark a long syllable in classical verse. See IONIC.

soliloquy /sa-**lil**-*a*-kwee/

a speech by an actor that is made when alone on stage. It is delivered by the character to the audience in order to reveal thoughts or feelings, to give personal information, to explain motives or perhaps to reveal personality.

A soliloquy can add tension to the drama because from that point the audience will have information and an understanding that other characters in the play do not have. The soliloquy was at its most popular in Elizabethan times and was often used by Shakespeare. In his plays *Macbeth* and *Hamlet* the soliloquies are particularly effective. **soliloquize** verb.

solution = DENOUEMENT.

song

a lyric poem set to music. Some are written as poems and the music is composed for them later, others have been written to be sung.

John Dowland composed many exquisite songs at the height of the period of Elizabethan drama and Shakespeare included beautiful songs in many of his plays; songs inside plays were very popular up to the closure of the theatres in 1642. Although songs by Dryden and others revived this device, poets abandoned the theatre – except for operetta and a few amusing contributions in comedies such as Sheridan's bawdy part song in his *School for Scandal* (1777).

Modern playwrights have revived the inclusion of songs, especially Irish writers such as Sean O'Casey and Brendan Behan. Musicals, especially later ones with the songs fully integrated in the text, are dramas in which songs are an essential element. See MUSICAL.

Songs are not a separate genre from verse. After all, the Chorus in ancient Greek theatre began as lyric poems that were sung by a group of actors. Later the Chorus, like the text that gradually took over as the principal element, was recited rather than sung.

Traditional ballads are narrative poems that can either be recited or sung to a simple tune. Lyric verse often has the form and rhythm of a song.

Most songs can be written down and used as poetry, though some are more successful as poems than others because they contain poetic elements such as imagery, rhythm and alliteration. Indeed, some modern composers like Leonard Cohen and Bob Dylan have published the text of their songs as poetry.

There have also been interesting modern examples of the close relationship between reciting and singing. The best-known example is Robert Prescott's spoken *You've Got Trouble* (with the song's tune in the background) in the musical *The Music Man* (1957). A later fine example is Rex Harrison as Dr Higgins in the musical *My Fair Lady* (1956) in which his spoken form of songs such as *Why can't a Woman be more like a Man?* expressed the emotional state and social attitudes of the character he was portraying far better than any tune could have done. See RAP, an excellent example of lyrics intended to be recited, not sung.

song cycle

a set of songs from the Romantic period, usually written by a named poet, with a central theme or with an identifiable storyline.

sonnet

a kind of lyric poem that contains fourteen lines. Sonnets first appeared in Italy in the 13th century and became popular with Dante (1265–1321) and later Petrarch (1304–1374). In the early 16th century, the sonnet spread into France, where it was popularized by Ronsard (1524–1585), and then into England where it was used by Thomas Wyatt (c.1503–1542), the Earl of Surrey (1517–1547) and Edmund Spenser (c.1552–1599).

Elizabethan poets enjoyed sonnets enormously; some of the most celebrated sonnets in English were written by Shakespeare. Soon after, it faded from popularity but was revived in the early 19th century by the Romantics; Wordsworth (1770–1850) and Keats (1795–1821) wrote many splendid sonnets. Gerard Manley Hopkins (1844–1889) was also fond of the sonnet form. Several poets have written sets or series of sonnets on a particular theme, usually love. Among the best known are those by Spenser, Shakespeare, Donne, Wordsworth and Elizabeth Barrett Browning.

Apart from a few experiments, the sonnet has not been used in the present century.

There are several types of sonnet although all are written in iambic pentameters.

The **Petrarchan** or **classical sonnet**, also referred to as the **Italian sonnet** or **Italian form**, was developed by Petrarch. It is divided into an octave (eight lines) followed by a sestet (six lines). The octave usually introduces an idea which is developed and contrasted in the sestet. The octave may itself be divided into two quatrains (four lines) and the sestet into two tercets (three lines) or three pairs of lines. The rhyme scheme is *a b b a a b b a* in the octave: the sestet is *c d c d c d* (or *c d e c d e*, or *c d c d c d*). Keats' sonnet *On First Looking into Chapman's Homer* (1816) is a classic example of the Petrarchan sonnet, with an *a b b a a b b a c d c d c d* rhyme scheme.

The **Shakespearian sonnet**, also referred to as the *English form*, was developed by Wyatt and Surrey and used with enormous success by Shakespeare. It is divided into three quatrains with the rhyme scheme *a b a b c d c d e f e f* followed by a couplet *g g*. This couplet often provided a comment on the rest of the sonnet. Here is a well-known example by Shakespeare:

> As an unperfect actor on the stage,
> Who with his fear is put besides his part,
> Or some fierce thing replete with too much rage,
> Whose strength's abundance weakens his own heart;
> So I, for fear of trust, forget to say
> The perfect ceremony of love's rite,
> And in mine own love's strength seem to decay,
> O'ercharg'd with burden of mine own love's might.
> O, let my books be, then, the eloquence
> And dumb presagers of my speaking breast;
> Who plead for love, and look for recompense,
> More than that tongue that more hath more express'd.
> O, learn to read what silent love hath writ:
> To hear with eyes belongs to love's fine wit.

The **Spenserian sonnet** was developed by Edmund Spenser and also consisted of three quatrains and a rhyming couplet but with the rhyme scheme *a b a b b c b c c d c d e e.*

The **Miltonic sonnet**, introduced by John Milton (1608–1674), is very similar to the Petrarchan sonnet but has no separation between the octave and the sestet.

More recently, the Chilean poet Pablo Neruda has also written many sonnets each divided into two quatrains followed by two tercets. His *100 Love Sonnets* (English version 1959) are extraordinarily beautiful even in their English translation.

See CROWN OF SONNETS, CURTAL SONNET.

sonneteer
a person who writes sonnets.

sons of Ben = TRIBE OF BEN.

sophistry
a way of arguing which seems clever or plausible but is actually based on misleading or unsound premises.

speech marks   See QUOTATION MARKS.

speech, part of   See PART OF SPEECH.

Spenserian sonnet   See SONNET.

Spenserian stanza

a form of stanza created by Edmund Spenser (c. 1552–1599) for his *The Faerie Queene* (1589–1596). It consists of nine lines, the first eight in iambic pentameters and the last in iambic hexameter, and it has the rhyme scheme *a b a b b c b c c*. Here is the opening stanza of *The Faerie Queene*:

> It falls me here to write of Chastity,
> That fairest vertue, farre above the rest;
> For which what needs me fetch from *Faery*
> Forreine ensamples, it to haue exprest?
> Sith it is shrined in my Soueraines brest.
> And form'd so liuely in each perfect part,
> That to all ladies, which have it profest,
> Need but behold the pourtraict of her hart,
> If pourtrayd it might be by any liuing art.

Several poets have used the Spenserian stanza, including Byron for his *Childe Harold* (1812–1818), Shelley for his *Adonais* (1821) and Keats for his *The Eve of St Agnes* (1820).

spine

the edge of a book where the pages are fixed together. The spine can also refer to the part of the book's cover that is fitted over this area.

spiral binding

a form of binding pages using a coil of wire, or a specially designed plastic tube, that fits into holes made in the pages.

split infinitive

the infinitive form of a verb, e.g. *to smile*, used with another word between *to* and the verb, as in *to warmly smile* or *to not enter*. It has been a traditional grammatical rule to avoid using split infinitives but in many instances it has become acceptable, as in *She is determined **to really try**.*

spondee

a metrical foot with two stressed syllables (‾ ‾). See METRE, PYRRHIC.
spondaic adjective.

spoof

an amusing piece of writing that satirizes a literary style, a historical event or person, a dramatic or literary style etc.

spoonerism

any statement or expression in which the initial letters or sounds are transferred in order to create an amusing phrase or sentence. The term is from Reverend W A Spooner (1844–1930), Warden of New College, Oxford, who created many memorable examples, such as the following (each paired sequence of underlined letters has been transposed, e.g. 'tasted' and 'worms' should be 'wasted' and 'terms'):

> Sir, you have tasted two whole worms; you have hissed all my mystery lectures and have been caught fighting a liar in the quad; you will leave Oxford by the next town drain.

spy fiction

novels, stories and plays in which the plot includes espionage.

Although the spy has been included as a character in earliest literature, it was not until the present century, with the emergence of government intelligence agencies and professional spies that espionage became an identifiable form of fiction with its own identifiable characteristics.

These characteristics include a clever and complex plot, a command of detail, sophisticated characterization, highly exciting action and, perhaps more important than all of these, an unpredictable twist to the storyline that encourages suspense and interest.

Joseph Conrad (1857–1924) helped to establish the spy novel with his *The Secret Agent* (1907) and *Under Western Eyes* (1911). The two World Wars of the 20th century provided great opportunities for plots, John Buchan's *The Thirty-nine Steps* (1915) being probably the best known from the earlier war. A notable feature is the respected, right-wing and nationalist hero of these novels and, although authors such as Somerset Maugham (1874–1965) and Graham Greene (1904–1991) were able to portray more realistic and critical images of espionage, products of the Second World War generally returned to superficial and unimaginative nationalism.

Ian Fleming (1908–1964) dominated the 1950s with his series of James Bond novels but the 1960s saw a return to the critical portrayal of the spy and his work, especially in the work of Len Deighton, as in his *The Ipcress File* (1962), and John le Carré, as in his *The Spy who came in from the Cold* (1963). Authors like Ian Fleming and John le Carré had direct experience of how organizations like MI5, the CIA and the KGB operate and used this information very effectively in their novels.

The background to these recent works has been the atmosphere of suspicion and fear between western and eastern Europe. The recent collapse of communism in eastern Europe will force authors to find new settings for spy fiction.

square brackets

the punctuation marks [and] used at the beginning and end of a text such as

a a comment, e.g. [passim], [q.v.] or [sic].

b a word that identifies a person or thing in quoted text when it would otherwise not be clear, e.g. 'It was ... his [Rowe's] edition published in 1709 ... ' or ' ... supporting Mrs T[hatcher] and her cabinet ...'.

c a separate unit in a complex mathematical expression.

standard

describes the form of grammar, spelling or structure used by most educated speakers and generally accepted as the correct form. See KING'S ENGLISH, NONSTANDARD, SUBSTANDARD.

stanza

a number of lines of verse in a particular pattern that forms a unit of a poem. It can be compared to the paragraph in prose. See BALLAD, ELEGIAC and SPENSERIAN STANZA.

statement

any sentence that affirms or denies something, e.g. *You're beautiful* or *He's not right.*

stative verb

a verb used to describe a state or condition rather than an activity, e.g. *know*, *seem*, *believe*, *hope* and *want*. Most of these verbs cannot be used in any of the continuous tenses and cannot have an imperative form. See DYNAMIC VERB.

stem

the form of a word without any inflections or affixes, e.g. the stem of 'loving' is *love* and the stem of 'unhelpful' is *help.*

stock

all the plays prepared by a repertory company for performance.

stock character

a type of character who by convention is included in a particular kind of literature. For example, in pantomime the *Dame* (played by a man) is a stock character.

story

an account of a series of events written in prose. See SHORT STORY.

storybook

a book of short stories written for young children.

storyline

the series of incidents and episodes that make up the plot of a story, play or narrative poem.

strawboard   See BOARDS.

stream of consciousness   See CONSCIOUSNESS.

street theatre

dramatic performances to entertain passers-by in public areas of a town or city such as a shopping centre.

stress

1 emphasis given to a syllable when speaking. See PRIMARY and SECONDARY STRESS.
2 = ACCENT.

strip cartoon = COMIC STRIP.

strong form

the form of pronunciation of a word when it is emphasized or spoken carefully. For example, *I can do it* can be spoken with the *a* as the 'a' in *candle* (strong) or as the 'a' in *appeal* (weak). See WEAK FORM.

strong verb

a verb with forms that have a vowel change for tenses, e.g. **sink**, *sank*, *sunk*. See WEAK VERB.

strophe   /stroh-fee/

the first of three sections of a Pindaric ode (see ODE) based on the movement and chants of the Chorus in classical Greek tragedy. During the strophe, the Chorus moved in a circle from right to left. See ANTISTROPHE, EPODE.

structuralism

the method for studying literature using a linguistic approach; it relates structural linguistics to poetic structure. Language is considered to be a system of signs that only have meaning in relation to each other, and structural linguists examine the rules by which these signs work and

how they relate. It is possible to break down a text, especially a
narrative, into its various components in the way that a sentence can be
broken down. It is also possible to examine opposites and contrasts
such as 'light' and 'dark'. **structuralist** adjective and noun.

Structuralism claims that literature has no reality outside its own
structure and therefore the individuality of the reader is not essential;
the reader is an impersonal decoder of the text.

Structuralism is a complex subject. For more detail, read Saussure's
Course in General Linguistics (1916), Jakobson and Lévi-Strauss'
analysis of Baudelaire's poem *Les Chats* (1962), and Roland Barthes'
S/Z (1970). See DECONSTRUCTION.

structural linguistics

the analytical study of the structure of a language, including grammar,
phonology and semantics, and not its historical or comparative features.
See STRUCTURALISM.

structure

1 the arrangement and relationship of the various elements of a
sentence.
2 the arrangement and relationship of the various elements of a literary
work. See STRUCTURALISM.

style

the way of writing that an author uses to express herself or himself in a
literary work, contrasted with content and meaning.

Each writer has an individual style just as each writer has an individual personality. It is therefore not easy to give style a precise definition.
However, a critical appreciation of a writer's style must start with an
assessment of whether the chosen one is suited to the subject-matter.
For example, Milton's *Paradise Lost* (1667) is formal and grand, an
appropriate style for the content.

In assessing style, we can identify certain broad categories for describing how the text is written, for example by historical reference such
as scholastic, neoclassical or Romantic or by comparison to established
classic authors, for example Miltonic (after John Milton) or Spenserian
(after Edmund Spenser). We may be able to identify a characteristic
language, for example journalese, scientific or emotive. We can also
examine the text to judge whether it is formal or informal, majestic or
comic, conventional or experimental etc. And we can consider aspects
such as imagery, rhythm, vocabulary and sentence structure, tone and
emphasis.

stylistics

the study of language according to how it is used by individuals or social groups in particular situations. It examines choices in vocabulary, syntax and speech sounds in order to obtain a particular effect.

stylized

describes a piece of writing expressed in an obvious conventional or established style, and therefore perhaps not natural or personal.

subheading

a heading for a section within a main division of a text, for example within a chapter.

subject

a noun, noun phrase or pronoun used to show who or what does the action stated by the verb or who or what is described by the verb. In an affirmative sentence, the subject comes before the verb, e.g. *The boy stood on the burning deck* or *The Moon shines bright on the sea*. See PREDICATE.

In a passive structure, e.g. *The house was burned down last night*, the subject of the verb is either implied or understood from earlier information (e.g. the owner is known to smoke in bed and is careless) or it is not of most importance when making the statement. In a passive structure such as *The house was burned down by Henry* the choice of the passive to place 'Henry' at the end may have been done deliberately for emphasis, e.g. to emphasize that Henry was responsible, not somebody else. See OBJECT.

subject complement

a noun or noun phrase that identifies or completes the sense of a subject by describing or explaining it, as in *That woman is my younger sister* or *He became a pop star*. See OBJECT COMPLEMENT.

subjective

the form of a noun or (more often) a pronoun when it is the subject in a sentence, as in *I have read the book*. See OBJECTIVE.

subjectivity

the qualities of a literary work related to the thoughts, feelings and attitudes of the author rather than the subject-matter. See OBJECTIVITY, SYMBOLISM (2).

subject tag = REINFORCEMENT TAG.

subjunctive or subjunctive mood

the form of the verb used to refer to events that ought to happen, or that we hope will happen or want to happen, as in *I would ask for help if I were you*, *We'd rather he came late than not at all*, *If only she believed in her own ability*, *I wish I were able to write like that!* and *I propose that the idea be accepted for the agenda*.

The subjunctive is not often used except in formal situations or in structures similar to the above examples, especially with *wish*, *if only* or *would rather*. See IMPERATIVE, INDICATIVE.

subordinate clause or dependent clause

a clause that cannot be used by itself as a sentence, as in *Because he works well, he'll pass the exam easily*, *The car that I'd like to own must have lots of room for luggage*, *Darkness fell as we drove home* or *If I wanted to, I could go tomorrow*. See COORDINATE and MAIN CLAUSE.

subordinating conjunction

a conjunction that joins a subordinate clause to the main clause in a sentence, e.g. *although*, *because*, *when*, as in *Although she didn't say so, I know she likes it*, *I'm much happier now because the exams are over* or *When he first came, there was no-one at home*. See COORDINATING and CORRELATING CONJUNCTION.

subplot

a secondary plot in a literary work. It is usually connected with the main plot in some way, for example by the relationships between the characters or by mirroring features of the main plot.

Subplots can add enormous interest and complexity as well as contribute to our appreciation of the supporting characters, and therefore of the total storyline. There are fine subplots in all of Shakespeare's plays, for example in *King Lear* the subplot of Gloucester and his two sons mirrors the main plot of Lear and his daughters. Long and complex novels by writers such as Tolstoy are built up by many interrelated subplots. A short story rarely contains a subplot.

subscript

a letter or number that is below the normal line of letters in a printed text, as in H_2O. See SUPERSCRIPT.

substandard

describes a form of speaking or writing that may be used in very informal contexts but is considered incorrect, e.g. *the book what he wrote* or *me and me brother* (instead of *the book that he wrote* and *me and my brother*).

substitution

a way of avoiding repetition or of abbreviation when speaking or writing, as in *A huge dog appeared. It ran towards us*, 'Can I borrow your pen? I need **one** to sign this cheque' or 'We arrived here in 1989.' 'How old were you **then**?' See PRO-FORM.

subtext

the unspoken elements in a play such as deliberate silence or pregnant pauses. This subtext can contribute significantly to meaning and atmosphere.

Subtext can now also refer to any extra elements in a speech or written text that are not apparent on the surface but that can be inferred from it or from other outside contexts.

subtitle

1 a secondary title given to a literary work, e.g. *What You Will* is the subtitle of Shakespeare's *Twelfth Night*.
2 a written translation of the dialogue of the screenplay of a film. It appears on the bottom of the picture as the film is being shown.

suffix

a group of letters (an *affix*) put at the end of a word to make a new word which has a different meaning or becomes a different part of speech, e.g. *-ship* in *leadership*, *-ly* in *softly* or *-es* in *peaches*. See PREFIX.

summary

a short account of the general content of a literary work. A summary contains the main or important points; it leaves out details and does not try to use the style or vocabulary of the original work. **summarize** verb.

superhero

a main character in a comic strip who has superhuman qualities and often wears a special costume. He or she is usually highly moral and confronts evil villains boldly and eventually successfully. *Superman* is probably the world's best-known superhero.

Some major characters of literary series are described as superheroes, e.g. *James Bond*.

superlative, superlative degree or superlative form

the form of an adjective or adverb used to show that the quality mentioned is of the highest or strongest degree. When a word is short, especially with one syllable, its superlative form is usually made by adding *-est* (or *-st*, *-iest*), as in *shortest, largest, earliest*. For other words use *most ...* as in *most enthusiastic*. Some words have irregular forms such as *best* or *worst*.

superordinate

a word whose meaning includes the meaning of another word, e.g. *blue* is a superordinate of *azure*, *indigo* and *turquoise*.

superscript

a letter or number that is above the normal line of letters in a printed text, as in a^2. See SUBSCRIPT.

suppl.

an abbreviation of *supplement*.

supplement

a magazine, or a separate section, produced with a newspaper or periodical.

surface structure

a presentation of words in a sentence that are marked to show syntax and are in the order in which they appear. See DEEP STRUCTURE.

Surrealism

a movement that encouraged literary works which examine the frontiers between conscious and subconscious experiences. It is noted for imaginative and provocative presentations of dreams and hallucinations using contradictory images and illogical sequences to mirror our subconscious.

Surrealism began in the 20th century and the best-known writers are French, including André Breton, Paul Éluard and Louis Aragon. The movement has had a strong influence on modern drama, evident in the literary works of Jean Genet, Samuel Beckett and many others. **Surrealist** adjective and noun.

suspense

a deep feeling of uncertainty and anxiety about the outcome of a plot, especially before the climax. The writer often uses diversions, irrelevant clues, the introduction of several possibilities, threat to the safety of the hero or heroine, mysterious events and many other devices to delay and obscure the eventual conclusion.

suspension of disbelief

the effect produced by a writer that makes the reader or audience incapable of questioning the logical or physical possibility of events.

S T Coleridge first used the phrase in his *Biographia Literaria* (1817): *that willing suspension of disbelief for the moment, which constitutes poetic faith*. It is crucial to many literary works that the plot or episode, however absurd or unlikely, is believed and keeps our attention so that we continue to feel deeply involved and concerned.

syllable

a part of a word that has one sound only. For example, 'sweet' has one syllable, 'sweetly' has two syllables. **syllabic** adjective.

Syllabic verse is classical verse measured according to the number of syllables in each line and not by stress or the duration of speech sounds. Strict measurement allows only a certain number of syllables, for example in a pentameter. See IONIC.

syllepsis   /sil-**lep**-sis/

a sentence in which one word, often the verb, is related to two or more other words but has a different meaning with each one, as in *Yesterday I got into trouble and a temper.*

syllogism

a way of presenting a logical argument using three parts; a major proposition and a minor proposition and then a conclusion that is true if both propositions are true. A typical example is:

Major proposition: *Fish can swim.*
Minor proposition: *A herring is a fish.*
Conclusion: *Therefore, herrings can swim.*

But! Are such arguments always true? Consider:

Major proposition: *Birds can fly.*
Minor proposition: *An ostrich is a bird.*
Conclusion: *Therefore, ostriches can fly.*

sylvan

describes a scene, situation or characteristic that is connected with woods or forests, especially one that is an idyllic portrayal of a simple rural life. See PASTORAL.

symbolism

1 the use of an object, animal, shape, colour, action etc as a symbol of a quality or idea. **symbolic** adjective. **symbolize** verb.

A pair of scales is often used as a symbol of justice, white symbolizes purity and a star is often symbolic of success. In Shakespeare's *Macbeth*, there are repeated references to clothes, all of which are symbolic of Macbeth's unsuitability to be king of Scotland.

2 (also **Symbolism**) the movement in France at the end of the 19th century that concentrated on the free expression of the poet's state of mind rather than an objective view of the real world. It preferred impressions, feelings and intuition to objective description. Symbolist poetry has a musical quality that the movement believed to be very important.

Stéphane Mallarmé with *L'Après-midi d'un faune* (1876) and Paul Verlaine with *Romances sans Paroles* (1874) were the leading figures. Arthur Rimbaud (1854–1891) and Paul Valéry (1871–1945) were also associated with this movement. A Symons in his *The Symbolist Movement in Literature* (1899) describes symbolism as a reaction against naturalism and realism. Symbolism influenced many English poets, including T S Eliot and W B Yeats, and also encouraged a separate movement among Russian poets between about 1895 and 1910 including Alexander Blok (1880–1921). See FUTURISM. **symbolist** adjective.

symbolist

1 a poet who favoured symbolism.
2 See SYMBOLISM (2).

symposium

(two *symposiums* or *symposia*)
a formal meeting in order to discuss a particular subject, especially a meeting of academics.

In ancient Greece, men would meet over a meal or drinks and enjoy a serious conversation about a social or philosophical topic (the Greek word *sumposion* meant 'drink together'). Symposium later referred to any meeting organized for a serious discussion.

synaeresis   /si-**nere**-i-sis/

the combination of two vowel sounds to produce one syllable. It was often used by earlier poets and dramatists in order to obtain the desired metrical pattern in a line, as in *is't* for 'is it'.

syncope   /**sing**-ka-pee/

the omission of a vowel or consonant from the middle of a word, as in *ne'er* for 'never'. See ELISION.

synecdoche /si-**nek**-dɑ-kee/

a figure of speech in which a part is used for the whole, as in *Many hands make light work* (*hands* is used for helpers or workers). The successful use of synecdoche relies on the use of a part that is the most closely related to the meaning of the whole, e.g. **guns** for *armed soldiers* or *count* **heads** for *count people present*.

synonym /sin-ɑ-nim/

a word that is similar in meaning to another word. *Big* and *large* are synonyms. See ANTONYM. **synonymous** adjective.

synopsis /si-**nop**-sis/

(two *synopses*)
a brief summary; it usually contains full sentences rather than a series of notes. See OUTLINE.

syntax

1 the rules for the grammatical arrangement of words to make phrases, clauses and sentences.
2 the study of the ways words form phrases, clauses and sentences. See MORPHOLOGY.
syntactic adjective.

synthesis

the act of combining two or more elements to make a complex whole. In the study of literature, this may be a combination of several characteristics in order to present a particular idea, or the act of relating or comparing features to support a point of view.

systemic grammar

a way of describing grammatical relationships as units in separate levels that provide choices according to intended meaning. See TRANSFORMATIONAL GRAMMAR.

T

tableau

(two *tableaux*)
a pause in the speeches and actions during a performance on stage when all the actors remain completely silent and still.

tabloid

a newspaper with a small page size. It usually has many photographs, and concentrates on short sensational stories about well-known personalities as well as ordinary people, rather than on political or economic news and comment. See BROADSHEET (1).

taboo word

a word that is unacceptable or forbidden because it is obscene, offensive or vulgar.

tag

a word or short clause added to a sentence. See QUESTION, REINFORCEMENT and SUBJECT TAG.

tailpiece

1 a decoration at the end of a chapter or section in a book.
2 an addition or appendix used to complete an essay, poem, speech etc. See CURTAL SONNET.

tale

a simple story. The term is used more often than 'story' when referring to traditional, fairy or folk tales.

tall story

a lie, or an excuse, boast etc that is exaggerated and incredible.

tanka

a form of Japanese verse that uses thirty-one syllables in five lines – five syllables in the first and third lines, and seven syllables in the other lines. See HAIKU. Here is an example by Dominic Dowell:

> *Tree*
>
> Swaying in the wind
> I catch the people's attention

I begin to wave,
They never wave back to me
I think nobody likes me.

tapestry

a word used of writing that contains a variety of elaborate and integrated images, phrases, descriptions, words etc. For example, we can refer to the rich tapestry of Shakespeare's vocabulary evident in his plays and sonnets.

taste

a personal view of the quality of a literary or artistic work.

Taste can be considered as almost entirely subjective since appreciation depends on a personal liking of qualities such as subject-matter or style. Other critics consider that taste should be based on an informed appreciation of the work, including an objective examination of the contents, the writer's purpose, the cultural background, the social mood, the historical context etc.

Taste is so often confused with what is fashionable at any time that critics prefer to find ways to make objective judgements; a piece of writing may not be to one's taste, but it can still be judged as possessing fine qualities.

tautology

the use in a statement of unnecessary vocabulary, of words that simply repeat what has already been conveyed by another word, e.g. *a pair of twins* or *splendid and magnificent costumes*. **tautological** adjective.

technical term

a word used only in a particular field of study or professional group, e.g. a scientific, computer or medical term that is not familiar to other people.

telestich   /ti-**les**-stik/

a poem in which the last letters of each line form a word. See ACROSTIC.

tense

a category of verb forms used to show the time when an action or situation happened. See FUTURE, PAST and PRESENT TENSES.

tension

a deep feeling of anxiety and fear about the fate of the characters in a literary work.

tercet /**ter**-sit/

a stanza, or section of a poem, with three lines. See SONNET.

term

a word or phrase used for a particular person, thing or idea.

Term is often used to refer to the vocabulary used by a group, profession or subject, e.g. *computer terms*, *medical terms* or *literary terms.*

terminology

the vocabulary used by a particular group, profession or subject, e.g. *literary terminology.* **terminological** adjective.

testament

a document or piece of writing that declares or confirms the beliefs or wishes of a person or group. The term is most often used in the phrase *will and testament*, the document that sets down a person's wishes for the disposal of assets after death (it can also contain statements on beliefs and opinion). Testament is also the name given to each of the two main divisions of the Bible.

There have been many literary works entitled Testament, including Thomas Usk's *The Testament of Love* (1385), the modern *Testament of Beauty* (1929) by Robert Bridges, and Vera Brittain's unfinished autobiography, *Testament of Youth* (1933) and *Testament of Experience* (1957), with *Testament of Time* uncompleted when she died in 1970.

tetrameter /te-**tram**-i-ta/

a line of verse with four metrical feet. See METRE. These lines in Peter Morgan's *Neap Tide* (1983) are tetrameters:

> Today | the rock | does not | concede |
> To sea. | The sea | does not | recede |
> From rock | which wor|ries through | the weave, |
> An el|bow through | a thread|bare sleeve. |

tetrastich /**tet**-ra-stik/

a stanza or poem with four lines.

text

1 the words in a book including the headings but not the illustrations, captions, footnotes etc, and usually not the front or end matter.
2 (also **set text**) any book used in a course of study, for example a play that must be studied for an examination.
3 the exact wording in a formal document.

textbook

a book that has been written and published for an educational purpose and provides the information needed to complete a course of instruction or to pass an examination.

texture

the general quality and nature of a piece of writing, especially a poem, formed by elements such as rhythm, imagery and sounds.

that-clause   See CLAUSAL OBJECT, INDIRECT SPEECH.

theatre

1 a building, or part of one, where plays and operas are performed.
2 any profession connected with the performance of plays.
3 a type of drama, as in *theatre of the absurd*.
4 an open air building in ancient Greece and the Roman Empire, made by a circle, or semicircle, of stone steps that are used as seats.

Theatre, the

the first building in England to be erected specially for performing plays. It was a wooden construction opened by James Burbage in 1577 in a district called Shoreditch to the east of what was then London. Shakespeare often performed at the Theatre until 1592 when all venues for public entertainment were closed because of the plague (a highly contagious and dangerous disease that spread through London).

In 1598, the Theatre was dismantled by James Burbage's son Richard Burbage and reassembled in 1599 on the south bank of the River Thames (Southwark) in central London as the Globe theatre.

theatre-in-the-round

(two *theatres-in-the-round*)
a theatre in which the stage is surrounded by the audience. The Globe theatre in Elizabethan London where Shakespeare's plays were performed was a theatre-in-the-round.

From the early 17th century this design was replaced by Inigo Jones's proscenium stage, the standard design since theatres reopened at the Restoration. A few modern theatres have been designed as theatres-in-the-round.

theatrical

describes behaviour that is exaggerated or far too emotional so that the feelings expressed do not seem genuine.

theatricals

dramatic entertainment, especially amateur drama.

theme

the central idea or ideas of a literary work. Although the theme may not be actually stated, it is usually easy to identify and simple to label. For example, the theme of Shakespeare's *Macbeth* is ambition. A major theme of E M Forster's *A Passage to India* (1924) is the relationships between the English and the Indians. Most literary works have more than one major theme.

thesaurus

(two *thesauri* or *thesauruses*)
a dictionary that contains lists of related words such as synonyms and antonyms. The best-known in English is P M Roget's *Thesaurus of English Words and Phrases* (1852) that is frequently revised and updated.

thesis

(two *theses*)
1 a detailed account of a piece of academic research, especially one prepared for the award of a doctorate. See ESSAY.
2 an idea or proposition that has yet to be proved.
3 the position taken by a writer or speaker towards a particular problem and supported in a formal essay or speech.

thesis drama = PROBLEM PLAY (2).

thesis novel = SOCIOLOGICAL NOVEL.

thespian

describes work or people connected with the business of producing or performing plays. The term is also used as an amusing or pretentious alternative to 'actor' or 'actress'.

think piece

an article or essay that is well researched and includes a careful analysis and commentary.

third conditional

the structure of a conditional sentence used to talk about past situations that did not happen.

if-clause PAST PERFECT TENSES	main clause *would have* + past participle
If I *had known about it*,	I *would have helped* you.
If you *had been listening*,	you *would have heard* what I said.

In some cases you can use *might have* and *could have* in the main clause, as in *If I had known about it, I might have been able to help* or *If I had known about it, I could have helped.* See FIRST, SECOND and ZERO CONDITIONAL.

third person

the form of a pronoun or verb used to refer to the person or thing, or people or things, being spoken about, as in *He is wrong.* See FIRST and SECOND PERSON.

threnody

a song or poem that expresses sorrow or grief about death, for example Tennyson's *In Memoriam* (1850). See DIRGE, ELEGY, LAMENT, MONODY.

thriller

a novel, story, play or film with a plot that involves crime, espionage or mystery. The action is fast, complex and exciting and there is always a strong element of suspense.

Thrillers developed in the 19th century: Wilkie Collins' *The Woman in White* (1860) and *The Moonstone* (1868) are still studied in schools, and Anthony Hope's *Prisoner of Zenda* (1894) continues to be popular. Edgar Wallace's novels such as *The Four Just Men* (1905) and plays such as *The Case of the Frightened Lady* (1931) dominated the genre in the first part of the 20th century.

Together with detective and spy fiction, thrillers now enjoy enormous popularity with numerous successful novelists such as Graham Greene, Len Deighton, Frederick Forsyth, John le Carré and Ruth Rendell, and some classic drama including Knott's *Dial M for Murder* (1952).

Because the plots and characters in thrillers are so clearly drawn, they make excellent material for film adaptations.

tie-in

a book etc produced as a direct link with a film or television serial or series. For example a book on the history of Russia may be published as a tie-in to a television documentary. A tie-in need not be a book; it may be a tape, record, video, magazine etc.

tilde

the mark ~ placed above a letter, especially 'n' in Spanish, to show a nasal form of pronunciation. In the Spanish word *señor*, *ñ* is pronounced /sen-**nyor**/.

timbre   /**tam**-b*a*/

the quality in tone that distinguishes one vowel sound from another.

time-free conditional = ZERO CONDITIONAL.

title

the name of a literary work, painting, musical composition etc. Successful titles of books or plays direct attention to a major theme or character.

title page

the page at the beginning of a book that contains the title, author and publisher.

to-infinitive

the infinitive form of a verb with *to*, as in *I ought **to go***. See BARE INFINITIVE.

tome

1 a large book, especially an academic work.
2 one volume of a set of books, especially encyclopaedias.

Tom Fool

a name used for a man who is mentally retarded, probably from the man who in earlier times was the 'village idiot' in rural communities. Tom the Fool is simple but well-meaning. He was a familiar character in medieval folk drama including the well-known mummery *Plough Monday Play*. He is also a character in Shakespeare's *King Lear* – Edgar, disguised as a fool, describes himself as *poor Tom*.

tone

1 the particular quality and pitch of sounds in speech. For example, a rising tone is used when speaking questions in English.
2 the general effect of the mood of a literary work that depends on style, imagery, moral perspective etc. Tone in literature can be compared to colour and shading in artwork or with the various tones of

voice when being kind, unpleasant, ingratiating etc. For example, tone in writing can be achieved by using words or phrases that have particular sounds, e.g. soft as in *z* or hard as in *t*, or by using sentences of varying length, e.g. long and gentle or short and abrupt.

tone colour

In literary criticism this term is used to describe the mood or tone produced by the sounds or meanings of words. For example, *sombre* with its deep sound expresses a feeling of darkness and sadness.

Tone colour is more often related to music than to speech or vocabulary.

tongue twister

a phrase or sentence that is very difficult to say quickly, e.g. *My sister Sheila's short.*

tonic

of or concerning stress, especially primary stress, in a spoken word. See ATONIC.

tour de force

(two *tours de force*)
a literary work that is the best example of the skills of a great writer. *Faust* (1808, 1832) is Goethe's tour de force.

tract

a pamphlet on a moral, religious or political issue, especially one produced in support of a particular point of view.

trade edition

the ordinary edition of a book that is sold in bookshops, not a special edition produced for a special occasion or particular market and not a cheap edition produced for schools or mail order.

tragedy

a serious play in which the main character (called the *protagonist*) becomes involved in conflict with disastrous results – usually through a combination of a course of events that cannot be changed and because of personal failings.

Classical Greek tragedy seems to have developed out of festivals in honour of Dionysus, the god of vegetation and fruitfulness, later the god of drama. The plays had a fixed structure: the prologue (called *Prologos*) that introduced the theme and set the hero's character, and sometimes other main characters; the entrance of the Chorus (called

Parodos) in which future events were often foreshadowed; episodes dramatizing the action of the plot (called *Epeisodia*) with each one separated by verses from the Chorus; the conclusion (called *Exodos*), usually a speech by a messenger and the appearance of a god with the power to save the hero from disaster. Later classical Greek dramatists experimented with this structure and introduced significant changes (see CHORUS).

Aristotle, in his *Poetics* (4th century BC) described the nature and purpose of tragedy as

a having a continuous plot with events that are a consequence of earlier ones, some plots involving a sudden unexpected change in events or an unexpected discovery of information (a 'complex' plot) and others not (a 'simple' plot). See UNITIES.

b concerning a hero whose misfortune is caused by an error in his character (called *hamartia*), not because of 'vice or depravity'. See TRAGIC FLAW.

c having the effect of arousing pity and fear in the audience. See CATHARSIS.

Aristotle has been so influential that there have always been attempts to apply his theories to subsequent tragedy. This is misguided because this is obviously not what Aristotle had intended.

Apart from the plays of the ancient Roman philosopher Seneca (d. 65 AD), significant examples of tragedy do not appear again until the 16th century, especially during the reigns of the English monarchs Elizabeth I and James I. Seneca's plays became the model for the very popular revenge tragedies which were sensational and often horrific; Webster's *The Duchess of Malfi* (c. 1614) is a typical example.

Shakespeare's genius was flowering at this time and he wrote many superb tragedies, the greatest of which are considered to be *King Lear*, *Othello, Macbeth* and *Hamlet*. He used some of the ideas of ancient Greek tragedy, especially the notion of the tragic flaw in the hero's character, but introduced many of his own. He abandoned the influence of the gods and gave his heroes the free will to choose their actions, although the audience is in no doubt that a tragic end is inevitable. Unlike the Greek tragedies, Shakespeare examines the heroes' state of mind; in his finest works such as *Hamlet* this is the central feature of the play.

Lope de Vega (1562–1635) established drama in Spain by writing about 1800 plays, many of which are tragedies that followed the classical model. His work had a profound influence on European drama, especially in France where tragedy flourished; Corneille wrote his masterpiece *Le Cid* (1636) and later Racine provided several great tragedies including *Phèdre* (1677) and *Athalie* (1691).

More recent examples of tragedy are dramas in which the main character is defeated by a combination of social and psychological circumstances. Fine examples are the plays of the Norwegian writer Henrik Ibsen, e.g. his *A Doll's House* (1879), whose portrayal of a corrupt society is very powerful.

The 20th century has seen a further move away from Aristotle's concepts; tragedy now deals with the lives of ordinary men and women, not influential people such as royalty or warrior leaders. Two classic examples are from American playwrights: Tennessee Williams' *A Streetcar Named Desire* (1947) and Arthur Miller's *Death of a Salesman* (1949).

tragic flaw

the aspect of the tragic hero's character that causes his downfall. In Greek this is called *hamartia* as defined in Aristotle's *Poetics* (4th century BC). See HUBRIS.

A tragic flaw does not make the hero an evil person; it is simply a human weakness or failing that we all possess but which can have fatal consequences. Macbeth's flaw is, as he confesses, 'vaulting ambition'.

tragic irony

a situation whereby the audience of a tragedy is in possession of information that other characters do not have; this ignorance will contribute to the tragic outcome. The whole of the ancient Greek writer Sophocles' *Oedipus the King* (5th century BC) is tragic irony; the audience perceives the truth long before Oedipus does. The Irish writer Sean O'Casey's plays are also filled with tragic irony as in his *Juno and the Paycock* (1925).

tragi-comedy

a drama that contains elements of both tragedy and comedy. In his preface to *The Faithful Shepherdess* (1610), John Fletcher wrote his definition of tragi-comedy: *A tragi-comedy is not so-called in respect to mirth and killing, but in respect it wants* [i.e. lacks] *deaths, which is enough to make it no tragedy, yet brings some near it, which is enough to make it no comedy . . . .*

We can use the term to refer to any literary work, but usually drama, whose general theme seems tragic but where a tragic outcome is converted into a happy one at the last moment. Shakespeare's *The Merchant of Venice* is a good example.

trans.

an abbreviation of *translated (by)*, *translation* or *translator*.

transcript

a recorded or written copy of the text of a drama, speech, debate etc.

transformational grammar

a grammatical description of a language using rules that relate deep structure to surface structure, an examination of the fundamental equivalent value of sentences that have different structures; *He scored the goal* has the equivalent *The goal was scored by him*. See GENERATIVE, PRESCRIPTIVE and SYSTEMIC GRAMMAR.

transitional element

a word or phrase that leads to a different sequence of thought, e.g. *however* as in *We took a taxi to the airport. **However**, we missed our flight*, or *now* as in *The contract was signed without too much difficulty. **Now** we could plan changes to the building*.

transitive

describes a verb that uses a direct object, as in *We **played** tennis this morning* or *Did she **get** the job?* See INTRANSITIVE.

translation

a text that has been rewritten in a different language. A **close translation** is one in which each element is presented in the translated text. A **free translation** allows for imaginative equivalents that express the ideas and mood of the original but without exact word-for-word translation.

transliteration

the representation of a word in one alphabet in the corresponding letters of another. For example, the Greek 'Μωτσαρτ' is a transliteration of 'Mozart'.

travel book

a book that reports and describes a journey. It can be an account of an expedition or exploration, or a guide to travelling in a country or region.

travelogue

a book, film, brochure or speech about experiences of travelling.

Among many examples are CM Doughty's splendid *Travels in Arabia Deserta* (1888) and Freya Stark's accounts of her journeys in Persia, Arabia and Turkey (1930–1970). Freya Stark wrote of her love of travelling, *the beckoning counts and not the clicking latch behind you*.

treatise

a formal and systematic examination of the principles and conclusions of a subject, especially philosophical, mathematical, scientific or literary subjects. It is aimed at a specialist academic reader. See ESSAY.

triad

a group of three; in literature it refers to the three lyric stanzas of classical Greek verse, *strophe*, *antistrophe* and *epode*. See CHORUS.

tribe of Ben or sons of Ben

a group of 17th century poets who were admirers of Ben Jonson (1572–1637). They were Robert Herrick with Thomas Carew, Sir John Suckling and Richard Lovelace. See CAVALIER.

Jonson's main influences were the encouragement to study classical literature and the use of conventional poetic forms such as the ode. The tribe of Ben used epigrams and satire in their lyrics and expressed enjoyment in living as well as having a serious critical view of poetry.

trilogy

a series of three plays, novels, operas etc that are related by the characters or storyline. Shakespeare's *Henry VI* is a well-known example.

Examples of modern trilogies by a novelist are the two written by Joyce Cary (1888–1957), one with art as a theme, the other about politics; the better-known trilogy is the first, *Herself Surprised* (1941), *To Be a Pilgrim* (1942) and *The Horse's Mouth* (1944). A modern dramatic trilogy is Arnold Wesker's *Chicken Soup with Barley* (1957), *Roots* (1959) and *I'm Talking about Jerusalem* (1960). A more recent trilogy in fiction is J R R Tolkien's novels that comprise his *Lord of the Rings* (1954–1955).

trimeter

a line of verse with three metrical feet. See METRE. The 2nd and 4th lines of the following verse from the traditional ballad *Sir Patrick Spens* are trimeters:

> Our king has written a braid letter,
> And sealed | it with | his hands |
> And sent it to Sir Patrick Spens
> Was walk|ing on | the strand. |

triple measure

a metrical foot with three syllables. See ANAPAEST. Here are examples in these lines written by William Cowper (1731–1800):

> From the cen|tre all round | to the sea |
> I am lord | of the fowl | and the brute. |

tripody   /trip-*a*-dee/
a metrical unit in poetry with three feet. See TRIMETER.

tristich   /tris-tik/
a stanza or poem with three lines, e.g. this stanza from *Lady Lazarus* (1965), Sylvia Plath's poem about her attempts to commit suicide:

> Dying
> Is an art, like everything else.
> I do it exceptionally well.

trochee   /troh-kee/
a metrical foot with a stressed syllable and an unstressed syllable (‾ ˘). See IAMB, CHORIAMB, METRE. **trochaic** adjective.

trope
a word or expression used with a figurative meaning. All metaphors and similes are tropes. This verse from Wordsworth's *To the Same Flower* (1802) contains a series of tropes (in this case metaphors) for the daisy:

> A nun demure of lowly port;
> Or sprightly maiden, of Love's court,
> In thy simplicity the sport,
>   of all temptations;
> A queen in crown of rubies drest;
> A starveling in a scanty vest;
> Are all, as seems to suit thee best,
>   thy appellations.

troubadour
a lyric poet who was paid to entertain the noble families of southern France in the 12th and 13th centuries.

Troubadours composed and sang lyrics about love, gallantry and chivalry. See COURTLY LOVE. Many troubadours, such as Arnaut de Mareuil, became famous throughout a wide region. Their songs had an enormous influence on the development of lyric verse and even on the sonnet. See MINSTREL.

truncation
the omission of a syllable at the beginning or end of a line of verse. See CATALECTIC.

Tudor
the period of English history from 1485 to 1603 when the monarchs

were members of the Tudor family (Henry VII, Henry VIII, Edward VI, Mary I and Elizabeth I).

turgid prose
pompous and pretentious writing.

turning-point
the point in the plot of a literary work when there is an important change of direction or reversal of fortune. From this moment it is clear that the action will move towards its denouement. See CLIMAX, FREYTAG'S PYRAMID.

turn of phrase
(two *turns of phrase*)
a particular or personal way of stating something, especially using a particular idiomatic phrase or figure of speech.

U

umlaut /**um**-lout/
the mark ¨ placed above a vowel in some languages, especially German, to show that it has a particular sound value, as in Schiller's *Die Künstler*. The umlaut was also used in Old English. Now it occurs rarely in English, e.g. in names such as Brontë.

unaccented
describes a syllable in a line of verse that is not stressed or emphasized. The symbol ˘ indicates an unaccented (unstressed) syllable, as in this line from John Fuller's *A Railway Compartment* (1961):

Ăgainst | the crim | sŏn arm- | rĕst leaned | ă girl |

See ACCENT.

unauthorized
describes a biography or article prepared and published without the involvement or permission of the person who is the subject.

A biography of this kind is usually advertised as unauthorized because readers have the impression that it will contain controversial or intimate personal details.

uncial

of, about or written using majuscules, especially in ancient Greek and Roman manuscripts.

uncountable noun or mass noun

a common noun that cannot be used with *a* or *an* and that does not have a plural form, e.g. *bread, furniture, information, happiness, solitude, humour, enlightenment.*

Some nouns can be uncountable with one meaning, e.g. *rhyme* as in *verse written in rhyme,* or countable with another meaning as in *I can't think of a rhyme for 'London'.* See COUNT and DEFINITE NOUN.

underground literature

literature that uses techniques and themes which are highly experimental, especially literature that rebels against the social or literary conventions of the period. The late 1960s publication *IT* (International Times) followed by *Oz* and *Rolling Stone* are typical.

understatement

a kind of irony in which something is stated as being less significant or special than it really is. See LITOTES.

unexpurgated

describes a text that has not had obscene or offensive elements removed. See BOWDLERIZE.

unique reference

the fact of being a reference to only one example. All proper nouns have a unique reference because they are names of particular people, places or things. Other nouns can also have unique references if they refer to a single concept, e.g. *nature, science* or *heaven.*

unities, the

the principles of action, time and space in dramatic structure.

Although Renaissance academics considered that the ancient Greek philosopher Aristotle had established these principles, in reality he had dealt only with the **unity of action**; he maintained that drama must have a clear beginning, middle section and conclusion. These academics found in Aristotle's writings what they interpreted as principles for the other unities. His reference to *a single revolution of the sun* was interpreted as **unity of time** – within one day – although some scholars preferred a period of daylight or even the period of the duration of the performance. Similarly, reference to Aristotle's writings provided interpretations for **unity of place** – the same city.

These three principles were not strictly followed by English dramatists (although Shakespeare's *The Tempest* observes all three), but unity of action has always held its importance in dramatic construction, especially before the influence of the Romantics.

universal grammar

grammatical limitations related to deep structure and meaning that are common to all human languages. This fundamental grammar makes it possible for a person to learn any language and allows for translations between different languages.

unstressed

a syllable in a word that is not emphasized in speech; in *appeal* the first syllable *a* is unstressed, /*a*-**peel**/.

unvoiced

describes a speech sound made without any vibration, e.g. /k/, /p/. See VOICED.

upper case

capital letters in printed text. See LOWER CASE.

usage

the conventional or established way of using a word, phrase or construction to express meaning.

Since language is always developing and adapting, usage can never be fixed or permanent. There is a constant flow of new usages to express contemporary concepts, inventions, discoveries, ideas, behaviours, social atmospheres and geographical settings. Equally, many terms and structures lose their usefulness and are gradually dropped.

Although many academics seek to establish a standard usage (one that is generally in use by educated people) it is pointless to interpret correct usage rigidly.

Utopia

an imagined place or situation that is ideal, especially a nation in which there is complete social, legal and political harmony.

There have been many attempts to describe such a country. The ancient Greek philosopher Plato's *Republic* (c. the early 4th century

BC) is the classical example but there have been many others since then. The term was coined by Sir Thomas More in his political essay *Utopia* (1516).

utterance
something produced from the mouth using the voice and breath, including speech, a whisper, a cry or growl and even a cough or sigh. **utter** verb.

v. = VIDE.

vade mecum   /vaa-di **may**-kʌm/
a small reference book that can be carried in a pocket or bag so that it is available if needed.

vanguard
the position in front of others, especially as the best example. See AVANT-GARDE.

vapours, the
In the 16th century, medical knowledge was limited and it was believed that depression, fits or hysteria were caused by gases (*vapours*). These gases were produced in the stomach or nearby internal organs and then travelled to the head and affected the brain. See HUMOURS.

The vapours often appeared in literary works during the 18th century, in particular to explain the behaviour and mood of young heroines.

variant
a form of spelling or usage familiar to a particular group such as American variants of English.

variety
a form of light entertainment that contains a set of short unconnected acts (*variety acts*) such as comic sketches, singing, dancing, acrobatics, juggling.

Variety became popular as live entertainment at the end of the 19th

century and still attracted large audiences until the 1930s. It continues
to be popular as television entertainment but is no longer performed
live in a theatre except for single productions using groups of established stars. See BURLESQUE (2).

vaudeville

the North American name for *variety*.

Veda   /**vay**-d*a*/

one or all of the ancient sacred Hindu writings. They include prayers,
hymns and rules for public worship.

vellum

1 the prepared skin of a calf, lamb or kid used as parchment.
2 = PARCHMENT (2).

verb

a word used to refer to the occurrence of an action or condition, e.g.
breathe, speak, come, wait, exist, hope. See AUXILIARY, FINITE, MODAL
AUXILIARY and NONFINITE VERB; INTRANSITIVE and TRANSITIVE.

verbal or verbid

a form of a verb that is not used to show person, mood or number.
There are three kinds of verbal:
a the infinitive used as a noun, as in *To **write** is not as easy as it seems.*
b a participle used as an adjective, as in *a grown man.*
c the -*ing*-form as the subject of a sentence, as in ***Shouting** makes my
head ache.* Verbal also describes the *ing*-form used as a noun followed
by a noun phrase, as in *the careful **washing** of lettuce. Washing* refers
directly to the action of the verb 'to wash', therefore it cannot be
replaced by another word. See DEVERBAL.

verbalize

to express something in words, especially one's feelings or thoughts, or
an opinion or idea.

verbatim   /ver-**bay**-tim/

a Latin word meaning 'exactly as it is written or spoken', i.e. using
exactly the same words. See LITERATIM.

verbiage

the use of too many words, many of which are obviously unnecessary.
See VERBOSE.

verbose

describes speech or writing (or the speaker or writer) that is boring because it contains far too many words (see VERBIAGE); it uses strings of adjectives or phrases in descriptions when one or two well-chosen words would be much more effective. Miss Bates in Jane Austen's *Emma* (1814) is verbose. See OTIOSE. **verbosity** noun.

verb phrase

a verb made up of several words, e.g. *would have come* or *would have been being washed.* See PHRASAL VERB.

vernacular

the language or dialect used as a first language in a particular country or region.

verse

1 poetry. See ALTAR POEM, BALLAD, BALLADE, CLERIHEW, ECLOGUE, ELEGY, EPIC, HAIKU, LAMENT, LIMERICK, LYRIC, MOCK-EPIC, ODE, SONNET, VILLANELLE; BLANK, CHAIN, ECHO, FREE, HEROIC, LIGHT, MACARONIC, NARRATIVE, NONSENSE, OCCASIONAL, SERPENTINE, SICK and SYLLABIC VERSE.
2 a stanza.
3 a set of metrical feet that forms a line of poetry.

verse epigram   See EPIGRAM.

versification

1 the type of metrical composition of a poem.
2 the act and practice of writing poetry.

vers libre = FREE VERSE.   /vair **lee**-bra/

verso

a lefthand page of a book; it always has an even number printed on it. See RECTO.

Victorian

describes the period when Queen Victoria (1837–1901) was on the throne. It was a time of enormous social, economic and scientific change.

The literature of the period reflected these changes, and also mirrored the prudish and hypocritical attitudes so characteristic of that time. See BOWDLERIZE. Scientific advances challenged established religious belief. The industrial revolution saw the emergence and rise of the middle classes and the abuse of position and power in public life and in the judiciary. There was a rapid increase in population causing urban squalor as well as poverty among the farmworkers. At the same time, financial and political encouragement was given to art and literature to satisfy the demands of an expanding wealthy and educated elite.

This period witnessed the birth of new ways of increasing the spread of literature, particularly the periodical and its inclusion of novels as part works. Dickens' novels such as *Oliver Twist* (1837–1838) and *Great Expectations* (1860–1861) and William Thackeray's *Vanity Fair* (1847–1848) were first published as part works.

There was very little serious dramatic work of importance during this time, perhaps because of the suffocating effects of prudish attitudes. But prose flourished, especially political and social essays and the hugely popular novels of Charles Dickens which often portrayed the social effects of the industrial revolution. Thomas Hardy's novels appeared later on and the period closed with writers who questioned the social and literary values of the period, including Oscar Wilde (1854–1900) and A W Pinero (1855–1934) who helped to revive drama.

The Victorian age also saw the establishment of the British Empire and many writers, among whom Rudyard Kipling (1865–1936) is probably the best known, took their themes and inspiration from overseas experiences. See EDWARDIAN.

vide
/vie-di/

a Latin word meaning 'see', used before a reference to another part of a text, another book etc.

Vide is often abbreviated to **v.** or **vid.**

vignette

1 a small decoration or illustration placed at the beginning or end of a chapter, section or book.

2 a short descriptive essay or sketch, for example about a place, activity or person. It can be a single item or one of a set.

A **vignette performance** is a thoughtful and attractive performance of a brief role in a dramatic work. It has become common for aging established actors and actresses to delight audiences with a vignette performance in a major theatrical production.

villain

a wicked and vindictive character in a literary work; the villain is usually the antagonist to the hero or heroine.

Villains first appeared in 16th century drama and became major characters in Elizabethan times. Iago is considered by many to be the most complex and evil villain in Shakespeare's plays.

villanelle

an elaborate verse, French in origin, probably from the 16th century. It has nineteen lines divided into five tercets followed by a quatrain with the rhyme scheme $A b a\ a b A\ a b a\ a b A\ a b a\ a b A a$ (A and a are repeated lines and form a refrain).

Some English poets have tried it including Oscar Wilde (1854–1900) and W H Auden (1907–1973). But here is a superb modern example, Dylan Thomas' *Do not go gentle into that good night* (1946):

> Do not go gentle into that good night,
> Old age should burn and rave at close of day;
> Rage, rage against the dying of the light.
>
> Though wise men at their end know dark is right,
> Because their words had forked no lightning they
> Do not go gentle into that good night.
>
> Good men, the last wave by, crying how bright
> Their frail deeds might have danced in a green bay
> Rage, rage against the dying of the light.
>
> Wild men who caught and sang the sun in flight,
> And learn, too late, they grieved it on its way,
> Do not go gentle into that good night.
>
> Grave men, near death, who see with blinding sight
> Blind eyes could blaze like meteors and be gay
> Rage, rage against the dying of the light.
>
> And you, my father, there on the sad height,
> Curse, bless me now with your fierce tears, I pray.
> Do not go gentle into that good night
> Rage, rage against the dying of the light.

virgin play   See MIRACLE PLAY.

virgule = SOLIDUS.

virtues, the or the cardinal virtues

the seven aspects of moral excellence: (natural) *justice, prudence, fortitude* and *temperance*, and (theological) *faith, hope* and *charity*.

vituperative

describes a piece of writing that uses harsh abusive language to criticize or complain.

viz.

an abbreviation of the Latin *videlicet* meaning 'namely', used in front of a list of examples, detailed items or possibilities etc.

vocabulary

words, phrases and expressions, especially when considered as the total number that form a language, or the number or range used by a person, profession etc.

vogue word

a word that is very popular for a short time, often with a meaning that changes because of too much use. A current example is *democratic*.

voice

the form of a verb used to show the relation between the subject and the verb, i.e. *the active voice* and *the passive voice*. See ACTIVE, PASSIVE.

voiced

describes a speech sound during which you can feel a vibration, e.g. /m/, /n/. See UNVOICED.

vowel

a speech sound made without an audible stop of breath, or the letter used to represent it, e.g. *a, e, i, o, u* that have twelve speech sounds between them. See CONSONANT, DIPHTHONG.

vowel rhyme

a kind of rhyme in which the vowel sounds of words rhyme but the consonants at the beginning or ends of the words do not, e.g. *thumb* and *fun*.

vulgar

1 describes a word or phrase used in coarse or obscene speech. The use of vulgar words such as swearwords and obscenities shows a lack of culture and taste. However, some people who have very strict and rigid social attitudes think of some words and phrases as vulgar when these are acceptable to others as informal but not offensive.
2 describes the form of a language, especially Latin, used by ordinary people and in ordinary situations. A more formal and conservative form is reserved for special occasions and publications.

vulgate

1 informal speech used daily by ordinary people. See VULGAR (2).

2 the usual accepted version of a text.

3 (**Vulgate**) the version of the Bible produced in the 4th century, and known from the 13th century, by revising the Latin version of the original Greek and translating the original languages.

waffle

vague terminology used in speech or writing to make it seem to be more academic or authoritative. See PADDING.

weak ending

an ending to a line of verse that is stressed in the metrical pattern but is not stressed if the same group of words is normal speech. See FEMININE ENDING.

weak form

the form of pronunciation of a word in normal speech when it is not emphasized or spoken carefully. See STRONG FORM.

weak verb

a verb that has forms using additions, e.g. *-d*, *-ed* or *-ied*, and not a vowel change. See STRONG VERB.

weepy

a sentimental or melodramatic play, novel or film.

werewolf   /**wair**-wawf/

a person said to be able to assume the body of a wolf, especially during nights when there is a full moon.

A werewolf appeared as a character in ancient folk tales, often in superstitious tales as someone who has been put under the spell of a wolf. Werewolves commit evil and brutal acts but the person who has been bewitched cannot remember having committed the acts.

West End

the district in central west London where most of the city's principal theatres are located.

whimsical

describes writing or speech that expresses impulsive thought and is full of fancy and strange ideas. It is often amusing or mischievous and can make a valuable contribution to light verse, dialogue or characterization.

white paper

an official government report that states the results of an enquiry and its recommendations.

whodunit

a literary work about the solving of a crime.

willing suspension of disbelief   See SUSPENSION OF DISBELIEF.

wit

the ability to use contrasting and unlikely associations to express a clever and amusing idea. Oscar Wilde was notable for his excellent wit, including this gem from his *The Importance of Being Earnest* (1895):

> I never travel without my diary. One should always have something sensational to read on the train.

witticism

a witty remark, e.g. Dorothy Parker's remark after seeing Katherine Hepburn in a Broadway play, *She ran the gamut of the emotions from A to B.*

word blindness = DYSLEXIA.

wordbook

1 a short book for younger people that contains words and their meanings. The words need not be in alphabetical order; for example, they may be grouped thematically.
2 the libretto for an opera.

wordbreak

a point where a word can be divided at the end of a line of writing or printed text. See WORD DIVISION.

word division

the act of dividing a word when it is too long to fit at the end of a line of printing. The first part of the word is put at the end of the line with a hyphen; the second part begins the next line.

Many people prefer not to divide words at all unless the word has a hyphen (and so is divided at the hyphen) or the word is made of two other words, e.g. *backache* (and so is divided between the two words), or has a very common prefix, e.g. *un-* (and so is divided after the prefix). It is unusual to divide other kinds of words when writing by hand.

There are four fundamental considerations for a typist or key-boarder when dividing words:

a Divide the word according to its syllables, as in *guar-an-tee* when – shows acceptable wordbreaks.

b Divide a word between two identical consonants, e.g. *ap-pear*.

c Divide a word after a prefix, e.g. *anti-*, or before a suffix, e.g. *-fully*.

d Divide a word so that both parts are sensible and can be spoken or read so that the complete word is understood. For example, avoid *not-able* or *no-table* for *notable* and *no-thing* for *nothing*.

And here are three rules for word division:

1 Never divide a word with fewer than five letters.

2 Never divide a word so that one part is a single letter. For example, *a-bandon* or *exemplif-y* are not acceptable.

3 Never divide a prefix or suffix. For example, *an-tisocial* or *probab-ly* are not acceptable.

word-formation

the way in which a word is formed, e.g. by combining parts

a that can relate to meaning, e.g. the prefix *un-* combined with *usual* to form *unusual*,

b that shows person, number or tense, e.g. *-es* added to *box* to form *boxes*,

c that changes a part of speech, e.g. the suffix *-ness* added to *great* to form *greatness*,

d that makes a new word by combining two other words, e.g. *air* and *mail* to form *airmail*.

word perfect

describes a person who is able to repeat a speech, poem, part of a play etc from memory without looking at the text.

wordplay

a witty exchange using ambiguous meanings of particular words. R B

Sheridan's comedies, e.g. *School for Scandal* (1777), are full of wordplay.

wordy

describes writing or speech that uses many words when a concise and tight style would be much better. See PADDING.

Y

yarn

a long and complex story, usually one that is an exaggerated and unlikely account of an experience or adventure.

yearbook

a book that contains reports (and photographs) of activities that took place during the previous year.

Yellow Book, the

a quarterly periodical that was produced between 1894 and 1897, a period of the relaxing of strict Victorian morality.

It contained verse, stories and drawings from a group of writers and artists who were determined to break away from the rigid conventions and prudish attitudes of the period. Henry James (1843–1916), Aubrey Beardsley (1872–1898) and Max Beerbohm (1872–1956) were notable contributors.

Z

zero article

an instance in a grammatical construction when there is no definite or indefinite article, e.g. *I drank coffee* (the statements *I drank a coffee* or *I drank the coffee* have different meanings). Many common pairs have no article before the second item, e.g. *a knife and fork.*

zero conditional

the structure of a conditional sentence used to talk about things that are true.

if-clause PRESENT TENSE	main clause PRESENT TENSE
*If you **mix** yellow and blue,*	*you **get** green.*
*If I **read** a lot,*	*my eyes **get** sore.*

Note that *when* or *whenever* can replace *if*, as in *Whenever I read a lot, my eyes get sore.* See FIRST, SECOND and THIRD CONDITIONAL.

zero plural

a noun that has the same form when singular or plural, e.g. *sheep* as in *That sheep has two lambs* and *Two sheep have died.*

zeugma = SYLLEPSIS.   /**zyoog**-ma/

An outline of British literary heritage

This can only be a brief guide in chronological order to principal writers set in literary periods and major movements. The entries in this dictionary give further information on the characteristics of various periods. Alongside the British chronology are significant writers, episodes and movements from Europe, North America and the rest of the world. This outline ends at the start of the 1920s since a brief guide to later writers would inevitably omit so many people as to become meaningless.

BRITISH LITERATURE

Period		Principal writers and major movements
Old English	c.450-1066	Bede, Grammaticus, *Anglo-Saxon Chronicle, Beowulf*
Middle English	ANGLO-FRENCH c.1066-1350	Geoffrey of Monmouth, Paris
	ANGLO-SAXON c.1350-1500	Chaucer, Langland, Usk, Malory
	MEDIEVAL DRAMA c.1000-1500	See MYSTERY, MIRACLE AND MORALITY PLAY
	MEDIEVAL ROMANCE c.1100-1500	*King Horn, Sir Gawain and the Green Knight, Troylus and Cryseyde, Le Morte Darthur*

INTERNATIONAL LITERATURE

Significant writers, episodes and movements

SCHOLASTICS c.1000-1500 Abélard, Lombard, Aquinas

TROUBADOURS IN S. FRANCE c.1100-1400: *chansons de geste*

Dante

Petrarch, Boccaccio

MINSTRELS IN EUROPE, ENGLAND c.1400-1500

Period	Dates	Writers	European context
SCOTTISH CHAUCERIANS	c.1450-1550	King James I, Dunbar, Henryson, Douglas	Villon
Modern English	c.1500-		BEGINNING OF RENAISSANCE, REFORMATION Erasmus Machiavelli, Luther Rabelais, Cellini
Tudor	1485-1603 (or 1558)	Skelton Wyatt, Surrey, Leland, Foxe	Ronsard
Elizabethan	1558-1603 (or 1611)	Deloney, Lyly, Marlowe, Heywood Kyd, Spenser, Jonson, Shakespeare Dekker, Campion, Bacon	Cervantes, Vega
Jacobean	1603-1625	Webster, Donne, Middleton, *Authorized Version of the Bible*	'LE GRAND SIÈCLE' – 17th CENTURY IN FRANCE Descartes, Corneille
Caroline	1625-1649	Herbert, Milton Crashaw, Herrick, Vaughan CAVALIERS Carew, Suckling, Lovelace See TRIBE OF BEN	
Commonwealth	1649-1660	Milton, Waller, Browne, Cowley Vaughan, Taylor, Marvell, Hobbes Walton, Bunyan See PURITANISM	Molière, Spinoza
		METAPHYSICAL POETS Donne, Cowley, Herbert, Crashaw, Vaughan	
Restoration	1660-1714	Pepys Wyckerley, Behn, Newton, Locke Congreve, Rowe, Berkeley, Defoe	La Fontaine, Racine ENLIGHTENMENT IN EUROPE c.1680-1800 Leibniz
	NEOCLASSICISTS	Goldsmith, Dryden Steele, Pope, Addison, Swift, Johnson	
Georgian	1714-c.1830	Fielding, Richardson, Gray, Hume	Le Sage, Voltaire

Rousseau
Kant, Goethe, Schiller, Richter
Gorki, Staël, Grimm brothers, Leopardi
Hegel, Pushkin, Manzoni, Lamartine
Kierkegaard, Balzac

Smollett, Sterne, Walpole, Burke
Sheridan, Gibbon, Cowper, Burns, Paine
Leigh Hunt, Austen, Southey, Peacock

ROMANTICS (ENGLISH)
c.1789-1830

Blake, Wordsworth, Coleridge, Lamb
Byron, Scott, Hazlitt
Keats, Shelley, de Quincey

Victorian 1837-1901

Hugo, Heine, Stendhal, Marx
Anderson, Gogol, de Musset
Sand, Longfellow
Dumas, Irving, Whitman, Gautier
Baudelaire, de Lisle, Flaubert, Hawthorne
Emerson, Alcott, Zola, Verlaine, Turgenev
Verne, Dostoevsky, Tolstoy
Nietzsche, Ibsen, Mallarmé
Maupassant, Cable, Twain, Rimbaud
Strindberg, Schreiner, Burnett, Wilcox
Maeterlinck, Chekhov

Dickens, Tennyson
Poe, Brontë sisters, Gaskell, Thackeray
Brownings, Arnold, Kingsley, Darwin
Mill, Trollope, G. Eliot, Hughes

Swinburne, Blackmore, Lear

SYMBOLISM BEGAN IN FRANCE c.1880
Mallarmé, Verlaine, Rimbaud, Valéry

Carroll, Hopkins, Bridges, Hardy, Meredith
Stevenson, Pinero, Jerome, Housman
Conan Doyle, Wilde, James, Potter

PRE-RAPHAELITES
c.1860-1890

Rossettis, Morris

CELTIC REVIVAL
c.1885-1940

Yeats, Synge, Joyce

EXPRESSIONISM IN EUROPE c.1900-1930
Gide, Colette, Henry, Blok
Pascoli, Pound, Mann, Tagore

Edwardian 1901-1912

Conrad, Barrie, Shaw, Galsworthy
Wells, Forster, Bennett

BLOOMSBURY GROUP
c.1907-1935

Woolfs, Forster, Keynes, Strachey

IMAGISTS IN USA c.1910-1920
Frost, Ford, Lowell, Valéry, Cocteau
O'Casey, Pirandello, Proust, Stein,
Fitzgerald, HD, Brecht, Kafka, Lorca

Later Georgian 1912-1922

Brooke, de la Mare, Lawrence, Owen
Sassoon, Drinkwater, Graves, Maugham